Under Fire
with ARVN Infantry

Under Fire with ARVN Infantry

Memoir of a Combat Advisor in Vietnam, 1966–1967

B̲ob W̲orthington

McFarland & Company, Inc., Publishers
Jefferson, North Carolina

ISBN (print) 978-1-4766-7436-0 ∞
ISBN (ebook) 978-1-4766-3444-9

LIBRARY OF CONGRESS CATALOGUING DATA ARE AVAILABLE

BRITISH LIBRARY CATALOGUING DATA ARE AVAILABLE

Front cover photograph of the author on his last combat operation
for his first tour in Vietnam (author's collection);
artist's rendering of Vietnam combat ribbon; ERDL camouflage pattern

Printed in the United States of America

*McFarland & Company, Inc., Publishers
Box 611, Jefferson, North Carolina 28640
www.mcfarlandpub.com*

To four women in my life,
Anita, Susan, Julie, and Karen.
They have always been there for me.

In memory of
Monte Doeren (1946–2017),
student, best friend,
and fellow Vietnam warrior.
Combat Infantryman Badge,
Silver Star, and Purple Heart

Acknowledgments

For more than 36 years this book has undergone numerous permutations in the process of becoming more readable. Different friends have read different versions of the manuscript or various chapters to provide feedback to improve my work.

A young man, Chris Leathers, provided valuable insight as to what would appeal to his generation and what parts were plain boring.

Tom Heilpern read the book and gave his opinion, which varied from mine, but evoked a response, on my part, to do better.

Bruce Edwards read the entire book and, as he finished each chapter, emailed suggestions to improve the flow.

And of course, my greatest cheerleader, Anita, who remained behind to keep the home fires burning, during each of my three combat tours, and encouraged the completion of this book. She typed and proofread the original manuscript and subsequence versions, never faltering in her quest to encourage me and to keep me motivated.

Special thanks goes to everyone at McFarland who helped bring my story on combat advisors to the public.

I thank all the above for their contributions to my efforts and especially Anita, my partner for more than 60 years.

Table of Contents

Preface

As long as there have been armies, there have been military advisors. Often professional soldiers from larger, stronger armies were loaned to mentor and help train newer, smaller, less professional armies.

The war in Vietnam probably used more professionally trained military advisors than any other war previously or since. During the war in Vietnam, from 1945 to 1973, 115,427 American military men served as advisors. Of these, 66,399 were combat advisors. There were 1,393 combat advisors wounded in Vietnam and 378 killed. Eleven combat advisors were awarded the Medal of Honor for conspicuous bravery in Vietnam.

Yet, for the most part, their stories have never been told. America's remembrance of the Vietnam War consists of TV images of U.S. combat forces fighting, books, movies, and ill-conceived documentaries. There is nothing about the role of combat advisors (except for a very few books, written by combat advisors). This book is one attempt to share with readers what a combat advisor did and what his role in the Vietnam War was.

In the U.S. military, there has been a long, distinguished, and dynamic history of the employment of advisors in military operations. In 1775, the Continental Congress of the American Colonies authorized the creation of a Continental Army to be commanded by Major General George Washington. The colonies never had a unified army, and help was needed. Professional military commanders from several foreign countries came to Washington's aid to provide training and leadership in this newly formed army. Among these men were Major General Louis L. Duportail, an engineer, and Major General Gilbert du Motier, Marquis de La Fayette, both from France; Major General Johann de Kalb from Germany; and Major General Friedrich von Steuben from Prussia. The colonists won the Revolutionary War due in large part to the assistance of these foreign advisors. From this time forward throughout U.S. military history, advisors have played important roles in wars in which the United States has been engaged.

During World War II, our Office of Strategic Services (OSS) sent advisors to all theaters of operations to small resistance organizations fighting for their freedom against the invading forces of Germany and Japan. In 1945, the OSS sent equipment and advisors to Vietnam (then called Indochina) to the Viet Minh, who were fighting the Japanese and led by a middle-aged man named Ho Chi Minh.

In the early 1950s, after the French regained possession of Indochina (Vietnam) after World War II, the U.S. stepped up its military involvement in Southeast Asia by providing equipment, weapons, and vehicles to the French, along with American military technical advisors to train the French in their usage and maintenance.

When, in 1954, the French lost the decisive battle at Dien Bien Phu and left Vietnam for good, the country was divided in half, with the Viet Minh remaining in the north and the south becoming the Republic of South Vietnam. U.S. advisors now began to advise the new military of the Republic of South Vietnam. As the war between the north and south escalated, the number of U.S. advisors increased, and their role changed significantly from a mostly technical advisory effort to include tactical advising and even engagement in combat with Vietnamese troops.

Over time, there has been a variety of advisors who have served in many different functions. In the 1950s and early 1960s, they were generally regular army non-commissioned officers (NCOs—senior enlisted men) and officers who taught technical skills to untrained soldiers and their leaders. As the Vietnam War expanded, U.S. combat arms NCOs and officers were assigned to Vietnamese combat units. Army infantry advisory teams joined Army of Vietnam (ARVN) in the field. U.S. Marine advisors joined Vietnamese Marines, U.S. Navy advisors assisted Vietnamese Navy units; and U.S. Air Force pilots and maintenance crews trained the Vietnamese air force.

Perhaps the best known of military advisors are the U.S. Army Special Forces "A" teams (or Green Berets), thanks to Barry Sadler's songs and John Wayne's movie *Green Berets* as well as numerous books which elevated the Special Forces into a prominent position among U.S. military advisors.

For many combat advisors assigned to Military Assistance Command, Vietnam (MACV), training was specialized and intense. Most of these advisors were trained in counter-guerrilla, counter-insurgency warfare at the U.S. Army John F. Kennedy Special Warfare Center and School at Fort Bragg, North Carolina. After completion of that training, many of these officers and NCOs were sent to the Defense Language Institute in Monterey, California, for extensive training in the Vietnamese language.

As more U.S. combat units were assigned to Vietnam, military leaders realized the value of creating small advisory teams to assign to local Vietnamese combat units in their tactical area of responsibility (TAOR) operations.

In 1966, the U.S. Marines created their Combined Action Program in which experienced combat Marines were assigned to live and work with local Vietnamese combat units. A year later MACV established their Mobile Action Teams (two officers and three senior NCOs), where experienced combat veterans were assigned to local Vietnamese combat units.

U.S. involvement in the Vietnam War began and ended with an advisory role. As U.S. units left Vietnam, U.S. advisors were still working with the Vietnamese military, and when South Vietnam fell in April 1975, some of the last Americans to leave were advisors.

Today, the U.S. military still has advisors serving around the world, training foreign troops and fighting their battles with them. Fighting terrorism has recalled lessons learned from the Vietnam War. By the early 2000s the U.S. military realized that combat troops can win battles, but then what? As in Vietnam, winning the war was only half the battle. The foreign troops had a great need to learn to survive on their own, and for this they needed assistance. Even though it took 16 years, finally the U.S. Army has traveled back in history to formally create a professional corps of military advisors as it did for Vietnam as well as create its own Military Assistance Training Academy, as it had during Vietnam.

In January 2018, the U.S. Army activated, at Fort Benning, Georgia, the 1st security Force Assistance Brigade, a six battalion, 500-person unit of senior officers and NCOs, trained as combat advisors, which deployed in Afghanistan in March. Their mission is to work with foreign indigenous security forces to achieve national security using U.S. combat advisors to train, advise, assist, and enable a foreign country. The 1st SFAB is the first of six planned advisory brigades, five for the active army and one for the National Guard.

The 2nd SFAB is located at Fort Bragg, North Carolina, with the 3rd, 4th, and 5th SFABs to be stationed at Fort Hood, Texas; Fort Carson, Colorado, and Joint Base Lewis-McChord, Washington. The headquarters for the National Guard SFAB will be in the Indiana National Guard with its battalions in five other National Guard states. Indiana National Guard units have deployed since 2001 overseas, conducting training and advising missions.

This book is about my training and experiences as a combat advisor during my first tour in Vietnam from 1966 to 1967 and my perceptions of the Vietnam War's impact on the people of that country and on me.

CHAPTER 1

U.S. Marine Corps and Army, 1957–1964

As a nineteen-year-old Dartmouth College sophomore in 1957, I was at a crossroads in my life. I was flunking out of college and not sure what to do next. By the end of the first semester of my freshman year, I was on probation due to low grades. Working hard got me off probation by the end of that academic year. However, at the beginning of my sophomore year, I joined a fraternity which led me to focus more on parties and girls and less on academics. At this time in my life, I was not good college material, so joining the military seemed like a very good idea. Consequently, just before my first semester final exams in January of my sophomore year, I enlisted in the U.S. Marine Corps. A two-year leave of absence from Dartmouth for military service was approved. A couple weeks' delay before beginning active duty allowed me to take my final exams and get my affairs in order. After my final grades of two Bs, a C+ and two Fs, I was expelled.

On 14 February 1957, I began my tour with the U.S. Marine Corps. An uncle, who was a Marine sergeant, advised me to keep my eyes and ears open and my mouth shut throughout boot camp at Parris Island: good advice I followed to the letter. After boot camp, I completed advanced infantry training at Camp LeJeune, North Carolina. My assignment was to the Operations (S-3) Office of the Tenth Marines, the division artillery regiment of the Second Marine Division at Camp LeJeune. Since I had enlisted in the U.S. Marine Corps for adventure, excitement, and travel, I wanted to be in the infantry. But the Marines believed that, with some college, I was better suited to be a clerk.

Fortunately, my gunny sergeant agreed I was not suited to be a clerk and arranged my transfer to the newly formed U.S. Marine Force Recon (the Marines' answer to the U.S. Army Special Forces). I passed all their tests and was transferred to the Recon unit. The first day there, my first sergeant called me into his office and said I was going to Fort Benning, Georgia, to attend the

5

Army parachute school as he handed me papers to sign, which I did. Then he pushed more papers to sign, explaining that to attend jump school I had to extend my enlistment another year. I said no way would I extend and was immediately sent back to the S-3 office.

Again, my gunny understood my frustration, so he arranged for me to be assigned to a 4.2-inch mortar battery which was to be attached to the Second Marine Infantry Battalion of the Second Marine Regiment soon to depart on a Mediterranean cruise: a plum assignment. The Med cruise was a six-month tour where the Second Marine Infantry Battalion would be the reinforced infantry landing battalion for the Navy amphibious force as part of the U.S. Navy's Sixth Fleet presence in the Mediterranean Sea. We left the United States in April 1958.

Things were hot and getting hotter in Lebanon. Outsiders claimed the conflict was an internal civil war between Christians and various factions of Muslims, while the government of Lebanon stated it was an attempt by the Arabs to take over the country. It turned out that Egypt was trying to do just that.

On 15 July 1958, the Second Marine Infantry Battalion arrived in Lebanon, making the first combat amphibious assault on foreign shores since Korea. Fighting lasted a few weeks, and then "under the table" agreements brokered by the United States generated new presidential elections in Lebanon, with the war ending after the elections. While the U.S. Marines' part in the war had been primarily to ensure peace, some 5,000 people in Lebanon had died during the several months of war. My unit left Lebanon two months after we made our amphibious assault on the Beirut city dump. Soon after returning to the States in October, the unit prepared to go overseas again. Since I had less than three months left on my enlistment, I couldn't stay with the unit, so I was assigned to be a coach on the rifle range at LeJeune until my release from active duty on 13 February 1959.

After release from active duty I obtained a job on a civil engineer company's survey crew. I contacted the admissions office at Dartmouth and asked what I had to do to be readmitted to the college. The college's policy after flunking out was expulsion for one year, but then one could reapply. In my case, though, before I was expelled, I had already been given a two-year leave of absence to do my military service, so I hadn't actually been formally expelled. I was told I could return any time I wanted and did so, beginning with the 1959 spring term.

In addition to my professional life, my personal life was also being transformed during this time. While in the Marines I had dated and became engaged to a Washington, D.C., woman, Anita Elliott, who was a year younger than me and studying at a local junior college. We married on her twenty-first birthday, just before the beginning of my junior year at Dartmouth, in

September 1959. I transferred from the Marine Reserves to the Army Reserves, so I could enter Army ROTC. From 1960, until I graduated from Dartmouth in 1961, I was a police officer with the Hanover Police Department. Due to the birth of our first daughter, Susan, in August 1960, I was able to delay ROTC summer camp until after I graduated. After summer camp, I was commissioned a second lieutenant and assigned to Fort McClellan, Alabama.

Our son, Scotty, was born in mid–1962, and in early 1963, I received orders to a rifle company in the Second Infantry Division at Fort Benning, Georgia. After reporting to my new company, I received orders to attend both ranger school and parachute school simultaneously. I choose parachute school because I would earn jump pay while in

Anita Elliott, my future wife, and me (then a USMC corporal), Christmas, 1958, in my family home in Roxbury, Connecticut. In October 1958 I had returned to the States after my first combat tour in the Middle East in 1958.

school. On my third jump, I did a parachute landing fall (PLF), a specific way to roll upon landing to minimize impact on the body, and broke my hip on a rock. I was pinned together during a lengthy operation and the injury kept me out of the infantry company for a year while the hip mended. After three months in the hospital, I was transferred to the battalion headquarters as the assistant S-1 (personnel) with an additional duty as coach and captain of the battalion pistol and rifle team. On the day of the Fort Benning post pistol and rifle matches, one of my pistol shooters was absent so I shot in his place. I won the pistol match, and, as a result, was reassigned to the division marksmanship detachment as executive officer and pistol shooter.

My year as an army shooter was fun. We traveled all around the country competing. In December 1963, we had another daughter, Julie. In 1964, I won the Third Army .22 Indoor Pistol Championship and earned the top NRA competitive pistol rating of Master. That summer, I returned to another infantry battalion as the assistant operations officer (S-3). During the next year, the battalion focused on counter-guerrilla, counter-insurgency training, conducted by a Special Forces B Team assigned to our battalion. This training was to have a profound impact on my military goals and aspirations, ultimately influencing my application for assignment to Vietnam as an advisor. I wanted a combat tour and to earn the Combat Infantryman Badge.

CHAPTER 2

Preparing for Duty
in Vietnam

I had a great desire to experience combat again, but this time as a leader to learn about my own physical, emotional, and psychological capabilities, and to determine what I was made of. I wanted to succeed while serving a cause larger than myself, beyond my current horizons.

In November 1964, I withdrew my application for a Vietnam advisor assignment because our son, Scotty, had died of a viral infection. In early 1965, I reapplied for the Vietnam assignment. In mid–1965 the Second Infantry Division became the First Cavalry Division Airmobile. My unit became the Second Battalion, Seventh Cavalry (Custer's old unit and later of Ia Drang Valley fame). I was scheduled to become commander of C Company as I made captain in May 1965.

On 28 July 1965, the First Cavalry Division Airmobile received orders to Vietnam. I was removed from the division because I was finally on orders to Vietnam as an advisor. In August, the division departed for Vietnam, and I began my own preparations for a tour in Vietnam.

In September, I was to report to the U.S. Army Special Warfare School at Fort Bragg, North Carolina, for the Military Assistance Training Advisor (MATA) course and then to the Defense Language Institute (DLI) at the Presidio of Monterey in California to learn Vietnamese. I was to arrive in Vietnam in January 1966.

Reporting to the John F. Kennedy Special Warfare Center, where the MATA course was taught, I received a pile of textbooks. Our assigned reading included dozens of books ranging from Bernard Fall's *Street Without Joy* to the Department of the Army's *Area Handbooks for North Vietnam and South Vietnam* to Army manuals on small-unit tactics, psychological operations, civic action procedures, and military firearms to textbooks on the Vietnamese language. For the next six weeks, I learned quite a bit about Vietnam, including its geography, history, government, religions, people, customs, and military.

Our schedule was to have Vietnamese language instruction in the morning and then study how to be a combat advisor in the afternoon. Our teachers for the language training were all native Vietnamese, men and women, from both North and South Vietnam. We quickly learned that the dialects of each area were different, like the difference between Brooklyn natives and residents of Atlanta.

In our class were about a hundred non-commissioned officers and junior officers, mostly infantry captains. All of us were in school because of individual orders, with our final destination being the Military Assistance Command, Vietnam. Most of us were also on orders to continue our language training in Monterey, California. None of the officers had any real problem with the language training at Fort Bragg, but several senior NCOs had no interest in it and were not motivated to exert themselves, so they were not required to continue at the DLI.

Seminars on the duties and skills needed to be an advisor were taught by knowledgeable instructors (many Vietnam veterans), and most of us eagerly absorbed all we could. To be effective we had to know about the people we would be advising and about the war we would soon be joining. Most of us had had several years of experience in small-unit infantry tactics as platoon sergeants or platoon leaders, and some captains had also been company commanders. Even a few of us had already been exposed to combat, some in Korea (mostly the NCOs), Lebanon (like me), the Dominican Republic, or in Southeast Asia in countries such as Cambodia, Thailand, or Vietnam. We knew how the infantry was supposed to operate; now we had to learn to use this knowledge to advise foreign troops to fight. Our main concern was how could we teach soldiers with five, ten, or even 20 years of experience fighting in Vietnam how to fight, when we ourselves had never fought in their war. As captains and senior NCOs, we would be working with the battalion commanders, their staff, and their company officers. It soon became clear that our value as advisors to experienced Vietnamese combat soldiers would be based on our common sense, our own personal military training, and our knowledge of the Vietnamese, both the Army of Vietnam and the enemy. While the Vietnamese had more experience in fighting, we had been better trained in planning and executing coordinated operations. Plus, we had the ability to access U.S. resources, such as artillery support, helicopters, close air-ground support, and helicopter medical evacuations.

The Vietnamese military weapons were those the United States had used in World War II, mostly M1 Garand rifles and M1 carbines. Vietnamese troops also carried the Thompson .45 submachine gun. The weapons of the enemy were a real hodge-podge of communist weapons of the 1940s and 1950s. We spent about a week on the range learning about U.S. World War II weapons as well as those of the enemy. As combat advisors in Vietnam we would be issued the weapons of our Vietnamese counterparts, so we would familiarize ourselves with them, spending time shooting, disassembling, cleaning, and reassembling these weapons.

We also devoted a lot of classroom time to understanding the civilians of Vietnam and what we could do to win them over to the Vietnamese government's side. This involved both psychological warfare operations and civic action projects like hosting Medical Civic Action Programs (MEDCAPs) using local U.S. or Vietnamese military medical personnel to visit rural villages and hold medical clinics to treat the local population, especially the children.

One big training event was the school's program to requalify all military parachutists. A sign-up sheet was passed around one day for all airborne qualified MATA students who wanted to make a training jump one evening. Because I had broken my hip on my third jump at Fort Benning, I still needed one more jump to get my wings, so I signed up. But the day of the scheduled jump an NCO told me that my personnel records had no documents testifying that I had completed jump school and asked me if I was airborne qualified. I replied no but then explained what I hoped to do. I was informed that this was not jump school but a requalification jump, only for men who already had their wings, so I couldn't jump that evening and was never able to make my fourth jump.

We also spent a lot of time learning how to get and use the various elements of close combat support such as tactical air, artillery, and naval gunfire, aware that a major key to battlefield success in Vietnam was outside firepower from aircraft and artillery. We were taught what kinds of support were available in Vietnam, how to coordinate their use, and how to adjust the various types of fire missions and close-in combat support. We also learned what types of aircraft were available, what the capability of each was, and from whom we could get support, such as from our Army, Marines, Navy, or Air Force. The class ended on 21 October, and we all went our separate ways until we rejoined each other at Monterey, California. During my stay for the MATA course I had my family with me—my wife and two daughters. We drove to Monterey, California, pulling our travel trailer, and we soon found an apartment, within walking distance of the DLI, where we enjoyed living.

At DLI our Vietnamese classes were held in old World War II barracks that had been converted to classrooms. We were issued Vietnamese language books and a reel-to-reel tape deck with boxes and boxes of Vietnamese language tapes to aid in our practice of the language. We had already completed 120 hours of language training at Fort Bragg and would get another 240 hours at Monterey. Upon completion of our course, we would be awarded a language competency level designation for our personnel record as well as college credit from the University of California for two years of language courses.

We were in class three hours each morning and three hours in the afternoon. At night we worked several hours with tape decks, practicing what we had covered during the day and preparing for the next day's lessons. I worked hard in class each day and studied three to four hours each night. For me, learning a foreign language was not difficult. In high school I had taken two years of Latin and two years of French. In college, I had taken two more years of French and had also used the language while overseas in the U.S. Marine Corps.

About three weeks into our eight-week language course, through various official channels and the *Army Times*, we learned that the First and Second Battalions of the Seventh Cavalry were in big trouble in Ia Drang Valley in the Central Highlands of Vietnam. The reported casualties reached more than 300 killed or wounded in action. What the First Cavalry Division had endured reminded us that the war was heating up and was changing from one in which the United States played a largely advisory role to one in which large U.S. units were being engaged by similar major North Vietnamese units.

Me as a 28-year-old infantry captain and my wife, Anita, with our daughters Susan (right) and Julie at the Muscogee County Airport at Columbus (Fort Benning), Georgia, on 21 January 1966, on the first leg of my trip to my first combat tour in Vietnam.

Despite these troubling signs pointing to an escalation of the war, I continued my language training and attained the highest level of reading and speaking proficiency in Vietnamese when I graduated on 21 December 1965. I took my family back to Columbus, Georgia, where they planned to stay during my year in Vietnam. In January 1966, I prepared to depart for Vietnam. I was to fly from Columbus, Georgia, to San Francisco via commercial air and take a bus to Travis Air Force Base for the military flight to Vietnam. After saying good-bye to my daughters and wife, I boarded a plane for the West Coast. I was finally on my way to the war in Vietnam.

CHAPTER 3

Going to War, Finally

My flight from Columbus, Georgia, to San Francisco was uneventful. Upon landing at San Francisco, I met with some of my MATA and DLI classmates. The Air Force provided transportation to Travis AFB, some 40 miles northeast of the city.

When we arrived at base, we were told our flight to Vietnam would leave early the next morning, so we checked into the visiting officers' quarters (VOQ) and went to the officers' club for dinner.

The next day we went to the Air Force passenger terminal at 5:00 to board our flight to Vietnam. The flight never came due to mechanical problems. By noon, we were told to go to lunch and report back for our delayed flight, but the plane never showed up that day.

The U.S. Air Force (USAF) was to dispatch two Lockheed C-141A Starlifters each day from Travis AFB to Vietnam, each of which would hold more than 150 men, totaling a little more than 300 men sent to Vietnam every day. Since no planes had flown during our first day at Travis AFB, the USAF now had more than 300 individual soldiers waiting. The first plane had a mechanical breakdown, as did the second plane, so Travis AFB put in a call to McGuire AFB in New Jersey for more C-141s. We checked back in the VOQ.

The next day we reported again to the Air Force passenger terminal and discovered that we were not going to fly out that day either. A Marine unit from Camp Pendleton, California, was scheduled to depart for Vietnam that day from Travis AFB, and units had travel priority over individuals. By the end of the second day, there were well over 600 individual soldiers waiting to fly to Vietnam. Several C-141s were en route to Travis AFB from Germany and McGuire AFB, but now the order of soldiers going overseas would start with the latest group to arrive and the last to leave would be our flight.

During this ordeal, five of us infantry captains formed a group. One, who had been assigned to Hawai'i in the Twenty-Fifth Infantry Division for three years before MATA and DLI, still had many military contacts in Hawai'i.

He explained to us that it would be several more days before we could leave Travis AFB, and that he knew of a regularly scheduled Air Force supply flight from Travis AFB to Hickam AFB on Oahu that he could get us on. On 24 January, the five of us were on that flight to Hawai'i; we were warriors seeking our war, and if we had to hitchhike across the Pacific, so be it.

On landing at Hickam AFB, the knowledgeable captain took us to flight operations to see what we could catch to Vietnam. Nothing was scheduled for the next couple of days, but the operations NCO said there were always unscheduled planes landing at Hickam going to Vietnam. We were advised to check into the VOQ and to report back to the passenger terminal at 6:00 each morning to wait for a ride. Our savvy captain explained to the sergeant that we would instead check into the U.S. Army Rest and Recreation (R and R) Center at Fort DeRussy, on Waikiki Beach. We would not be waiting at his office at 6:00 each morning but would call him at 6:00 each morning; if he had a flight, we would report to him post haste.

We arrived on a Monday, and by mid-week I was running out of money, so I called my wife to wire me some. This was a not-so-pleasant surprise to her as she had been expecting me to be in Vietnam. She reluctantly said okay, warning me that there would be no more money later, so I had better get to the war instead of lying on the beach. As there were no military aircraft going to Vietnam via Hickam AFB we had to come up with an alternate plan. Again, the captain came through, but only for three of us. Through his local contacts, he learned that a commercial airliner, chartered by the U.S. government, would be stopping in Honolulu and dropping off three passengers, leaving three seats vacant for its continuing flight to Bangkok, Thailand. He booked himself, me, and one other captain on that plane.

On Friday, 28 January, we departed Hawai'i for Vietnam via Bangkok. While over the Pacific, we were talking to one of the stewardesses who asked if we had U.S. passports. When we replied, "Of course not—we're on military orders," she explained that without passports we couldn't land in Bangkok legally. She said she would talk to the captain and see what could be done. The captain said he could land in the Philippines at Clark AFB and from there we could easily get a flight to Vietnam. After landing at Clark AFB we checked into operations and were told to return the next day and wait until something showed up, as there were numerous flights each day to Vietnam. To avoid further delays, the three of us decided to split up and make our way to Vietnam individually. I signed up for a backseat in a jet fighter to Saigon the next day.

Arriving at base ops to board the jet to Saigon, I was told that I had been bumped by a colonel flying to Saigon for an overnight trip. I discovered that anyone remaining more than 24 hours in Vietnam would draw combat pay for the month, and as a result many senior officers scheduled 36-hour temporary duty "business" trips to Saigon to qualify. The next day, a C-47, a World War II twin-engine prop cargo plane, was scheduled for a mail run and had plenty of room. Sitting on canvas bags of mail, I arrived in Vietnam on Sunday, 30 January 1966, having spent nine days hitchhiking across the Pacific to go to war.

After landing at Tan Son Nhut airport, reportedly the busiest airport in the world, I made my way to the MACV check-in counter next to the main terminal. An old, beat-up, blue USAF bus transported me to Koelper Compound in downtown Saigon. Koelper was a bachelor officers' quarters (BOQ) for in- and out-processing MACV-assigned officers. The structure of the bus was our first indication we were in a war zone; all windows were covered with a steel mesh to prevent hand grenades from being thrown inside the bus. I and 26 other officers would be spending a week here, in-processing, and getting our final orders, drawing our combat gear, and being briefed on various facets of the war effort.

The excellent briefings added depth to all we had learned at MATA and to our role of the U.S. advisor to teach the Vietnamese soldiers how to use and maintain the equipment and weapons issued by the United States. The briefings began by explaining the U.S. military and MACV structure and the parallel government of Vietnam (GVN) and military structure from the top echelons down to lower Vietnamese military units. We were also educated on the current friendly military and enemy situations. Much time was devoted to the advisory efforts for both combat and combat support.

This was very useful information, especially given the fact that most Vietnamese officers just had a high school education and the enlisted men considerably less. We were also to advise the Vietnamese on proper tactical techniques and act as a liaison with various U.S. support units and resources.

During the middle of the week, MACV commander General William Westmoreland spoke to us and asked if any of the captains had attended West Point while he had been the superintendent from 1960 to 1963. Several men raised their hands, so he spoke personally to each one.

After General Westmoreland left, we received our assignments. Mine was to a sub-sector (a Vietnamese district like a county in the United States) in Quang Nam Province, in the middle of I Corps, the northernmost political and military geographical area in South Vietnam. I would be the assistant sub-sector/district advisor, working for a major, advising both the district regional and popular military forces (like our Army Reserves and National Guard) and working with the civilian government personnel running the district. I saw this as an ideal assignment as I would be working with the local people and thus get to use my Vietnamese language skills, but I would also be involved in combat operations with the local militia.

In I Corps, there were no U.S. Army units but some 40,000 men in the

III U.S. Marine Corps Amphibious Force and the Third Marine Division. There were several ARVN units throughout I Corps, with Quang Nam Province having two ARVN Ranger battalions and the ARVN Fifty-First Infantry Regiment.

On Thursday we drew our combat gear: jungle fatigues, jungle boots, web gear, camouflaged poncho liner, M1 semi-automatic .30-caliber carbine, and 90 rounds of ammunition. The next day I would fly out of Saigon to Da Nang, the largest city in I Corps.

Thus far living in Saigon was not vastly different from living in the United States. Our BOQ had hot and cold running water, a snack bar that served hamburgers, cheeseburgers, French fries, and milkshakes, a TV and three radio stations (U.S. Armed Forces Radio Vietnam and two Vietnamese stations), and three daily newspapers (the military's *Stars and Stripes* and two Vietnamese papers, all in English). The weather in Saigon in January and February was pleasant. While it was warm during the day it was not humid like in North Carolina and Georgia, and a cool breeze was often blowing.

During our ample free time, we began our introduction to Vietnam. The second night in town several of us ventured to a Vietnamese bar across the street from the BOQ. I didn't even buy a drink, but we watched as the bar's "B girls" hustled drinks from the U.S. servicemen in the bar. In about 30 minutes we crossed the street back to the BOQ. Another night I went to the Rex Hotel, a plush BOQ for officers stationed in Saigon. At the top of the hotel was a terrace bar that had a band playing American pop songs. It was fascinating to be leaning on the parapet, high above the city, sipping a cool drink, listening to familiar music while watching the war being fought outside the city. The steady stream of gunship tracers, night bombing runs, artillery strikes, and small-arms ground fire were brightly visible at night, although seeing them seemed unreal, more like watching a movie than viewing actual combat.

All we had read and been told about Saigon described the city as the pearl of the Orient. While this may have been true in the past, the war and influx of displaced refugees had spoiled the beauty of the city. It was filthy, with garbage piled up as high as six feet and open sewers running down the streets. Public works endeavors, such as garbage collection and street maintenance, had been curtailed due to the fighting. Men, women, and children simply urinated in the street gutters, regardless of how many other people were walking around them, and they left a foul smell. It reminded me of another war-torn city in which I had fought my first war: Beirut, Lebanon.

The conditions in Saigon were directly attributable to the surge of people who had been unable to find affordable or habitable housing and had been forced to live in makeshift cardboard and plastic sheet hovels in the alleys. Saigon appeared to be a very moralistic city on the surface. Prostitution was prohibited and there were no pimps around as in some cities in Europe. On the other hand, there were steam baths and massage parlors where girls could be obtained, if desired.

Whenever I had enough time off between briefings during the day, I would walk about three blocks to Nguyen-Hue and Tu Do, two historical streets where shops and restaurants catered to both local residents and U.S. military personnel. On Nguyen-Hue was one of the two United Service Organizations (USOs) in Saigon where it was possible to relax and get some good American food. These walks also provided more opportunities to practice my Vietnamese.

Friday morning, I finished packing all my gear and went to the airport at noon for a C-130 flight to Da Nang, to arrive there about 5:30 p.m. Next, I would report to the headquarters of MACV Advisory Team 1 for two days of tactical briefings before reporting to my sub-sector. Finally, I would be a part of this war and could look forward to testing my skills and knowledge as a combat advisor and earning my CIB.

CHAPTER 4

Da Nang,
My First Assignment

Three of us on the Air Force bus, going to the Tan Son Nhut airport, were destined for I Corps: Mike Miller, a huge airborne-ranger weight-lifter type; Jason Calder, a thin, lanky, quiet man; and myself. We were all infantry captains and had attended MATA and DLI together. Mike was going to the Second Battalion, Fourth Regiment, ARVN Second Infantry Division as the battalion advisor to be stationed at Quang Ngai. Jason, like me, had an assignment as an assistant sub-sector advisor.

At the airport, I saw things I had evidently missed on arrival, what with the excitement of finally being in Vietnam. Air traffic at Tan Son Nhut, the busiest airport in the world, busier than Chicago O'Hare, Los Angeles International, and New York's JFK, was controlled combat style, unlike the smooth flow of traffic at airports in the States. Numerous planes of all types lined up and awaited their departure instructions. Aircraft at Tan Son Nhut varied from FAC O-1E Bird Dogs (forward air controller high-wing tandem two-seater Cessnas) to commercial 707s sporting the logos of Continental, Pan Am, Braniff, and Air France. Intermingled were mammoth USAF transports like the C-141s or the smaller C-54s, C-118s, C-119s, C-123s, and C-130s. Fighters of all sizes and shapes, F-4s, F-5s, F-100s, F-102s, and F-104s, were spread all over the airport, parked in their own protective revetment areas. Smaller olive drab green (OD) painted cargo planes, such as the Army's Caribous and Beavers, were sitting alongside Blue Canoes, the USAF U-3 small twin-engine staff transport and liaison planes, a military version of the Cessna civilian 310 executive aircraft. Helicopters flitted everywhere, from the boxy USAF Kaman HH-43 airport emergency helicopter to the omnipresent Hueys.

Planes departed, seconds apart, two at a time, while other planes were simultaneously vectored in for landings on the same runways. Approaches and departures certainly did not occur in the precise by-the-numbers manner common to America's civil airports. Incoming aircraft came in high, seemingly plunging at the last minute, almost right over the runway. Departing aircraft climbed high fast, making steep turns left or right to quickly move out of the airport control space to make room for more arrivals or departures.

When our turn to depart finally arrived, the old, combat-worn, OD-colored C-130 rumbled down the runway. Strapped into the web seats strung along both sides of the interior, we saw Saigon from the air, as the pilot banked hard left shortly after liftoff. The first leg was northeast to Cam Ranh Bay, then north along the coast to Qui Nhon, our first stop. After dropping off some supplies and people, we headed to our next stop, Da Nang.

At 5:30 p.m. we approached Da Nang, the second largest city in South Vietnam. Peering out a small side window, I saw a large green mountain to our right, jutting out into the deep blue-green South China Sea. South of the mountain was a thin strand of pure white beach, where the sea met the land in wave after wave of white breakers. Just north of the city I saw another large bay and, north of that, additional dark green mountains dropping straight off into the sea. Their tops were snuggled in brilliant white puffy clouds obscuring their uppermost slopes.

Beneath us the white beaches quickly gave way to endless flat rice paddies. Looking west, the fields, inundated with water, were intermittently broken up by either jungle or small hills. Further west were fewer rice fields, and the land had been overtaken by jungle and forest. The ground became steeper, rising rapidly to form the rugged Chaine Annamitique, the Annamite Mountain Range, which peaked at 8,500 feet and ran south along the Laotian border from North Vietnam to its terminus about 50 miles north of Saigon.

God, this is beautiful, I thought. This even had Hawai'i beat: the deep colors, the contrasts between sea and mountains. From 5,000 feet it was hard to fathom so many people were dedicated to only one thing: killing each other.

We approached Da Nang airfield high then dropped down hard and fast, flaring at the last minute rather than crashing onto the ground. Da Nang airfield was a joint U.S.–VN military-civilian facility that seemed like a miniature Ton Son Nhut. The USAF assets included more than 30 types of aircraft from small O-1E Bird Dogs, World War II C-47 transports, and A-1E prop fighters to the most modern fighter planes, such as F-102 Delta Daggers, F-104 Starfighters, F-105 Thunderchief fighter bombers, and F-4C Phantoms.

On the Vietnamese Air Force (VNAF) side of the field, less modern but no less deadly planes of war resided. The 41st VNAF Tactical Wing was based at Da Nang; it soon became the First VNAF Air Division, so designated because of its location in I Corps. VNAF aircraft consisted primarily of the same light observation aircraft as the USAF, C-47 transports, C-123s, and single-seat and two-seat Douglas A-1 Skyraider prop fighters, and several older model helicopters as well as Bell UH-1 Hueys. Several USAF pilots and crew members supported the VNAF as advisors, even flying combat missions with the VNAF. The Vietnamese I Corps headquarters was also located on the airfield on its east side.

A vehicle from the I Corps advisory team headquarters was waiting for us. As it was past 6 p.m., the driver said he would take us to the MACV billeting office and then to the transient BOQ, where we would be staying during our in-processing. Jason and I each had a single duffle bag. Mike had two; one similar to ours contained clothes and a second bag held 150 pounds of weights and a long metal bar for weightlifting. I knew what was about to happen because I had watched Mike get his bags in Saigon. Grabbing his clothing bag, Mike asked the driver to get his other bag. The slight Spec 4 couldn't lift it. Mike tossed the bag he was holding in the back of the Jeep as easily as one would a basketball, and then leaned against the Jeep, asking the struggling Spec 4 if he was having problems with the duffle bag. The poor driver, who couldn't get the bag off the ground, turned red from both the potentially hernia-producing strain and embarrassment. Mike, grabbing it with both hands, deftly deposited it in the back seat, and then nonchalantly climbed in next to it.

After signing for our rooms, we were taken to the transient BOQ, where we left our gear, and then the driver dropped us off at the Officer's Club for supper. Before leaving, the driver said he would pick us up at the BOQ at 8:00 the next morning.

After a supper of steak and French fries, we went to the bar. Our lack of tan and jungle fatigues (we were still wearing our regular fatigues until we got our name tags, patches, and insignia sewed on our jackets) announced to the crowd we had just arrived. The customers were an odd mix of officers from all branches of the military. Most were Army and Air Force advisors working with ARVN or VNAF forces and some were U.S. Navy support personnel providing logistical assistance for the United States Marine Corps (USMC) III Marine Amphibious Force (MAF) headquarters west of the air base. Less numerous were USMC officers in Da Nang on business from III MAF, U.S. Agency for International Development (USAID) civilians, and the press. The crowd ran the gamut from overweight, overdrinking rear-echelon field-grade advisors to the lean, tan young Marine platoon commanders getting a respite from the fighting.

After a few drinks and hearing a dozen different versions of the war in I Corps, we left. But it was scary getting back to our quarters. Here we were, combat-ready troopers in a city in a combat zone at night, yet not one of us was armed since we had been told to leave our carbines in our locked rooms. We were too embarrassed to acknowledge our anxiety to each other as we quickly and silently made our way down the street to our BOQ just a couple hundred yards away. As we reached our abode, we collectively relaxed and went to our separate rooms.

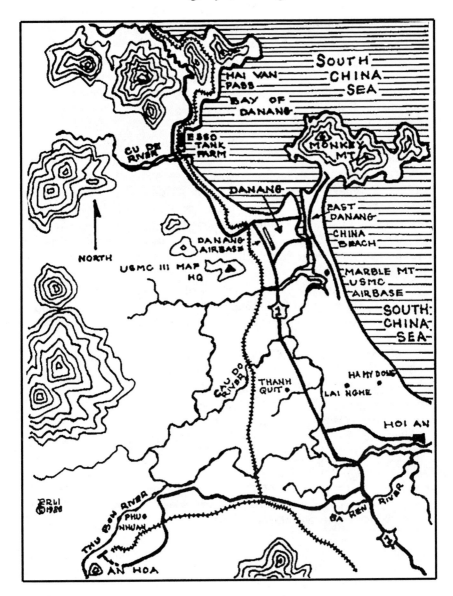

Da Nang Area

For my first night I met my roommate, a U.S. Navy officer who was on his way back to the States. After we exchanged names and backgrounds, I inquired about the safety of walking around Da Nang at night. Although he had not been stationed in the city, he guessed there was no real danger, especially around this end of town where most of the U.S. activities were located.

When I asked what kind of a weapon he had, he pulled out a large-frame, well-worn Smith & Wesson .38 Special revolver with a short barrel. He said the Navy had issued him an M-14 semiautomatic rifle, but it was too cumbersome, so he had bought the Smith & Wesson.

This is a neat gun, he offered, asking if I wanted to buy it.

Looking at the revolver, I recognized it as a square-butt version of the M&P model with a two-inch barrel, the same as those issued to our USAF pilots. I thought it would bring $50 or $60 back in the States.

Asking how well it shot, I knew what his answer would be. He replied he didn't know since he never fired it. The gun had a light covering of surface rust on it, common on weapons in the humid tropics. I pointed out it was pretty rusty, and the Vietnamese army, which I would be with, didn't have .38-caliber ammo, only .45. Putting the handgun back on his bunk, I told him I was not too sure about this gun because he didn't know how it shot so it was probably not worth too much. He said he would give me the gun, the holster, and about 50 bullets all for $5.

I almost fell off my bunk. If the rest of my tour turned out as good as this deal, I'd have it made, I thought. The officer passed the pistol, holster, and a sock full of ammo over to my bunk, and I gave him a five-dollar bill.

The next morning at 8:00 we were ready to be picked up by the driver. In addition to our normal fatigue uniforms, we wore our web belts, first aid kits, and magazine pouches, and we carried our carbines. We sure looked like we were going either bear hunting or off to war.

The Spec 4 driver, armed only with a .45-caliber service pistol, snickered as we jumped into the Jeep. Jason and I hopped into the back as Mike filled the entire shotgun seat in front. A massive man with biceps as big as my thighs, he turned slowly to the driver and deliberately asked him how many times had he gotten his ass shot up.

The young Spec 4 began to squirm in his seat, looking up at the giant captain glowering down at him and replied, stuttering, "Ah—ah—uh—never, sir."

Still looking fierce, Mike quietly explained that he had been shot at and he sure as shit didn't like it. So, he intoned, if the Spec 4 really didn't mind, Mike would just stay armed.

The driver mumbled, "Yes, sir," as he let the clutch out too fast and stalled the Jeep.

I saw the back of his neck and ears turn a bright red as he ground on the starter, trying to get us to I Corps headquarters and out of his hair as quickly as possible. I felt sorry for him, thinking that Mike had been a little hard on him.

Mike had been a company commander with the Eighty-Second Airborne

Division last year when they had gone into Dominican Republic. In the six weeks the U.S. Army and Marines were in the Dominican Republic, several small firefights had ensued resulting in the deaths of about 18 U.S. troops and the wounding of about 60 more. I had received my baptism of fire in another part of the world, in Lebanon, in 1958. The poor driver had no way of knowing that while Mike and I were neophytes to Vietnam we were not experiencing war for the first time.

Even though it was a Saturday, all the I Corps advisory team offices were open. I Corps headquarters, on the east side of the air base closest to DaNang, was in a beautiful old yellowish French compound trimmed in a reddish brown. The stately two-story quadrangle was a heavily guarded fortress. Concrete and dirt bunkers without tops were scattered around the compound, each designed to hold a single communications truck to protect it against shrapnel from a mortar attack or small-arms ground fire.

We would receive our briefings this morning and later meet with the I Corps deputy senior advisor, U.S. Army colonel Andy Hamilton. We were told that the war, as waged by U.S. and GVN forces, had two main thrusts in I Corps. One was to eliminate the enemy from the prime agricultural areas within the central lowlands along the coast. The second was to protect the land and the people from the enemy while supporting rural development. Essentially, the double thrust was to first, using military assets, destroy the enemy, and second, using both military and civilian resources, pacify and retain the area. The leaders at the top were Major General Lewis W. Walt, commanding general of the III MAF and I Corps senior advisor; Vietnamese lieutenant general Nguyen Chanh Thi, commanding general of the I Corps Tactical Zone; and Colonel Hamilton, I Corps deputy senior advisor.

Most of the units the USMC were facing were local Viet Cong (VC) guerrillas. There were, though, some major enemy units in I Corps. The 325A NVA Division was on the I Corps southern border, along with the Thirty-Sixth NVA Regiment and the First Viet Cong Regiment. Just outside of Da Nang was the R-20 or Doc Lap Viet Cong Battalion. Major ARVN assets in I Corps were the First and Second ARVN Divisions, the independent Fifty-First ARVN Regiment, and two ARVN light infantry ranger battalions. Altogether General Thi commanded some 60,000 soldiers consisting of 25,000 ARVN, 12,000 regional forces (RF), and 23,000 popular forces (PF).

The USMC assets were the III MAF, headquartered on Hill 327, just west of Da Nang, and all of its tactical and support units. These units included the Third Marine Division (the Third, Fourth, and Ninth Regiments), the First and Seventh Regiments (which joined the First Marine Division), seven artillery battalions, two armor battalions, a recon battalion, and separate recon company, three engineer battalions, a medical battalion, two motor transport battalions, and two service battalions. Air assets included several fixed-wing and rotary-wing squadrons based at Chu Lai, Da Nang, and Marble Mountain on the coast just southeast of Da Nang.

Our briefings on I Corps ended about mid-afternoon when we met with Colonel Hamilton. He had the personnel files of all three of us on his desk. He explained that as usually happens, Saigon was not up to date on the personnel needs in I Corps. The positions on our orders were no longer vacant. They were already filled. What advisory slots that were available for infantry captains, he pointed out, were the Third Battalion, Fifty-First Regiment at Hoi An; second, a different battalion in the ARVN Second Division; and third, the position of the deputy senior advisor for Da Nang garrison.

Addressing Captain Miller, he continued that he had read his personnel file and saw no reason why he should not join the Second ARVN Division as originally planned, except with a different battalion.

"Yes, sir," Mike almost shouted, happy to be with an ARVN combat unit.

Turning to Jason and myself, Colonel Hamilton explained about the other two assignments. The ARVN Fifty-First Regiment was an independent regiment consisting of three light infantry battalions. The ARVN First Division, probably the best ARVN Division throughout Vietnam, was in the top two I Corps provinces. The southernmost two provinces in I Corps were under control of the ARVN Second Division. Quang Nam Province, in the middle, was the combat area of the Fifty-First Regiment, based in Hoi An, about 20 miles south.

He explained that Da Nang garrison was a special organization. Da Nang had its own little army, because it is an autonomous city. Its mission was to provide security for the city.

Colonel Hamilton continued, stressing the fact that both positions fell under the advisory criteria MACV has established for being awarded the Combat Infantryman Badge (CIB). He asked Jason and I where each of us wanted to go.

Jason immediately began to tell the colonel why he should get the Fifty-First Regiment, describing in detail his background, experience, and special skills. As I listened, I realized that if the colonel had read my file he'd know that my background included a lot more than what Jason had just stated, and that my qualifications far exceeded his. Not wanting to brag I simply told the colonel I wanted the Third Battalion and that my record reflected my qualifications for the position. He asked Captain Calder if he wanted to say anything else.

Jason said yes and made his pitch a second time.

Laughing, the colonel told Calder he was convinced. Calder got the battalion and Worthington got Da Nang garrison.

I learned a lesson the hard way that day, one that has remained with me from that day forward: never expect someone else to promote you for

Da Nang garrison headquarters where I was senior tactical advisor to ARVN troops responsible for the security of the city.

something you really want but depend only on yourself to get it. I now know that that's how life works.

The next morning Mike got a C-123 flight down to Quang Ngai to join the ARVN Second Division. I never heard what happened to him after that. He was the only soldier I knew that went to war carrying 150 pounds of weights in a spare duffle bag.

Jason and I were transported to Hoi An via an armed Bell UH-1B Huey helicopter. In the morning we met with various Quang Nam Province staff advisors and the senior sector advisor, Lieutenant Colonel Cranston. Cranston explained that Jason's job would be a field assignment and he could expect to leave the battalion in about six months for a staff position. On the other hand, he said, I could also expect to leave Da Nang garrison in the same time frame and get a field assignment.

I asked how it could be a staff position when Colonel Hamilton said the garrison position was a job where I could earn the CIB. Lieutenant Colonel Cranston said the difference in a field or staff position was not as much what you did as where you did it.

The Da Nang garrison position, he explained, was by MACV directive a tactical position calling for an infantry captain to advise Vietnamese infantry units. As such one would be eligible for the CIB if the combat engagement criteria were met. He continued to explain the reason it was not a field assignment was because I would be living in a BOQ in Da Nang and eating in the officers' mess at the Da Nang officers' club. Calder, on the other hand, would be living and eating in the field with the ARVN battalion. What we had learned was that the field advisors found it difficult to remain healthy if they stayed with a Vietnamese unit much beyond six months.

My boss would be Major Braun, an artillery officer. He had been the senior advisor for Da Nang garrison for about seven months and most likely would stay in that assignment because there were no other field positions for majors at the time.

After Calder and I ate lunch we were escorted to the MACV advisors' lounge by a staff captain. This was the advisory team social hall, where most advisors congregated for relaxation when not busy at their job. In one corner was a bar made of bamboo and woven rattan. Bottles of hard liquor lined the shelves on the back wall, and cold beer and soda were stored in an ancient refrigerator in the corner behind the bar. A small Vietnamese man dressed in a white long-sleeved shirt, dark slacks, and sandals tended the bar. Instead of taking money for drinks, he kept a running tab for all the advisors.

The captain asked us if we wanted a beer or soda. After ordering with us, he told the bartender to put them on his tab. Two men in shower shoes, cut-off fatigues, and green T-shirts were throwing darts at a cork bulls-eye on one wall. One man was writing a letter and a couple more were reading. Some others were playing bridge.

Before we had finished our drinks, two majors came in laughing. One commented on how dark it was in here, asking why the lounge lizards didn't open some windows so the working class could see. One major ordered a beer for himself and his companion, then turned to meet the two new captains, reflecting that they must be the new meat.

I introduced myself to the major whose nametag said Braun. Jason introduced himself to his new boss. Small talk about our backgrounds and the States ensued while we finished our drinks. Major Braun announced that our helicopter would be leaving in a few minutes, so we should start going out to the chopper pad. Saying good-bye, Jason and I wished each other luck in our new assignments.

Moving beside my new major, I sized him up. His dark, close-cropped hair, thick five o'clock shadow, and name clearly suggested a European background. Later I found out he had been raised and educated in the East. He wasn't dressed in jungle fatigues; instead he wore regular fatigues with the sleeves cut off short and hemmed. His U.S. Army patch and name tag were black letters on OD tape. The oak leaf on his collar was gold cloth as was his field artillery insignia. Above his left pocket, over the U.S. Army tape, was sewn a blue and white cloth CIB. With his black-framed sunglasses and bright metal wristwatch, he did not seem to me to be dressed like a field advisor. A large man, about two inches taller than my five feet, ten inches, he appeared to have not lost weight during his tour of duty in Vietnam. Heavy jowls and a thick torso did not make him appear overweight, though: just well fed. Even white teeth and a flashing smile suggested he was an okay guy. If first appearances counted for anything, I thought we ought to get along well.

The helicopter took us back to I Corps Headquarters, where Major Braun kept his Jeep. I became aware that all the advisory and ARVN Jeeps were the same, but they weren't really military Jeeps. They were OD in color and had blackout drive lights, extra batteries for radio connections, and military non-directional tires, but they were actually civilian Jeeps built primarily as military aid program vehicles for export by the U.S. military to our allies who needed military equipment.

On the way back to downtown Da Nang, Major Braun explained my job. His first name was Rick, but I always called him major or sir. The major said that my position was presently occupied by a Marine infantry captain who was due to rotate next month. He would be with us for only one more week, then he had a three-week special assignment escorting the movie actor Robert Mitchum around Vietnam. When he completed that assignment, he would have less than a week left to out-process.

Major Braun explained that my job as deputy senior advisor for the garrison was one of assisting the senior advisor and advising the tactical elements of the northern command of Quang Nam sector. I would be responsible for assisting and advising in the planning and conducting of ARVN counterinsurgency operations in the area from Da Nang north to the border of Thua Thien sector. My counterpart would be the operations officer at Da Nang garrison, who was responsible for all military and police operations to ensure the security of Da Nang. The operations officer was Major Bich and his assistant was Captain Phiem. The ARVN operations officer had at his command six RF companies and 11 PF platoons, which occupied key defensive positions around Da Nang and along Route 1 up to the Thua Thien border at Hai Van Mountain Pass, a spur of the Annamite chain from the Laotian border. Another important part of my job would be to effect coordination with the Third U.S. Marine Division. Driving through the city, Major Braun went straight to Da Nang garrison where the Marine captain, Sam Prince, was waiting for me. Tall, blond, balding, lean and leathery, Captain Prince had to be at least 15 years older than me and I was 28, while Major Braun was in his early 30s.

Major Braun said Sam would take me to the MACV billeting office, where I would get a permanent BOQ. After some more kind words about being pleased to have me join the team, he left. Captain Prince had been a senior NCO in the Marines. In fact, when I was a Marine corporal in the late 1950s, he had been a staff sergeant. He had later received a commission and expected to make major next year. He had more than 20 years of active duty and planned to retire in a few more years. He seemed to be a friendly man and I didn't think we would have any problems.

Picking up my gear at the transient BOQ, we went back to MACV billeting so I could get a permanent room. Soon I was assigned a room at the opposite end of the city on Bach Dang Street which parallels the Han River. The BOQ, which had been a four-story French hotel, now housed American advisor officers.

After moving my gear into my ground-floor room, I found I had a roommate: an Air Force captain, Al Lorry, an advisor to the VN air force, who was out. Captain Prince asked if I had everything I needed, especially combat gear. I answered in the affirmative and inquired why he had asked. He replied that tomorrow morning he would pick me up here at 4:00 to go on my first operation. I spent part of the night feeling both curious about and eager to participate in whatever the next day would bring, hoping I was well prepared for any challenge.

CHAPTER 5

Duty in
Da Nang Garrison

At 4:00 a.m., Captain Prince was outside waiting in his Jeep. As we drove to the Da Nang garrison headquarters he explained that the operation this day would be a battalion-sized search and destroy mission south of the city. Two RF companies and two PF platoons would be used. The operation would be controlled by Major Bich, the Da Nang garrison operations officer. The role of the advisors (Captain Prince, me, one of our NCOs, and a USMC liaison lieutenant and his radio operator) would be to assist in any medical evacuations and to provide USMC artillery support.

At the advisory offices, I met our NCO, Staff Sergeant Billstone. The fourth member of the Da Nang garrison advisory team was Spec 5 Kurtz, who was not present. Our interpreter, Ham, a chunky Vietnamese sergeant, with long, unruly hair and a puffy body who appeared more like a street hustler than a soldier, was also there as were the Marine lieutenant and his radio operator. Ham didn't look military.

At 4:30 all the vehicles were lined up and ready to go. It was still dark when our small convoy left. The lead vehicle was a Jeep driven by Major Bich, to whom I had been briefly introduced before we departed. Next was Captain Prince's Jeep with our driver, Captain Prince, myself, and Sergeant Ham, followed by the Marine liaison Jeep with Sergeant Billstone. The last vehicle was an ARVN two-and-a-half-ton cargo truck loaded with soldiers from the garrison.

Our route took us out of town to a grassy area surrounded by tall trees where the major explained what the operation intended to accomplish. Using his map, he pointed out where the two RF companies were and the area they would sweep, mostly rice paddies. The two companies would follow parallel tracks in a horseshoe-shaped pattern. They would leave the road, move east, maneuver to the south, and then swing west back again to the road. The two PF platoons would go south down the road to pick up any stragglers trying to escape by the road. It was a one-day operation, designed to terminate by late afternoon.

Our position was initially about 1,000 meters away—so far, in fact, that we couldn't even hear any gunshots. There were no U.S. advisors with the maneuver units. The day was boring, not unlike a command post exercise (CPX) back in the States, the field exercise where a headquarters staff functioned as a command and control group based on radio message input from evaluators. The time was spent recording positions and situation reports as they were radioed in by the field units moving across the rice fields. Everyone performed their duties in an unexcited, detached manner, indicating that what was happening was a common occurrence. Events and times were logged, questions asked and answered over the radio, movements plotted on the operations map, and pocketbooks read.

Security for our command group was lax. Two ARVN soldiers armed with M1 Garand rifles lounged at the side of the road, ready to challenge anyone who might want to enter our small, tree-shaded area.

I observed, asked hundreds of questions, and formed some impressions of what was transpiring. First, we were apparently never in any dangerous position. Second, the operation was carried out just like the Fort Benning infantry school taught. And third, this was a dull way to fight a war with absolutely no action. I was extremely disappointed that there was no combat.

When I talked alone to Sergeant Billstone, who had been awarded his CIB, his suggestion was to relax and enjoy the war. Sure, it would very quickly become tedious, uninteresting, and repetitive, and, as he pointed out, it would be a safe way to earn my CIB.

I asked what he meant.

He commented about the MACV regs. He explained that U.S. advisors not assigned to ARVN combat infantry units would be eligible for the CIB if they served as part of an infantry unit, battalion-sized or smaller, that conducted combat operations and made contact with the enemy. To get the CIB you had to be in at least six of these operations covering at least 30 days.

For today, he continued, our RF companies had made contact at least twice—I had one operation down and five more to go to get my CIB. I countered that we were not in any danger. No one has shot at us. We were so far away we couldn't even hear any gunfire. So how could this be eligible for the CIB?

Exasperated, the sergeant pointed out that we didn't make the regs, we only went by them. We were advising the commander of a battalion-sized combat operation that had exchanged fire with the VC, so the operation counted toward the CIB. That's the way it was. That's how he got his CIB. That's how Kurtz got his and that's how Major Braun got his. In about four months, that's how I would get mine. Shaking my head, I left the sergeant to return to his paperback book.

Captain Prince saw the operation from a more stimulating perspective. While the advisors were not needed today, he explained in his professorial manner, in the event the maneuvering units came upon a tenacious foe desiring to engage the RF or PF troops, the advisors could then become a very important part of the battle by coordinating the use of American artillery or air support if it was needed to dislodge or defeat the VC. He continued to explain that if some ARVN soldiers were wounded and needed helicopter medical evacuation, we advisors would also coordinate that.

Obviously, Captain Prince did not view his role as an advisor the same way I did with my belief in doing everything personally possible to directly affect a fortuitous outcome. When pressed on how close the advisors actually came to the action, Captain Prince was silent momentarily.

Thoughtfully he reflected on his past. When he first arrived almost a year ago, most of the combat operations around Da Nang were carried out by these RF and PF units. As his tour had passed, the build-up of Marines in the area had decreased the type and amount of Vietnamese operations he went on. In the past four or five months he had not physically been with any unit from Da Nang garrison that had been shot at. To be perfectly honest, he said, he doubted if I would either.

By the time the operation terminated at 4 p.m., I had become quite disillusioned. The operation had resulted in four contacts with the VC, one RF soldier killed, and no VC killed, wounded or captured. I was so far removed from the action I had heard and seen nothing. It didn't seem fair. I had come so far to fight, and now I was being denied the opportunity.

The next few days were busy. One day I took a driver's test to get my Vietnam driver's license. That night I attended a Vietnamese version of our USO shows: a variety show for the local ARVN, RF, and PF soldiers with 20 acts, put on by the Central Cultural Group, a Vietnamese traveling theater group. The show was presented in the Trung-Vuong Theater in Da Nang with Lieutenant General Nguyen Chanh Thi, the commanding general of I Corps, acting as the master of ceremonies. As one of the garrison advisors, I was invited to attend as the guest of Lieutenant Colonel Tu, Da Nang garrison commander and Major Braun's counterpart.

The show was a highly professional program and entertaining. Even though it was totally in Vietnamese, my program was in English, so I had no problem understanding what was being done. The acts included songs, folk and Western-style dances, traditional Vietnamese music and some Western music as well as magic and comedy acts. The main purpose of such traveling cultural entertainment teams was political. They were used to foster support for the Saigon government by embracing traditional culture and by sharing it with the local people, many of whom had never seen live, professional theater. The actresses were young and pretty, while the actors were young and handsome. Their costumes reflected the traditional Vietnamese dress with "big city" or Western dress forbidden. Though the show was enjoyable, attending it certainly did not fit into my concept of the war in Vietnam.

One afternoon during my first week in Da Nang we received a tip that several VC would be meeting in a house in East Da Nang, just across the river, early that night. Immediately an operation was set up. RF troops would cordon off a large area of several blocks. The police, using boats, would begin a house to house search looking for people in the dwellings who didn't live there, ascertained by checking ID cards. I was asked to go along with the police and an ARVN captain from Da Nang garrison.

About an hour after dark, the soldiers had the target area sealed off. We loaded into small boats and crossed the river to begin our search. The quarter we were going to was a residential area for people from the urban upper lower class to the lower middle class: a segment of Vietnamese society that still retained most of the traditional customs of their lives. What I learned about the personal nighttime habits of the Vietnamese during the operation surprised me. We probably searched 20 to 30 houses, in which people were already asleep. Everyone was sleeping in the clothes they had worn during the day. No one was sleeping in their underwear, pajamas, or naked. Male occupants slept in one part of the house, females in another. Not once did we come upon any bed or sleeping mat where couples, male and female, were sleeping together. The men were found mostly in the front part of the houses, the living areas, while the women were found in the rear, the family sleeping areas. As was common in this culture, households held extended families with two or three generations sharing the same space.

Interpersonal family relationships as practiced by this class of Vietnamese were unlike anything I had known in the United States. Vietnamese marriages were more social than personal relationships, based on compatible horoscopes and the practical enhancements the couple would bring to their respective families. Courtship was more of a formal, businesslike ritual than a blooming of love. Consummation of the marriage might not even occur for several nights, reflecting the bride's reluctance. In fact, sometimes, once the marriage was consummated by intercourse, the bride would return to her parents until the husband wanted her again.

By the time our search was completed, we had arrested one young girl who had no ID, ten suspected VC, and two young men who did not belong in Da Nang. Despite the lack of the action during the operation on my first day, I hoped there would be more future operations to keep me interested and challenged. I now spent time acquainting myself with Da Nang and the

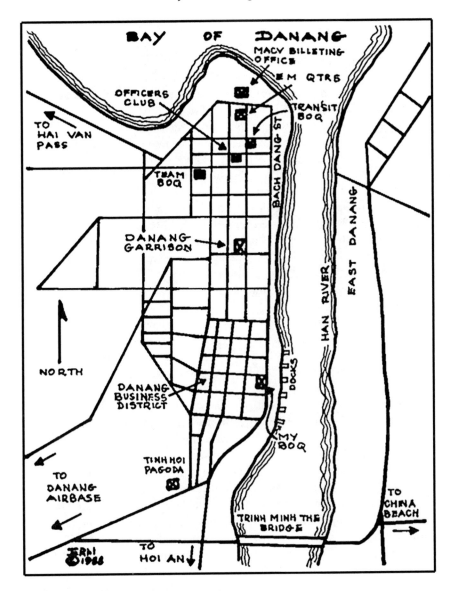

City of Da Nang

function of the Da Nang garrison, which was to protect the city and secure the railroad through the surrounding mountains.

I learned the following facts about Da Nang. The city, with a population of 300,000, lay at the southeastern corner of the large Da Nang Bay where the Han River joined the sea. The central part of the city was on the west bank of the river. Across the Han River was East Da Nang, where houses lined the riverbank; however, just east of the houses the area became rural farmland. Providing pedestrian and vehicular access between the two was the Trinh Minh The Bridge on the south side of Da Nang. The countryside surrounding Da Nang was beautiful, with almost every type of geographical feature found in South Vietnam lying within a few miles of the city.

Northeast of the city, north of the Han River estuary, was Tiensha Peninsula, a large, egg-shaped mass connected to the mainland by a narrow neck of sand. On the peninsula was Monkey Mountain, rapidly rising to a height of almost 2,300 feet. While populated mostly by monkeys, the mountain was still within the Da Nang city limits.

Western ships first visited Da Nang Harbor in 1535, but serious oceanic trading did not begin until the mid–1800s. In 1888, after sporadic fighting for more than 30 years, the French gained control of the city, renaming it Tourane. It remained under French control until the Japanese took the city at the beginning of World War II. After the war, the French returned in the mid–1940s. In 1950, under an international agreement, the city reverted to the Vietnamese.

Northwest of the city, on the northwest curve of Da Nang Bay, was another set of tall mountains, seemingly dropping right out of the sky into the bay on its south side and the South China Sea on its north. These mountains, Nui Hai Van (Mountains of Large Clouds), had been so named because the tops were often covered with clouds. Thickly forested, the steep mountains effectively separated Quang Nam sector from Thua Tien sector.

There were two major land transportation routes out of Da Nang: the national highway, Route 1, and the single track, narrow-gauge Vietnamese Railway. These two routes went in two directions, north to Hue or south to Hoi An and eventually to Saigon. This 689-mile route paralleled the coast from Dong Ha in the north, just south of the demarcation line, to Saigon in the south. The portion that was most operable was the line from Da Nang south to Nha Trang. The train ran occasionally from Da Nang north to Hue going through four tunnels to pass through the Hai Van Mountains northwest of Da Nang. In 1964 the Vietnam railway system moved almost 500,000 tons of freight and two million people.

Security of the railroad through these mountains was the responsibility of Da Nang garrison. U.S. Army Transportation Corps advisors had helped the Vietnamese plan the defense of the railroad. A three-dimensional system had been devised whereby defense up and down the track was provided by eight companies of civil guards, defense in height was provided by VNAF and USAF air support, and defense in depth, such as for bridges and potential ambush sites, was provided by local ARVN RF or PF units.

In addition, at the front of a typical eight- to 12-car train were up to three empty flatbed "sleepers," heavily weighted railway cars used to detonate any pressure-type along the track before the General Electric diesel-electric locomotives, valued at $133,000, passed over them.

Other sources of protection were wicker trolleys, armored, diesel-powered railroad vehicles armed with .30-caliber machine gun turrets on their tops that preceded the trains to provide security en route, a British innovation developed to safeguard Malaysian railroads during the Communist uprising.

From Da Nang, following the shore of Da Nang Bay to the foothills of the Hai Van Mountains, the railroad tracks and Route 1 ran side by side. At this point Route 1 went straight up the mountain through what the French called Col Des Nuages, Pass of the Clouds, while the railroad track moved around the mountain's eastern slope, passing through four tunnels before arriving on the northern side of the mountain. Even with several French fortresses and massive concrete bunkers guarding the bridges, passes, and tunnels, the 120 inches of annual rainfall made the vegetation so thick that concealment of enemy ambush positions was very easy.

I'm pictured here as tactical advisor for the ARVN troops responsible for the security of Da Nang with my counterpart, Capt. Phiem of Da Nang garrison, in charge of all the troops guarding the city.

Shortly after my arrival Captain Phiem, the Da Nang garrison assistant operations officer asked me to accompany him on a trip to the Two Hundred Fifty-First RF Company on the top of Hai Van Pass. The distance to the mountaintop was about 21 miles from Da Nang.

Captain Phiem, from a middle-class Catholic family, was of average size, his hair long enough to comb and neatly trimmed. He was well educated and multilingual, able to speak French, Vietnamese, and adequate English, and he had everything in place, looking like a nice, nonaggressive career staff officer in anybody's army.

Leaving the city, we passed by a large cemetery across from which was Red Beach, where the U.S. Ninth Marine Expeditionary Brigade had made amphibious assaults almost a year before. The invading Americans had been met by attractive young ladies dressed in flowing ao dais (trousers worn with a tight top with long, flowing front and back panels) proffering flowers. What had been planned as an inconspicuous entry of U.S. Marines to Vietnam had become an international Associated Press story as the combat troops had been greeted by the young ladies and their chagrined, flower-bedecked commander, Brigadier General Frederick Karch.

About eight miles further, beyond another extensive cemetery, we encountered the first contingent of Vietnamese forces. A PF platoon was stationed at the Nam O Bridge over the Cu De River to protect the vehicular traffic bridge, the railroad bridge, and a nearby ARVN artillery unit. Located on the far side of the bridge, the artillery unit had two 155 mm Howitzers. Its mission was to provide fire support for Vietnamese operations in the Hai Van Mountains.

Almost two miles north of the Nam O Bridge was the ESSO gasoline depot at Lien Chieu, a very vulnerable target that was heavily guarded by a PF platoon. In addition, two massive old French concrete bunkers built on Hill 358 (so named because the top of the hill was 358 meters above sea level, 1,164 feet), overlooking the ESSO depot, were home to a platoon of the Two Hundred Fifty-First RF Company, commanded by Warrant Officer Sang.

While showing me around, Warrant Officer Sang, speaking in English, pointed to a mountain stream flowing past the bunkers, explaining that the VC would come down the stream to ambush soldiers of his company. But yesterday, he continued, his soldiers saw and shot a big "con meo."

Not understanding what he was talking about, I voiced my confusion. Sang then hunched his back, made hissing and growling noises as he pawed the air, forming his fingers into claws. I thought, con meo—Vietnamese for cat. I asked if he meant a tiger—like a big cat? "Yes," he said, grinning and pleased I could understand his English as well as understand his language. He explained that his soldiers shot at a big tiger but missed, so the tiger ran away.

An aerial view of the top of Hai Van Pass. The ARVN outpost is seen in the middle right of the photograph. The division on the road, separating the traffic from each side of the mountain, is seen at the top left.

As we walked back toward the drive where our Jeeps were parked I noted several small grass structures about the size of U.S. Army pup tents and asked what they were. Warrant Officer Sang explained they were shelters in which the soldiers slept. When it rained, they covered them with clear plastic.

Climbing into the back of Captain Phiem's Jeep, I said good-bye to

Warrant Officer Sang and thanked him for the tour. As we continued up the mountain to the top of Hai Van Pass, I reflected on how my ability to speak Vietnamese was an advantage in Da Nang. Of the five advisors on the team, I was the only one who had had any formal Vietnamese language training. Major Braun spoke no Vietnamese or French; Captain Prince only knew a few phrases of Vietnamese; and the two NCOs spoke only a little Vietnamese. I had soon discovered, as I had in both the Middle East and in southern Europe when with the Marines, that people here had more respect for Americans who had taken the time to learn their language. Eight years before I had been fairly fluent in French. My efforts to speak Vietnamese had been richly rewarded as soldiers, their families, merchants, and even the BOQ maids had taken time to help me improve my ability.

The view from the ARVN outpost (an old French fort) at the top of Hai Van Pass. The buildings were mostly small restaurants. The road crossing the mountain was narrow, just a single lane, so traffic went up the mountain on each side at the same time, stopping at the top of the Pass. Then, while traffic was stopped at the bottom of the mountain on each side, the traffic at the top began its journey down the mountain on each side. The danger was that the Viet Cong would ambush the traffic about halfway up or down the mountain, making it very difficult for rescue troops to get to an ambush site. The road to the right in this photograph, going down the mountain, is where an ambush killed several American military advisors and their weekend girlfriends. I was with the ARVN reaction force (but we were too late and never caught the VC).

The Vietnamese commander of all ARVN troops providing security for Hai Van Pass, shown here at the top of the Pass. The restaurant behind him is where I ate all my meals when visiting the troops at the Pass.

Halfway up the mountain we became part of a line of vehicles waiting for the southbound traffic to stop. Once the steep and curvy road was clear, the soldiers motioned the vehicles forward to go up the mountain. The scenery was breathtaking; we saw clouds touching the tops of the peaks on both sides. At the top was a small community with traffic flowing up or down on both sides of the mountain simultaneously. Thus, southbound traffic could begin its ascent from the northern side of the mountain while northbound traffic ascended from the south. When all traffic from both sides of the mountain had reached the top, the southbound convoy went down the south slope while the northbound traffic descended the north side. The soldiers stationed at Hai Van Pass controlled the traffic flow.

Nine restaurants were available at the top, catering to the travelers as well as a hand-operated lumber mill, its wood provided by the thick jungle forests. On the eastern side of the roadway, above the lumber mill and restaurants, was an old French fortress with numerous stone, brick, and concrete buildings surrounded by multiple rings of barbed wire fences and rolls of concertina wire. On sunny days this fence became a community clothesline as uniforms, socks, and underwear festooned the perimeter.

Within the fortress were machine gun towers equipped with light .30-caliber machine guns mounted on tripods. An 81 mm mortar was in a pit in the middle. Inside the back of the fortress was a fire arrow, a four-foot-long board shaped like an arrow with small cans of sand on it. During an attack, the cans of sand were filled with gasoline and lit, with the point turned toward the attackers to let gunships know where the enemy was. Just beyond the rear of the fort, on top of a hill, the ground was leveled for a heliport. Many of the soldiers' wives and children lived at the pass, and some spouses worked in the restaurants or the lumber mill.

After a noodle soup lunch in one of the restaurants, I toured the fortress with First Lieutenant Lieu, the commanding officer of the Two Hundred Fifty-First RF Company and the pass commander. He explained to me that on the other side of Hai Van Pass, on the north slope referred to as Hai Van II, was a second RF company with its own commander who reported to Lieutenant Lieu when he acted in the capacity of pass commander.

Lieutenant Lieu claimed that he had never heard of the fortress being attacked. Instead, the VC ambushed convoys going up the mountain since the vehicles ascending moved slower and were easier targets. The VC also mined the railroad tracks and ambushed the trains.

The job of the RF company was to secure the highway and railroad, protect the top of the pass, and react to VC ambushes. Protection was provided by constant sweeps of the mountain on both sides of the roads and the rail tracks.

The biggest problem the company had in reacting was maneuvering through the rugged terrain. Even if an ambush occurred only a mile away, it could take the reaction force 20 minutes or longer to get there. By then the enemy would be up one of the stream beds that led back into the mountains. Pursuit was generally a waste of time, and men in helicopters couldn't see through the dense foliage to detect enemy movement. The best defense seemed to send out small roving patrols to keep the attacks down, but such patrols did not eliminate the harassment entirely. That afternoon, after expressing admiration for the excellent defensive posture of the company, we returned to Da Nang.

The next morning Captain Phiem took me to East Da Nang. We went to the PF headquarters, a concrete block and stucco building with a tin roof surrounded by a tall concrete fence. Since much of East Da Nang was an extension of the beach along the South China Sea, most roads and the terrain were very sandy, the entrance was manned by a guard armed with an M1 carbine, hanging on his shoulder by a sling.

We visited the other PF units, all located in nice buildings, many surrounded by large shade trees. Most rural hamlets in East Da Nang had a PF platoon. I noticed that any land that was not sandy or didn't have buildings erected on it was planted with rice.

Captain Phiem explained that this area was fairly secure during the day-time, but at night the local VC controlled it. Platoon- and company-size operations were common in this area because a village could be easily surrounded in the dark hours of early morning, allowing the police to search every household, looking for people without proper IDs or with weapons, ammunition or enemy documents.

As we drove down to the sea, Captain Phiem pointed out China Beach, a long stretch of pure white sand disappearing beneath the frothy white-capped waves of the clear, green water. On the road running along the beach were several nice-looking restaurants with bars. Shrimp or fish dishes served with cold beer seemed to be the main fare. Also along the beach were the small but expensive-looking vacation homes belonging to Da Nang's wealthier citizens. Among these was the cottage of Marine General Walt.

After eating lunch in one of the local restaurants, Captain Phiem said we would next go to Cau Do, the Red Bridge on the Cau Do River about two miles south of Da Nang air base. The bridge was guarded by a platoon from an RF company, but a U.S. Marine platoon was also stationed on the bridge to provide security for a marine water purification plant next to the river.

The long metal bridge on Route 541 carried both vehicular traffic and trains. Route 541 branched off from Route 1 at the northwest corner of Da Nang air Base, ran south on the east side of the airfield, and rejoined Route 1 two miles south of Red Bridge.

With our inspection of Red Bridge completed, Captain Phiem informed me that I had now visited all the defensive positions controlled by Da Nang garrison, the RF companies at Hai Van Pass, the several PR platoons in East Da Nang, and the RF platoon at Red Bridge. The other RF companies were assigned specific guard duties at strategic points within the city and used as a reserve force for combat operations.

Captain Phiem said he was pleased I had been assigned to Da Nang garrison as he would be promoted to operations officer next week. Major Bich was going to Dalat to attend the Vietnamese command and general staff school. The following week Major Bich left for Dalat, and Captain Prince left for Saigon to begin his tour with Robert Mitchum.

During my second week in Da Nang, the VC ambushed a civilian convoy going up Hai Van Mountain. In the middle of the southbound convoy was an ARVN two-and-a-half-ton truck loaded with about 20 soldiers and some members of their families. Behind the truck were two Jeeps from a sub-sector in Thua Thien containing three American advisors, one Australian advisor, and their Vietnamese girlfriends, all bound for Da Nang for a short R&R visit. The truck was blown up by a command-detonated mine buried in the road. Flanking machine gun fire and hand grenades had wiped out all survivors in the truck as well as all the people in the two Jeeps in less than four minutes.

The first reaction force to reach the ambush site was an ARVN Ranger company, but by the time they arrived the attackers were gone. Then Captain Phiem took his Jeep and a two-and-a-half-ton-truck to the ambush site. I went with him to report on the ambush of the Americans and the Australian and to make arrangements for their bodies. Captain Phiem's men took care of the Vietnamese women who had been with the advisors.

At 6:30 the next morning, one of the RF companies from the garrison left to conduct a five-day sweep along the railroad track beginning at the first tunnel near Hill 358. The operation was scheduled to end at the fourth tunnel on the north side of Hai Van Mountain. During this same time, the ranger company would sweep the mountains from the ambush site on the north side of Hai Van south, ending in the vicinity of the RF platoon on Hill 358. The operation would be controlled by Captain Phiem from the French fortress at Hai Van Pass, including myself, SP5 Kurtz, a garrison warrant officer, Captain Phiem's driver, and several ARVN garrison NCOs. We drove up in two Jeeps and a three-quarter-ton truck.

As an advisor, there was little for me to do during this operation. I spent most of my time talking to the Vietnamese soldiers and officers. I was as curious about them as they were about me. Most of their contact with Americans had been distant because of the language barrier and the reluctance of most Americans to engage in discussions other than business.

The nights were spent on cots in one of the old French stone buildings. During the darkness, squealing mice ran all over, including over us, while we slept. One of us would turn on a flashlight, throw our boots, and they would scatter, only to return when the light was turned off. Apparently one boot hit a mouse: when we woke up one morning there was one tiny VC mouse, KIA, lying next to my boot. Another night we were invaded by two- to three-inch cockroaches crawling all over. They would run into the cracks in the walls when the flashlight went on, returning when the light went out. Our meals were purchased at the restaurants. We had chicken or beef noodle soup for breakfast, and different meats with various sauces, rice, and vegetables for supper. By the time the operation ended five days later we found nothing and had had no contact with the VC.

When not on operations, which wasn't that often, my days became a dull routine. I would usually eat breakfast in my BOQ room. Arriving at my office at 8:00, I'd stay there until noon. My office in the Da Nang garrison compound was a square whitewashed room with open windows, desk, chair, wood shelves, and telephone, with a map of our area on the wall. The midday siesta was from noon to 2:30, then I'd be in the office until about six o'clock. This routine quickly became so boring I began to schedule trips as often as possible to visit the various RF and PF units we controlled.

The furnished BOQ room I shared with Al Lorry, a USAF captain and

VNAF advisor, was fairly nice. It included a private bath with sink, toilet and shower. We didn't see much of each other because we often worked different shifts. There were several maids to wash and iron clothes, polish boots, make beds, and clean the rooms. Each officer contracted for his own ba, the Vietnamese term for married women whom we called the maids. Mine was in her 40s, honest, and efficient. Most maids worked seven days a week from 8:00 a.m. to 6:00 p.m. with siesta time off. For this, a ba was paid 600 piastras a month by each man, which was equal to five U.S. dollars.

I would usually receive mail from my wife and other family members in five to seven days. The army post office system worked well. According to General Westmoreland, commanding general of MACV, mail movement had the highest priority in Vietnam. When one considered the volume of mail processed in Vietnam, one couldn't argue with a five- to seven-day delivery time. The United States was divided in half by an east-west line, California to Washington, D.C. All mail above the line was sent to Seattle, while mail below the line was sent to San Francisco. The mail would then go to Hawai'i or Japan or the Philippines, where it was put on a Pan Am flight, because Pan Am was the only airline with a contract to fly mail into Vietnam. All mail addressed to the troops stationed in Vietnam went through the U.S. air mail terminal at Tan Son Nhut. The 140-man staff sorted it by APO, and within four hours it was on its way again, in-country. Sometimes USAF planes were used to shuttle mail from Clark AFB to Saigon.

During this time, periodic letters from Anita let me know all was okay there, except for one small problem with the state of Georgia (I had been stationed at Fort Benning in Columbus and my family lived in a house we owned in Columbus). When we had been in North Carolina while I was attending MATA at Fort Bragg, we bought a new 1966 Ford station wagon to pull our travel trailer across the United States to California for language school and then back to Georgia. We had paid North Carolina sales tax on the car and had it registered in that state. I had wanted Anita to have a new car during the year I would be gone so there would be less chance of car problems. Before I left for Vietnam I had registered the car in Georgia where we lived. Now the state of Georgia wanted my wife to pay a Georgia sales tax on the car. She had refused, and the state had become nasty and persistent. Finally, I suggested Anita tell them that since the car title and registration were in my name the state should demand I pay the additional tax. I then told the state to come to Vietnam to collect it, after which we heard no more from the state of Georgia.

Time passed slowly, and I began to tire of reading paperback books. At night there was a curfew in Da Nang and all bars and restaurants were off limits to American military personnel, including advisors. During Sunday, our day off, I could wander the streets of Da Nang, but soon I had seen everything.

I spent time improving my Vietnamese by talking to Vietnamese soldiers and in due time I also began teaching English to other military personnel. Using the books I had brought with me from DLI, I began to teach English, starting out with a single lieutenant and then a class of eight students. I would teach from 7:30 to 8:30 each night. Later, I obtained some English textbooks for my students from the U.S. Information Service Office in Da Nang.

Between 6:00 and 7:30 I went to the Da Nang officers' club for supper. My meals were the same as the food back in the States, except we didn't have milk, and I usually drank iced tea, soda, or juice. Eating in the officers' club cost me $40 to $45 per month. Breakfast there cost $0.50, lunch $0.65, and supper $0.85, except for the steak dinner with all the trimmings that cost $1.85. On Saturday night the club special was surf and turf, lobster tails and steak: an excellent meal. The "O" club also had a Sunday steak fry, where you cooked your own steak over a charcoal fire in a barbecue grill made from a 55-gallon drum cut in half along the long axis. In the evenings, it had a cash bar as well as a nightly free movie. With $5 for the maid, I usually spent another $20 to $25 each month on other odds and ends. Thus, my total living expenses for a month usually averaged about $70.

Most of the MACV advisors in I Corps were Army personnel. There were no American Army units in I Corps, though, only U.S. Navy and USMC. Logistical support became a problem. In early 1966, neither the Navy nor the Marines wore the same uniforms as army advisors. We wore jungle fatigues and jungle boots; therefore, it was difficult to obtain all the military clothing necessary for Army advisors. I needed a second pair of jungle boots, so I could alternate wearing different pairs, and I also needed more jungle fatigues, but they were not available in any military channels in I Corps. Sergeant Ham, our interpreter, took me to a commercial area of Da Nang in the southern part of the city where I could buy more jungle fatigues and boots on the black market. I also bought a rain jacket, made from a rubberized U.S. military poncho; the long-sleeved, waist-length, hooded jacket was tailored, right there, to fit me.

I even started drawing and painting again. I had been a commercial artist before I was commissioned in the Army and my college degree had been in art. Now I spent time sketching or painting a variety of Vietnamese scenes, mostly those with people.

One morning, the train was hit by a mine at Hai Van Pass, initiating another three-day operation. At 5:45 that afternoon we heard a loud explosion from the direction of the Nam O Bridge, south of Hai Van. We responded and found that a 105 mm artillery round, possibly fired by the USMC, had hit the bridge and blown up an ARVN truck. Two soldiers were still in the truck, alive when we arrived. I knew at first glance that one would die before he reached the hospital, as a third of his head had been splattered over the inside of the truck's cab.

The following day, still at the ARVN fortress atop Hai Van Pass, I had to radio a report back to Da Nang to Major Braun. My radio was mounted in the back of the Jeep. To use the radio without running down the battery, we'd put the Jeep in neutral and turn on the engine. The Jeep was parked on the edge of a small, ten-foot stone cliff inside the French fortress. I leaned inside the Jeep across the driver's seat and moved the gear shift lever into the neutral position. Half in the Jeep, with my arms and chest in and my lower torso and legs out, I turned the ignition key and started the engine. Somehow the Jeep remained in gear, and it ran off the cliff with me still half in and half out. I parted company with the Jeep in mid-air and fell ten feet to the ground, doing a PLF (parachute landing fall) to cushion the crash landing then rolling away from the falling Jeep. I was bruised and battered but had broken no bones. I had managed to turn off the key in flight, so the engine was dead when the Jeep landed. The Jeep was nose down but at a 45-degree angle to the ground, with its front bumper on the ground and its back wheels up against the vertical wall it had just come over.

My radio Jeep was parked on top of this stone wall. It was in gear, and when I leaned in to start it to supply power for the radio, it drove itself right over the wall, with me half in the Jeep, ending up nose-down. The concrete pad around the steps is where I ended up. This photo was taken after the Jeep took a dive (and reparked). Note the rock under the tire.

The Vietnamese soldiers thought that was the best thing they had ever seen an advisor do. Smiling, they told me that the flight my Jeep and I had taken was quite impressive. To get the Jeep back on all four wheels, we piled big rocks between the underside of the Jeep, the ground and the wall, and, using ropes, pulled it down the rock pile we had built. Every time I returned to that location thereafter, I was asked where I would park the Jeep and if I would please drive it over the cliff again.

On another day, Captain Phiem and I were at Hai Van on an inspection trip and decided against spending the night, even though it would soon be dark, and driving anywhere outside Da Nang after dark was dangerous. The road down Hai Van toward Da Nang was open so Captain Phiem decided make the trip fast. His driver was in the driver's seat, he was in the front passenger's seat, and I was in the back seat. We came down the mountain doing 40 to 50 miles an hour when we hit a huge pothole in the road. The Jeep went up, I went up; the Jeep came down, I came down, bashing my side on the back of Captain Phiem's seat, breaking six ribs. So far, the operations I had been part of from Da Nang garrison had been of limited scope and had offered little experience, although I had learned a great deal about the people, language, and terrain of Vietnam.

Chapter 6

Unrest in Da Nang

As February gave way to March I began to sense an undercurrent of unrest in Da Nang, although it was hard to put my finger on anything specific. The senior officers and NCOs in Da Nang garrison seldom discussed politics except in a very general sense. The young Vietnamese soldiers I had met in my travels around Da Nang had made comments on local current events, but mostly only vague references. My students and I at Da Nang garrison, however, had developed a good degree of trust that allowed us to be open and honest with our thoughts and feelings, so one evening after class I asked some of them about any potential unrest, particularly about rumors of bad blood between Premier Nguyen Cao Ky in Saigon and General Thi, I Corps commander. Five students, all in their mid to late 20s, and I were sitting around the G5 (Civil Affairs, responsible for military-civilian coordination in military operational areas) office that we used as a classroom. The three females, all from Saigon, were sergeants in the Vietnamese army and the two male lieutenants were from the Da Nang area.

In response to my question, Lieutenant Loc replied that Vietnam was divided many ways. Da Nang was far from Saigon and Premier Ky's government of generals. General Thi had a following in I Corps. Many government workers, merchants, and even Buddhists were becoming disenchanted with the Ky government. Sergeant Lien added that Saigon was too far away, but General Thi was here and he knew the problems, which Ky did not.

The problem, Lieutenant Hoa explained, was that General Thi was a powerful man in I Corps who had spoken against Ky for government corruption. General Thi was also a Buddhist. Sergeant Hanh continued, explaining that the United Buddhist Church leaders were anti-government and therefore supported General Thi. I asked what would happen, and Lieutenant Loc said that no one knew, but maybe General Thi would take over Ky or maybe Ky would get rid of Thi.

Sergeant Huyen listed the possible options. One, Premier Ky could fire

General Thi which would make trouble in I Corps. Raising a second finger, she stated that General Thi could try and overthrow Premier Ky and Chief of Staff Thieu, except General Thi didn't have much power out of I Corps. Raising a third finger she presented her last option that possibly no one could do anything. Premier Ky would leave Da Nang alone and General Thi would refrain from talking bad about the Saigon government, but she didn't think so, because she believed that neither Ky nor Thi could be quiet.

Silent for a moment, Sergeant Huyen leaned forward, as if to share a deep secret, and said quietly that she thought that Ky and Thi would fight right here in I Corps, in Da Nang. The others nodded in agreement.

Lieutenant Loc (right), a regional force and popular force G-5 (civil affairs) officer who was also one of my English students (I taught English at night to several ARVN soldiers, both male and female), with Lieutenant Hoa, also an English student. Note that both are holding the English textbook.

Lieutenant Loc explained that both men were strong and powerful. Premier Ky had his Saigon generals and General Thi had the Buddhists. No one would give in, so they must fight, and since General Thi would not go to Saigon, Premier Ky must come to Dan Nang. I wanted to know what kind of fight we were talking about.

Lieutenant Hoa answered that Premier Ky might send his paratroopers or rangers or marines up to I Corps to seize I Corps headquarters and then the local soldiers and Buddhists would fight for General Thi.

I questioned my students about what would happen to Da Nang garrison if Ky sent in his troops and what they would do.

Lieutenant Loc pointed

out that the battle would be between two powerful men and their armies. He didn't think Da Nang garrison would get in the fight. The garrison soldiers would not fight but would just wait and see who would win.

Thinking out loud, I asked why the Buddhists and the civil servants would be involved in this fight between two generals. Lieutenant Loc explained that the government of Vietnam was now run by generals, but many Vietnamese wanted an elected civilian government, not a military government. Lieutenant Hoa described how Premier Ky would stall because he wanted to remain premier, so no elections. Sergeant Lien added that the Buddhists did not want the military government; they wanted a civilian government.

I guessed that the Buddhists and many other Vietnamese wanted to hold a free election and have a civilian government, which Ky didn't want. Because Thi and Ky had their own personal differences over power, the Buddhists would support Thi against Ky.

That night I reflected on what I learned that evening and what I had learned in the past. Shortly after I arrived in Da Nang, I met Nguyen Cao Ky when he came to address the advisors in the Da Nang area. I was impressed with the man. Physically he personified the fighter pilot he was. He was trim and handsome with a pencil-thin mustache, and dapper in his black flight suit with purple scarf. Around his waist he wore a web belt with a holstered .45-caliber service pistol. His knowledge and use of English, his mannerisms, his confidence, and his convictions on how to fight communism were so persuasive that everyone in the room came away with a deep respect for the man. Ky was a charismatic leader, a credible fighter that one would support to the end. He very successfully projected the image of a man capable of leading his country in winning the war.

In the five or six weeks I had been in Da Nang, many changes had occurred, aside from the Ky-Thi issue. More of the Da Nang garrison tactical area of operational responsibility (TAOR, the geographical limits of a combat area) had been given to the Marines which meant we had less territory in which to conduct combat operations.

I began to question my value as an advisor and what I was contributing to the war effort. Nothing, I decided, unless one counted English lessons. Otherwise my presence had zero influence on the safety of Da Nang. I tried to talk to Major Braun about my feelings, but he wasn't interested. I would be here six months for my staff assignment and then I would go elsewhere for my six months field duty. He also pointed out I could earn my CIB while at the garrison.

My response that I wanted to earn my CIB the honest way, by fighting, didn't sit too well with him. I explained that I don't want to have someone give it to me because of paper operations. I wanted to fight and all I was doing here was putting in time.

Recognizing my frustration, he said he knew how I felt. He didn't want to fire me. He said I had been doing an excellent job as an advisor, out visiting the RF and PF units every week, making good suggestions to Captain Phiem on improvements. He mentioned I had the respect of all the Vietnamese in Da Nang garrison from the commander on down. The commander had told Major Braun how much he appreciated my English classes; his niece was a student of mine.

He explained that every advisor had a job to do, but not all were doing exactly what was desired. He said he wished he could be advising an ARVN artillery unit, but the garrison didn't have any artillery. At least the garrison had infantry units I could visit. He didn't even have that.

Major Braun and I saw this war and our positions totally differently. He was simply going along with events to not upset the applecart. He had his CIB, which was very unusual for an artillery officer, so he would just coast until his date expected to return from overseas (DEROS). By contrast I wanted to engage in combat, and my assignment at Da Nang garrison would not allow me to experience that. I wanted out to a combat unit.

The days passed by. Sometimes we cordoned off a hamlet in East Da Nang while RF troops and police searched houses for evidence of VC. Occasionally shots were exchanged; rarely was anyone hit. I never knew what was going on, as I was back with Captain Phiem. My requests to go with the ground troops were always denied because my place was advising Captain Phiem, not some RF company commander or platoon leader. Still, each operation counted toward my CIB if the units made contact. Typically, one out of three or four qualified by MACV regulations, but because of my personal feelings about this system being a sham, I never documented my attendance on these combat operations.

Saturday, 5 March, was a dead day, until we had an unusual surprise visit. We had been sitting around the office that afternoon, staring at the walls, when a Jeep with two men in it pulled up outside. I recognized the driver as Captain Sam Prince, the Marine I replaced. Climbing out of the passenger seat was a big American dressed in khaki pants and jacket and wearing an African-type bush hat. It was Robert Mitchum. We spent the next two hours asking Mr. Mitchum all kinds of questions about what it was like to be a famous movie star. He answered all questions graciously and honestly. He had turned a dull time into a very interesting experience.

Sam's next stop was the officers' club for supper, so he invited me along. Mitchum was the star attraction. He never needed to ask for a drink and I never saw him without one. The officers, though, were less interested in moviemaking and more interested in the sexual habits of Mitchum's female co-stars. That evening I learned three things about Robert Mitchum. First, even though he drank steadily all night, he never got drunk. Second, he never said an unkind word about any person with whom he had worked, and third, if he knew about any of the sexual exploits of his co-stars, he did not say. He was a fascinating person to talk to and listen to, having had led a most interesting life. The drinks continued to end up in his hands as he held the crowd spellbound, but eventually I became worn out, so I bid Sam and Mitchum good night and left.

On 10 March the events my students had predicted came true. Premier Ky announced the dismissal of General Thi. Nine members of South Vietnam's ruling National Leadership Committee had unanimously voted to oust their tenth member. Two days later General Thi was under house arrest. He was replaced by Brigadier General Nguyen Van Chuan, the highly regarded commander of the ARVN First Division. Beginning the day after General Thi's dismissal, Da Nang was off limits to all U.S. military personnel. Advisors and other military personnel living in Da Nang could travel from their quarters to work and to the enlisted or officers' clubs, but no other place. A few days later there were some mild protests against General Thi's removal, but these scattered demonstrations did not involve any Vietnamese military. Work continued as usual as far as the ARVN and U.S. Marines were concerned.

On 21 March, General Thi returned to Da Nang where he addressed the people at a public meeting, telling the crowd that he had to leave his position because he was sick, and that he was behind the Vietnamese government and that the people of Da Nang and all of I Corps should support Premier Ky and his government. He left for Hue in an armed convoy.

By late March, the only TAOR Da Nang garrison had left was Hai Van Pass, where two RF companies were located. Two more of our six RF companies had been turned over to the USMC for operational control. The remaining two companies were spread throughout Da Nang on guard assignments. When I had arrived almost two months before, we had had two RF companies for operational purposes and garrison reserve. Now we had only one for reserve, and, essentially, no area in which to operate.

As time passed, General Thi continued to hang around Da Nang. We advisors were on semi-alert and I was assigned the additional duty of coordinating, with both the ARVN and other U.S. advisors, the evacuation of Americans from Da Nang in case General Thi tried to start an uprising.

It really didn't make sense, I thought. Here the country is in a major war, fighting for its very existence, and the war effort was in jeopardy because of two little men with very big egos. Even worse was the dilemma in which the advisors found themselves. We were advising Vietnamese military units that were becoming more militant in their support of General Thi and against the government of Vietnam which the U.S. government was supporting.

Just who was the enemy here? I wondered.

Soon I discovered that apparently the Buddhists had become divided in their support for Premier Ky or General Thi. The dissidents were supporting public demonstrations against the Vietnam government. Because the U.S. government still supported Ky, much of the public's anger was also turned toward Americans. From Premier Ky's point of view, Da Nang was almost like a communist-occupied city. He denounced the mayor of Da Nang as a communist, and claimed ARVN troops were taking over and becoming disloyal to the government of Vietnam. Public parades and angry demonstrations became common. Public officials and Buddhist leaders became more vocal in their dissatisfaction with Premier Ky and his Saigon government. The situation in Da Nang was becoming increasingly hostile.

Co (Miss) Hanh, a Vietnamese military social worker, was one of my English students. She was 25 and engaged to a French college professor in Saigon, where she was from. She studied with me in class about seven hours a week, then another three hours in a class taught by an Australian captain and another four hours in a class taught by a U.S. major. This dedication to learn English I found to be typical among the young, educated Vietnamese.

In my attempt to return to sanity, I wrote Lieutenant Colonel John White, my former Seventh Cavalry Battalion commander, who was now the G1 (personnel officer) of the First Cavalry Division, telling him about my current situation and how I wanted to take over a U.S. rifle company, asking if he could help me get a transfer to the First Cav.

I continued to teach English at night. I had fun trying to teach the students the tongue twister "How much wood would a woodchuck chuck, if a woodchuck could chuck wood?" The students enjoyed it but had no idea what a woodchuck was, so I asked Anita to send me some pictures of the animal, which I shared with my students. Other tongue twisters I taught them included "Peter Piper picked a peck of pickled peppers."

During the Da Nang debacle, Army personnel had sent me a form asking what I wanted to do after my Vietnam tour. I requested to attend the Infantry

Career Course (at Fort Benning) and then be assigned to Hawai'i. I knew the request had been approved up through MACV. It had to be sent to Hawai'i for concurrence and then to DA for final approval.

Eventually, I heard from Lieutenant Colonel White who said he could arrange for me to get transferred to the First Cavalry Division but could not guarantee me a company. The battalion commanders had a lot to say about who would command in their battalions, and I didn't personally know any battalion commander in that division. If I joined the First Cavalry in July or August, many of the company commanders would be leaving so I'd be in a good position to get a company. If, however, I stayed with MACV, I knew I would get a field (combat) assignment in July. According to *Army Times*, the increase in U.S. forces in Vietnam was such that Army captains and majors currently serving in Vietnam could expect to return in less than a year for a second tour. If that was true, I could become an ARVN battalion advisor, go to the career course, or be assigned to Hawai'i for a year and return for a second tour as a company commander. I didn't know what I should do so I presented all options to Anita for her input.

Soon Anita replied to my letter, suggesting I stay with MACV and see about getting a battalion as soon as possible. One morning, with Major Braun's permission, I flew to talk to Lieutenant Colonel Cranston, the sector senior advisor. Sitting in front of him, I explained my situation and told him I wanted to be reassigned to an ARVN battalion or a sub-sector. I emphasized that there was no action whatsoever in Da Nang garrison and I wanted a field assignment.

He told me that Major Braun said I was doing an excellent job at the garrison. I insisted that I was an infantry officer and I wanted to be with combat infantry troops and explained that I couldn't do that in Da Nang. Becoming frustrated with my insistence on leaving Da Nang, he forcefully declared that unfortunately not everyone in Vietnam would get the exact assignment they wanted. He said there would be an opening for a battalion senior advisor in 45 to 60 days and he would consider me for that position. Standing and saluting, I thanked him, said good-bye, turned on my heel and departed to return to Da Nang.

As the weeks turned into months, I had quickly become accepted as the co van my (American advisor) who really cared. During my off-duty time I was with the Vietnamese, not staying in my BOQ or spending my time at the officers' club.

I was discovering that Vietnam was a beautiful country with all kinds of people: handsome and ugly, bright and dumb, rich and poor, kind and evil, dreamers and doers. I wanted to become accepted by the people, and teaching English had been one step toward this goal. Now, since I had spent considerable time with Vietnamese soldiers, I became a welcomed guest in their homes. Sharing meals with their families and playing with their kids added a dimension to this war that escaped most Americans in Vietnam. Not knowing or understanding the people and not speaking their language usually distanced American soldiers from the rural Vietnamese, and for their part, these Vietnamese could not relate to our modern world of automation, cleanliness, and electronic convenience.

Interaction with my students and the soldiers with whom I worked allowed me to know that their aspirations and their desires to live and be happy were not less than my own. The only difference was the cultural setting in which we existed. My close association with these people led to a deep respect for them and a desire to help them. I had an urge to learn as much about their customs as possible as well as a need to be accepted by them as another human being who cared about them. I brought flowers to the soldiers' wives who prepared the meals they shared with me and I made drawings for their children as they watched with amazement.

Back in the States I had collected old Jeeps and rebuilt them. I worked with the mechanics doing maintenance on my advisor's Jeep, something no other advisor had ever done, so I was eager to share tricks I had learned working on these vehicles over the years and learn from the Vietnamese mechanics.

In addition, while visiting the various outposts, I test fired my carbine and pistol weekly, and simultaneously I gave the Vietnamese tips on improving their marksmanship.

While my time in Da Nang so far had not been rewarding from a military standpoint, my interaction with the Vietnamese people had instilled such respect, trust, and love for them that I never feared for my safety. Unlike the Vietnamese soldiers who knew the people, the language, and the land, American troops did not always have the ability to communicate effectively with the Vietnamese, or completely understand the people, the culture or the area. Thus, there was no doubt in my mind that combat operations with the Vietnamese were less risky than with American troops.

On 2 April, we conducted another operation in Hai Van, this time on the southern slopes near Hill 358. During the night, one of the RF company squads on an ambush detail confronted a VC unit that had been moving supplies. Three VC were killed. The ambush unit also had some U.S. Marines with it. No friendlies were injured in the firefight, but when the VC bodies were pulled away to be searched, a VC grenade came loose and exploded, wounding three RF soldiers and one Marine.

In addition to their weapons and ammo, they also carried very crude homemade gas masks that looked like small brown plastic garbage bags with the slits for eyes covered with clear cellophane and the mouth area covered with white gauze filled with small particles of charcoal to provide a few moments of protection from tear gas. Somewhere, I figured, these soldiers had been in a tunnel: the only place they would have feared a gas attack.

In early April, the problems between Premier Ky and General Thi had escalated to near violence. The Buddhist-inspired demonstrations now included civil servants, laborers, and even some military. Premier Ky could no longer ignore the demonstrations, especially since they suggested that the government of Vietnam was losing control.

During the night between 3 and 4 April, three battalions of Vietnamese (VN) marines were flown into Da Nang. When I arrived at Da Nang garrison the morning of Wednesday, 4 April, the guards at the gates were VN marines. When I went into the Vietnamese operations office, Captain Phiem was no longer there, having been replaced by a VN marine, Captain Ai, a tall, heavy-set officer with a close-cropped burr haircut. He wore the dark green and black camouflage utility uniform common to VN marines. He was sharp and impressive, almost arrogant, and both his demeanor and appearance projected no-nonsense military. I spoke to him in Vietnamese, introducing myself and identifying myself as the Da Nang garrison military advisor.

Captain Ai, responding in English, smiled and stated he knew who I was and what I did. I asked if he was replacing Captain Phiem, and he said he would only be here temporarily. He explained that the Vietnamese marines arrived during the night and were now in control of Da Nang garrison. As such the VN marines had assumed responsibility for the security of Da Nang. The four regional force companies and all the popular force platoons would continue their assigned missions, but under VN marine control. He said that they had been sent by Premier Ky to restore order to Da Nang.

I asked if the VN marines were now in control of the garrison, then what was the role of the American advisors?

Captain Ai stated clearly in his excellent English that now the men and officers we had been advising would be taking their advice from the VN marines. He did not see any immediate need for our services and he said we could best help by letting the VN marines complete their mission without interference. He made it exceptionally clear that he wanted the American advisors gone. With my acknowledgment of his wanting the American advisors to just stay out of his way, he came to attention, ramrod straight, executed a perfect salute, stated he enjoyed meeting me and wished me good day. Returning his salute, I bade him good-bye and left.

Going into Major Braun's office, I found him, Staff Sergeant Billstone, and Specialist 5 Kurtz discussing the situation. I described my meeting the guy who was now the new ops officer and told them he didn't want any advisors at all. Major Braun said he had just got back from talking to Lieutenant Colonel Tu who said the VN marines had taken over Da Nang garrison and they did not need or want any U.S. advisors. He continued, saying that Colonel

Cranston said for us to just hang tight. He was talking to the deputy I Corps advisor, Colonel Hamilton, to find out what to do, so all we could do was just wait. We all wondered how long this would this last and what would become of our jobs. Who would we advise?

The situation in town was very tense. I updated our evacuation plan. All American military and civilian personnel in Da Nang would leave. The USAF advisors to the VNAF would move to the USAF facilities at Da Nang air base. All USMC, U.S. Army, and U.S. Navy personnel and civilians, including U.S. embassy employees and the press, would go by boat to the U.S. naval base at Camp Tiensha near East Da Nang or by helicopter to the USMC helicopter facility at Marble Mountain. The garrison advisors would remain where we were.

The evacuation plan was executed smoothly on 9 April. The bachelor officers' quarters and bachelor enlisted quarters and all MACV offices were closed and locked. Only those Americans defined as essential could remain, and then only where they worked, including the Da Nang garrison advisors, some I Corps headquarters advisors, and some U.S. Navy logistical personnel. With our weapons, ammo, sleeping cots, and C-rations, the Da Nang garrison advisors were set up for the duration.

The following day Premier Ky fired Major General Chuan as commanding general of I Corps and replaced him with a Saigon general, Lieutenant General Ton That Dinh. Chief of State Thieu, speaking for the Saigon directorate, promised free elections in three to five months as well as the possibility of a new constitution.

This announcement seemed to mollify the Buddhists, but now the U.S. government became concerned. Fearing that Premier Ky's government might be replaced by a neutral Buddhist faction, President Johnson's administration began to reassess the U.S. position in Vietnam. Undersecretary of State George Ball advocated against any further build up of U.S. forces in Vietnam. CIA analysts and Defense Secretary Robert McNamara supported a continuation of current U.S. policy. Clearly the United States was becoming divided on its position in Vietnam.

The Americans eventually returned to Da Nang, but the curfew and restrictions continued. The post exchange at Da Nang air base, which supported 35,000 U.S. troops, reopened for business. Da Nang continued to be the site of numerous demonstrations, especially by civil servants demanding Premier Ky, Chief of State Thieu, and other officials of the GVN step down. All these demonstrations were watched with interest by garrison soldiers and advisors alike from behind the stone and steel grated wall of Da Nang garrison.

Finally, Premier Ky had seen enough. At a press conference he stated angrily in English, "Da Nang is already held by communists and the government will undertake operations to clean them out. We will liberate Da Nang. The mayor of Da Nang is using public funds to organize anti-government demonstrations. Either this government will have to fall, or the mayor will be shot."

From my post in Da Nang, I didn't envision us as being trapped in a communist regime. The U.S. government was caught in the middle, and who it would back now was not clear.

CHAPTER 7

The Battle
for Da Nang

Premier Ky's verbal assault on the mayor of Da Nang only fueled more riots around Vietnam. For some unknown reason, Premier Ky then appeared to acquiesce to some of the Buddhist demands, promising to resign after an election of a civilian assembly, which would be held within five months. Consequently, the unrest then quieted down.

As advisors we had become used to the roller-coaster politics of the Saigon government changing direction every week or so, depending upon the personal whims of the generals involved. After all, in less than 60 days we had had three I Corps commanders. If it had not been for the presence of the U.S. Marines in I Corps, I believe the war effort would have collapsed. Despite the dissension among the government troops, especially the ARVN First Division and the government civilian employees, the war against the VC and NVA continued. The United States continued to support the Ky-Thieu regime, and the political ups and downs became just another aspect of life in I Corps. The next move by Premier Ky surprised almost everyone, especially his American supporters.

Premier Ky felt continued support from the United States would be based on his ability to retain control of South Vietnam. The U.S. troop commitment currently was more than 250,000 men. Premier Ky realized that he had to take firm steps to settle the problems in I Corps. He believed that the United States failed to understand not only his country's Buddhist problems but also all other competing influences that determined the direction of the country.

On 14 May, without informing Chief of State Thieu or any U.S. officials, Premier Ky held a top-level conference with his military chiefs at 3:00 a.m. Two hours later, a flight of VNAF C-47s, supported by a wing of VNAF fighter-bombers, landed 1,500 VN marines and airborne soldiers with tanks in Da Nang. The task force was initially led by the joint general staff, but eventually Colonel Nguyen Ngoc Loan took over. This was the same Colonel Loan who gained international notoriety two years later when an AP photograph of him shooting a VC prisoner in the head with a small revolver was published.

The task force took over Da Nang. The four battalions stormed the almost abandoned I Corps Headquarters on Da Nang air base. From there, strategic points within the city were quickly occupied by Premier Ky's troops: the radio station, city hall, police headquarters, and other facilities. The battle lines were clearly drawn. His marines and paratroopers were waging war in Da Nang against various rebel I Corps troops, including the Eleventh Ranger Battalion and some elements of the First ARVN Division.

As dawn broke over Vietnam on 14 May, we advisors became aware of the fighting in the streets. Using my PRC-10 radio (a backpack infantry radio used by field troops, an older model no longer used by U.S. troops referred to as a PRICK 10), I contacted Major Braun; the advisors were told to remain in the BOQ. We had plenty of food, potable water, and soft drinks. We went to the open BOQ rooftop to watch the war unfolding on the street below. As a precautionary measure, we dressed in our flak jackets and helmets, and we armed ourselves with our carbines before venturing out.

It was evident that the American military and their facilities were not a target of either the rebels or Premier Ky's forces. This was an internal war between the Vietnamese, and American advisors in Da Nang had no fear for their safety. In fact, armed ARVN guards from Da Nang garrison stationed themselves inside our BOQ courtyards as extra security. Two days later our maids returned to work.

Soon circumstances began to fluctuate. A new I Corps commander, Major General Huynh Van Cao, was appointed by Premier Ky to assume command of the operation, but his reluctance to clear dissidents out of the Buddhist pagodas in Da Nang rendered his command ineffective and of short duration. Colonel Loan again took charge of the operation. He had no reluctance to kill or capture the rebels. When the fighting ended a week later, approximately 100 rebels had been killed and several hundred people wounded, including some U.S. newsmen covering the story in Da Nang's Tinh Hoi Pagoda.

Marine General Walt was caught in the middle. As the senior American military man, he wore two hats; he was commander of the U.S. military forces in I Corps, and he was the senior advisor to the Vietnamese military units in I Corps. I was not a fan of General Walt. I had been a witness to many incidents which I felt showed him to have a two-faced nature. He also did not seem to hold MACV field advisors in very high regard, resulting in many Marine field-grade officers seeing us as riff-raff who could neither control nor influence our weak Vietnamese counterparts.

ARVN rebel soldiers from Da Nang captured by Nguyen Cao Ky's Saigon troops during the rebellion in I Corps in spring 1966. They were held at Da Nang garrison.

A good example of General Walt's hypocritical behavior occurred toward the end of my tour in Vietnam. Some NCOs in an American Marine unit came to me with a small black-and-white puppy asking if the U.S. advisors could take her. The Marines had raised her from a few weeks old to now, when she was probably six months old, and named her Hanoi Hannah after the female North Vietnamese propaganda radio broadcaster. Because the small dog was very friendly, playful and loving, I asked why they wanted to give up such a nice pet, and they exclaimed that General Walt just put out an order that no Marines could have any pets. They didn't want to turn her loose as she might end up as someone's supper. Ultimately some ARVN soldiers in the unit I was with heard about the problem and asked if they could have the dog for a pet and the Marines agreed. Six weeks later, when home on leave, I saw a *Life* magazine article on General Walt with photos taken at his China Beach villa. The caption under one photo explained how much he enjoyed playing with his pet dogs as shown in the picture.

General Walt's dual role placed him in some unusual positions in trying to defuse the rebellion. At the same time, childish behavior was evident on both sides. Too often the men charged with the duties of mature senior commanders displayed idiosyncrasies characteristic of one-upmanship. One time Premier Ky ordered VNAF planes to bomb the rebel outpost at the Tiensha ammo dump near a U.S. Marine compound. Rockets were fired, and U.S. Marines were wounded. In response, General Walt ordered two U.S. Marine jets to take off and fly on top of the VNAF propeller planes. He told the VNAF commander that if any shots were fired at the U.S. Marine compound, the USMC planes would shoot down the VNAF planes. The VNAF commander immediately dispatched four more VNAF planes to orbit above the two USMC planes. General Walt then ordered two more USMC jets to form a fourth layer, continuing this childish game. Eventually, the VNAF planes departed and the USMC planes landed.

About four days after Premier Ky's troops landed in Da Nang, I had to go to Saigon on business. The fact that I could leave Da Nang as if everything were routine underscored the reality that the conflict was very limited to only a few isolated locations and was conducted at a very high command level involving senior colonels and general officers. It almost seemed like a very small part of a large city was engaged in a minor civil disturbance that was totally controlled by the local authorities.

My trip to Saigon involved obtaining supplies for our advisory team, such as boots and uniforms, checking the personnel records of our two NCOs, and taking a break. While there, I experienced a relaxing three days sight-seeing and shopping for Anita and the girls. I bought some dolls for Suzi and Julie, and for me, three oil paintings done by a local artist whose work I had seen in a downtown gallery then later during a visit at his studio. I stayed with Major Brad Gentry, the USARV recreation services officer who had been my battalion executive officer in the Second Infantry Division at Fort Benning. He had come to Vietnam as the Second Battalion, Seventh Cavalry, executive officer.

One day, Major Gentry said that a friend of his, whom he had known as a football star at the U.S. Military Academy, would be coming by. The guy was now an infantry officer and an advisor with one of the Vietnamese airborne battalions stationed in Saigon as a mobile reaction force. That afternoon the guest appeared, tall and athletic with a dark tan, a lean appearance and short blonde hair that made him

A U.S. Army 1911A1 .45-caliber pistol taken from a dead VC and given to me. I accurized the pistol by removing the military slide (top) of the pistol and replaced it with a civilian model Colt target slide (the dark top half of the pistol with adjustable rear sight). This was the primary weapon I carried during my first tour in Vietnam.

a perfect subject for an Army enlistment poster. He was Pete Dawkins, U.S. Army captain, airborne, ranger, top West Point student, football hero, and Rhodes Scholar. He was being touted as a future Army chief of staff, the top general in the U.S. Army. Before I left Major Gentry gave me a model 1911A1 .45-caliber army pistol that a friend of his got off a dead VC officer in response to my expressed desire for a pistol with more punch than my .38 special.

I arrived back in Da Nang on Sunday afternoon, May 22. The next day, May 23, the rebellion in Da Nang officially ended.

CHAPTER 8

Good-Bye
to Da Nang

Following the rebellion in Da Nang, Captain Phiem and the other garrison officers reappeared at work, most having been in hiding during the last half of May, preferring not to take sides in the VN marine-paratrooper conflict with the I Corps rebels. Lieutenant Colonel Cranston, Quang Nam sector advisor, left to return to the States before doing anything about my reassignment to an ARVN battalion. I asked Major Braune to talk to Colonel Cranston's replacement, Lieutenant Colonel Fred Keppler. Colonel Keppler told Major Braune that I would get my battalion advisor's position sometime in late July when my six-month Da Nang assignment ended.

I was thrilled that I now had assurance that I would get a battalion. After informing me of Lieutenant Colonel Keppler's promise, Major Braune good-naturedly told me to please get off his back about my leaving. Grinning broadly, I promised that my lips were sealed, and I would not utter another word about wanting a battalion.

In August 1965, the Marines had created a joint USMC–VN unit called the Combined Action Company (CAC). USMC First Lieutenant Paul R. Ek had formed the first CAC under the supervision of the Third Battalion, Fourth Marines. CAC platoons and squads were assigned security duties within specific Vietnamese villages. A CAC platoon consisted of a local PF platoon augmented by a USMC rifle squad. The Marine squad's mission was to train the PF platoon to successfully fight the VC and defend their village. Probably more important to the Vietnamese than the training was the support available to the attached Marine squad and therefore the members of the PF platoon. Gun ships, artillery, automatic weapons, ammunition, medevacs, radios, C-rations, PX goodies, and, most important, reinforcements were available. In a fight, the USMC was not likely to jeopardize one of their own squads.

The CAC concept was introduced into the USMC Da Nang TAOR in

February but never really got off the ground due to the problems in Da Nang. In June, the program was revived, and the Da Nang garrison PF platoons in East Da Nang were targeted for integration.

The plan to be used in the East Da Nang area was a variation of the CAC, called the Combined Action Platoon (CAP). The concept was the same as the CAC with 30 PF soldiers and a USMC rifle squad of 12 men. Support responsibility for the USMC rifle squad would fall on whatever USMC battalion was operating in that portion of the USMC TAOR.

My job was to assist the Marines to become successfully assimilated into the PF platoons. From the Marines, I received a list of the technical requirements needed for joint placement. The term used for the integration of a USMC squad and PF platoon was "co-location." For each Marine squad, I was given their security requirements which Captain Phiem and I would go over with local PF platoon leaders.

When the co-location integration was completed, the PF units would still come under Da Nang garrison for logistical support and command purposes. Operational control, though, was to be under the USMC. Word got around fast that U.S. Marines would be stationed in East Da Nang villages. As Captain Phiem and I made the rounds of the possible PF platoons to be integrated, I noticed the blossoming of entrepreneurial activities by enterprising civilians and military personnel.

I watched considerable new construction going on in the areas surrounding the PF platoons. However, it did not appear that a lot of time, effort, or money were being spent on the erection of these new facilities, a situation I attributed to the vagaries of the war. But structures were going up in anticipation of the Marines' arrival and would be given American names and stocked with tape decks for

VN regional force headquarters at Da Nang East where the U.S. Marines started their combined USMC–ARVN combat units.

music, liquor, and prostitutes. The Vietnamese knew what kinds of local establishments would be patronized by American Marines.

As the Marine squads moved into East Da Nang, the area became more secure. I would take my Jeep and spend time swimming and sunning alone at the USMC R&R facility at China Beach. Events during the past few months had surely made a difference in reducing the danger around Da Nang. There was no longer any fear of ambush or sniper fire in the daytime, and at night the CAP patrols were encountering less VC activity.

As June progressed, I was totally involved in working out the CAP integration, not only in East Da Nang but also in the other parts of the city. Communication between the Marine squads and PF units was not a real problem. Although almost none of the Marines spoke Vietnamese and only some units had interpreters, most Vietnamese spoke passable to excellent English. My job was to ensure the security requirements met USMC specifications.

In late June, Major Braune said Lieutenant Colonel Keppler, the new Quang Nam Sector senior advisor, wanted to talk to me. I grabbed a helicopter courier flight, and, after I reported to him, he said he was glad to meet me, commenting on Major Braune's praise for the fine job I had been doing. Noting that I was quite adept working with the RF and PF units, and I was fluent in Vietnamese and French, he addressed my preference to be with an ARVN battalion.

I replied, "Yes, sir," hoping I would get a chance to really impress upon Colonel Keppler how strong my desire was. This time I wasn't going to let opportunity pass me by; I explained I was a well-trained infantry officer, having had several leadership and staff positions. I pointed out I had been in Vietnam almost five months. I knew the people and their customs. I'd had ample experience assisting in the planning and conduct of Vietnamese combat operations. I ended my spiel by emphasizing that my background and experience would allow me to do an excellent job as a battalion senior advisor. Smiling, Colonel Keppler asked how soon I could be ready. Puzzled, I asked how soon could I be ready for what!

To take over a battalion advisory team, he explained, asking again how long it would take me to finish my work at Da Nang garrison so I could become the senior advisor of an ARVN infantry battalion. My mind began to operate on triple overtime. What did I have to do? No major projects on tap. Today is Wednesday.... I could leave on Friday, I figured. I spoke up, confirming that I could be ready the day after tomorrow ... Friday.

Colonel Keppler glanced down at the calendar on his desk and said he could have orders cut, effective Saturday, 2 July. He said that he had already cleared this with Major Braune who said he'd try to cope with me being gone but also said that having to do my job would be better than listening to me bitch if I didn't get this assignment.

He asked if I knew Captain Jason Calder, senior advisor with the Third Battalion, Fifty-First Regiment, and I replied in the affirmative. He clarified that Jason was in the hospital with some kind of intestinal problem, had lost a lot of weight, and would not be able to return to the field for a while. I would be his replacement.

His personnel officer would need to get some information from me, and Captain Tony Stinson, the Fifty-First staff advisor, would fill me in on my new assignment. Colonel Keppler told me that Major Haines, the senior advisor, and Master Sergeant Wright, his NCO, would meet me when I returned on Friday.

Then, turning around, Colonel Keppler yelled out through open door for his staff officer, who led me out into another office, where he asked some brief questions about my background, date eligible to return from overseas (DEROS), shots, military occupational specialty (MOS), and so forth. Captain Stinson arrived and I went with him to the advisors' lounge. Captain Stinson was about my size and build but had dark hair. As the Fifty-First staff advisor, he assisted the regimental staff. In rapid succession, I asked where the Third Battalion was, what it did, what kind of leaders it had, how good it was, whether they got much action, and who was on the advisory team.

Laughing, Captain Stinson responded that I would find out soon enough. The Third Battalion was stationed in Hoi An, but as a mobile reaction force it could actually operate anywhere in Quang Nam sector. Currently, the battalion was between operations.

The battalion was good, he continued. It had good leaders. The battalion advising team was short a couple of people. Normally the advisory team table of organization and equipment (TO/E), the official authorization of personnel and equipment for a unit, calls for a captain, a lieutenant, and two NCOs. The lieutenant's position had been, until recently, filled by an Australian warrant officer. So that position was vacant. The only one on my team, he explained, was Staff Sergeant Curtis Bronson. The other NCO position was vacant. I asked Captain Stinson what Sergeant Bronson was like. Silent for a moment, Tony replied that he didn't look like a soldier. In fact, he sort of looked like the cartoon soldier Beetle Bailey, tall, stoop-shouldered, slouchy when he walked and a sloppy dresser, but a damn good man. He knew his stuff. Tony told me to wait on the rest of the questions until later. First, I would have to move my stuff into the advisory team room in Da Nang.

I would have to give up my place in Da Nang and go to MACV billeting and get a key to the advisory team room. I could take one of the empty hot boxes, an enclosed moveable clothes closet made of wood and with an electric bulb in it to ward off mildew. The team room was where Fifty-First Regiment advisors kept all their stuff except their field gear. The room was secure, and if advisors ever got a break they could always go into Da Nang for a little R&R, sleep in a room with sheets, use indoor plumbing, and take a shower.

I asked Tony how often he got to go to Da Nang to use this place and he replied that in the eight or nine months he had been with the regiment he never had any time off, so he had never been to the team room. It sounded like I would definitely be a lot busier on this assignment, with little time to read paperback books, and, hopefully, a more useful role in combat.

Going back to Da Nang I almost believed I could have kept the helicopter aloft by my sheer exuberance. I went directly to Major Braune's office and told him the good news. He acknowledged he knew about it and was happy I was finally getting my field assignment. I went to Captain Phiem's office and told him the good news. He too was happy for me.

I informed my students that Thursday night would be our last English class. When I told them why, they were both happy and sad. They decided Thursday night we would not hold class but have a little party instead. I protested but they insisted. I didn't like drawn out good-byes. I preferred to just say good-bye and leave. My students wouldn't accept that.

The next two days were spent making arrangements to leave. My responsibilities as our advisory team supply officer, classified documents officer, and intelligence fund expenditures officer were turned over to one of the NCOs or Major Braune. I moved out of the BOQ leaving my new roommate, John Black, an Army captain who was the I Corps USAF ground liaison officer, with the room to himself. John, working with the USAF, was able to obtain for me an Air Force survival knife. As a collector of various combat knives, I considered it my favorite.

Thursday night all my students showed up as did Captain Phiem, Major Braune, Staff Sergeant Billstone, SP5 Kurtz, and our interpreter Sergeant Ham. The Vietnamese provided the food, beer and soda. It was an impromptu good-bye party that we all enjoyed. Time passed quickly and soon it was over. Friday afternoon I boarded the helicopter to Hoi An, carrying my field gear. I was as excited as any kid on Christmas morning who got everything he ever wished for.

CHAPTER 9

Joining the Third Battalion, Fifty-First Regiment

When I arrived in Hoi An, Captain Tony Stinson met me at the helicopter pad with his Jeep. He welcomed me and took me to the advisory compound at Quang Nam sector headquarters where I would meet my new boss, Major Howard Haines.

Settling into the passenger seat of the Jeep, I inquired what Major Haines was like. Spinning the wheels in the soft gravel as he took off, Tony described the major as one who might be perceived, at first glance, as a hard-ass, by-the-book guy, always reminding his men of haircuts, shaves, clean boots, and squared away uniform. You know, always look like an officer and a gentleman shit. But that really didn't do him justice. He was honest and fair, and he would never ask one of his men to do anything he couldn't or wouldn't do himself, Tony concluded.

Gripping the wheel as he turned a sharp corner, Tony stated that the major didn't bother his field advisors. That is, he wasn't on their backs all the time asking for reports. That was Tony's job: to get the info from the guys in the field to prepare the reports. The major saw you as a combat advisor. When your battalion was in Hoi An, taking a break, he wouldn't be on your ass all the time with make-do busy work. When your battalion was in the field, you did your job. When you came in from the field, he expected you to first get everything ready to go back out, then relax. All in all, Tony thought that he was an okay guy to work for.

Tony slowed the Jeep at the front of the headquarters building, where the entrance had a covered, sand-bagged sentry box, above which an iron sign proclaimed TRAI PHAM-PHO-QUOC, "the military post committed to reconquer our country." Good first impression, I thought.

Tony drove across the open courtyard, passed two large white concrete buildings on our left, and at the end of the courtyard veered right, around a large raised concrete platform. On the other side of the platform was another fence with barbed-wire and sand-bagged sentry boxes and more Vietnamese guards who waved us through. This was the U.S. side of the sector headquarters. Stopping the Jeep next to a concrete volleyball court, he waved his hand toward a single-story, metal-roofed building; this would be my home. I would stay here when the unit was in from the field.

Grabbing my bag, Tony led me inside the large darkened room, not unlike a U.S. barracks. He told me to grab any bunk that didn't have gear on it. The room was the BOQ for the field advisors, and next door was the one for the NCOs. I could just put my stuff in one of the empty field lockers across the room. Following Tony's instructions, I removed the lock on my duffle bag, crammed the bag into the locker, and used the same lock to secure the locker.

We walked across the U.S. compound area and went into the lounge to meet the major. Tony said the advisory offices were in the Fifty-First Regiment headquarters which were not in this compound.

Inside I saw an older infantry major who appeared to be in his early 40s. He had short brownish hair and was clean shaven. His jungle fatigues were well worn but fit his muscular, compact body well. He was in good physical shape with leathery, tan skin indicating he had been around quite a while. Pushing back from the bar, the man extended a huge hand attached to a thick arm and greeted me and introduced himself.

I responded appropriately, stiffly grasping his outstretched hand as I said hello and gave him my name.

Before more could be said, Tony motioned for us to sit down and get comfortable as he moved toward a corner table with some chairs. After the three of us sat down, the major spoke first, getting straight to the point, asking about my background. It all came out in a rush, starting with dropping out of college at 19 and enlisting in the Marines. Leaving as a junior NCO in '59 to return to school and get married. Commissioned after graduation, ROTC, in '61. Being a platoon leader, S-3 air, assistant battalion ops officer, assistant S-1, executive officer of a marksmanship detachment, and battalion exec. I said I had been in Vietnam since January and just finished as the deputy senior advisor of Da Nang garrison. Haines chuckled, questioning why I was still only a captain with all that experience.

Haines got us back on track. The Third Battalion, the one I would to join, was presently on operational status. Right now, it was here in Hoi An, but Sunday it would be going out again. He explained that Captain Calder, the advisor I would be replacing, was doing a good job but he got sick and could no longer go on combat operations.

Nodding at Tony, the major continued, saying that the Fifty-First had the reputation of being one of the best ARVN units in I Corps. During this last political Chinese fire drill in Da Nang and Hue and Hoi An, the Fifty-

First stayed out of it thanks to their commander, Lieutenant Colonel Nguyen Tho Lap. He was a 20-year man who started with the French right after World War II. The Fifty-First had three battalions. One was stationed at An Hoa about ten miles west of Hoi An and another was operating in the field north of Hoi An, just southwest of Da Nang. The third battalion was what was called a mobile reaction force. Essentially it went where the trouble was. For the next few weeks it would be working in Hieu Nhon sub-sector with an RF company and a U.S. Marine battalion. Tony again jumped in, looking directly at me, exclaimed that I would like "Ding Dong" Bell. He speculated we two jarheads ought to get along really good.

Major Haines, looking exasperated, continued, explaining that Lieutenant Colonel Van Bell was the Marine battalion commander I would be working with. He was an old-time grunt, a dedicated infantryman, probably the most decorated Marine around. Besides that, he was an old Marine boxer and still built like one. He was one tough cookie. He didn't take any crap from anyone. His troopers called him "Ding Dong" behind his back. And, looking at Tony, Haines stated that I never had heard "Ding Dong" from them.

Tony, not at all chagrined by Haines's remark, added that Colonel Bell didn't care much for the Vietnamese, letting it be known that he felt they were lazy and not good fighters. He didn't hold American advisors in high regard either. Haines continued to reinforce how important it would be for me to work with him to positively represent us as U.S. Army advisors. I was told to do my best with him and not get him pissed off. I nodded that I understood.

Major Haines explained that about half of the Third Battalion operations were with the U.S. Marines, so we had to work with them. Most of our combat support came from the Marines. We depended on them for medevacs, artillery, gunships, close air support, and so forth. He expected that I should get along with them well, as one ex-leatherneck to another. Tony commented that at least I, as a former Marine, should be able to understand them because he sure as hell couldn't.

Getting back to business, the major explained that I would meet regimental commander Lieutenant Colonel Lap and the Third Battalion commander, Captain Van, the next day. Van was a good man. He was described as another old soldier who started with the French and should be promoted to major sometime soon, according to Colonel Lap.

My officer efficiency report would be done with Tony as the rater because he had date of rank on me and Major Haines would be my endorser. This way everything would be kept in-house. Major Haines emphasized that if I did a good job my OER would reflect it. If I fucked up, he would fire my ass in a New York minute. Tomorrow I would meet the Vietnamese commanders and Master Sergeant Wright, our NCO advisor.

My mind gushed a torrent of questions as I thought about when I would get briefed on the operation. When would I get an intel briefing on the area we were going into? When would I get a status briefing on the Third Battalion? When would I get with the Marine liaison for the operation?

Major Haines said that tomorrow morning Tony and Sergeant Wright would go over everything I would need to know on the Third Battalion and the area it would be working in. Tomorrow afternoon I would meet all the key players and attend the briefing on the upcoming operation.

That evening, after supper, I was rearranging my gear when I heard a knock on the door. I yelled for my visitor to come in. In walked a tall, dark haired, lanky young man, Sergeant Harry Cousins, an NCO I had met three months ago at Da Nang garrison. Cousins was on his third extension in Vietnam. He had served two previous field assignments and was now on his third with the Second Battalion, Fifty-First Regiment. I ad-

Me and my ARVN counterpart, Major Van, the commander of the Third Battalion, Fifty-First Infantry Regiment. When I first met the major, he was a captain, then was promoted to major.

mired the man. He was a good field soldier, the kind of man you'd want next to you in a fight. He knew infantry tactics and weapons, the Vietnamese, and the Viet Cong.

After mutual greetings I asked how his leg was. He replied it was doing okay. He had been shot in the calf a week ago in a firefight. The bullet went clean through the muscle, a nice neat hole. No damage to the bone. He said it just hurt like hell, but it was healing. The docs in MILPHAP were taking care of it pretty good and he would be back in the field in a week or two. MILPHAP was an acronym for Military Provincial Health Program, a joint U.S. military and GVN project to create or expand public medical facilities throughout South Vietnam. In Hoi An, the MILPHAP medical clinic was staffed by U.S. Navy medical personnel and located next to our BOQ. I spent the next few hours picking his brain; he was an excellent teacher and I was a very attentive student.

The next morning after breakfast Tony drove me to the office of Fifty-First Regiment advisors. As we entered, Master Sergeant Benjamin Wright rose and introduced himself. I liked him immediately. His smile was genuine and his grip firm. Here was an athletic, confident career soldier, a no-nonsense type who wasted no effort. With little prompting from me, the senior sergeant began telling me about the Third Battalion, Fifty-First Regiment, and the local VC.

Wright began by describing the ARVN unit as a typical ARVN infantry battalion with three rifle companies, a headquarters company, and a heavy weapons platoon for each of the rifle companies. The rifle companies had about 100 to 110 men each. The headquarters company also had about 100 men. Overall the total battalion strength was close to 430 men. Most riflemen were armed with an M1 Garand or an M1 carbine. Some had Thompson .45-caliber machine guns. Each rifle company also had a weapons platoon with a 60 mm mortar and three .30-caliber air-cooled light machine guns. Each company also has six M79 grenade launchers. The battalion heavy weapons platoon had two 81 mm mortars and a couple of 57 mm recoilless rifles. He also commented that the ARVN firepower was not what we were used to in a U.S. battalion.

I agreed, recalling that a U.S. infantry rifle company had 162 M14 semi-automatic rifles, 29 M79 grenade launchers, 18 M60 machine guns, nine 81 mm mortars, three 3.5-inch rocket launchers, three portable flame throwers, 18 90 mm recoilless rifles, and four 106 mm recoilless rifles. An ARVN rifle company had even less firepower than one of our infantry companies had during World War II.

Tony began to describe the people of the Third Battalion, starting with the CO, Captain Van, a good man. I would meet him in the afternoon. He began his military career as a private in the French forces right after World War II. He had fought all over North and South Vietnam for the French, and now he was an officer for the South Vietnamese army. He had been the battalion commander for several years and probably had at least one of every combat decoration the Vietnamese government ever handed out. He was an easy-going guy who was admired by both the Vietnamese and the advisors. He spoke some English and excellent French.

The battalion executive officer, Sergeant Wright added, was a real junkie, a hophead, a druggie who took dope and didn't do a damn thing for the unit. Captain Van was trying to get rid of him. He was fat, lazy and selfish, and he never went on operations. The sergeant major was number one. He'd be a good top sergeant in any army. All the men liked him, and he did a good job. He liked advisors and got along with them really well. The staff officers were all okay. The company commanders were all experienced and did a good job. The CO of the Second Company, First Lieutenant Phong, also served unofficially as the battalion XO when in the field. The headquarters company CO, First Lieutenant Pham, was probably the friendliest officer in the battalion and the most helpful in the unit for knowing what was going on. He was the one the advisors worked with mostly to get information for reports.

Sergeant Wright expounded on my going to a good unit. They had good leaders and liked to fight. If I didn't have my CIB yet, I would certainly earn it in my first 30 days with the battalion. I inquired about the local VC.

This area was mostly local VC guerrillas, Tony explained. There was at least one VC main force unit, the Doc Lap Battalion. The VC had concentrated their efforts against the GVN by attacking and killing village and hamlet officials. The VC had a parallel government which replicated the local GVN. Their continued terrorist tactics of killing and kidnapping and taxation put fear in the local peasants. All the local people were fully aware of what the VC were doing, according to Sergeant Wright, but too scared to do anything. During the night the VC entered the hamlets and did whatever they pleased, with no interference. The VC would take village chiefs and their families out of their huts during the night. Sometimes they would just cut them up a little with knives as a warning. Other times they would slit their throats or disembowel them right in front of their wives and kids and let them bleed to death. Unless the GVN could provide protection, the VC would continue to have free reign.

Most of the VC activity, Sergeant Wright said, consisted of terror raids against the rural areas. The local guerrillas were supported by main force units. The ARVN and the Marines had been working together to locate these bigger VC units and destroy them. It was hard work because they moved around so much, but last year, the Ninth Marines had come up with a good idea: their county fair operations.

The county fair concept initiated by the Ninth Marines was originally designed to use a combination of U.S. and Vietnamese military and civilian government personnel to identify and destroy the Viet Cong infrastructure found within the Vietnamese hamlets and villages. The military forces were used to surround the targeted hamlet or village, usually before dawn, and hopefully trap everyone inside the cordon. The civilian forces, police, intelligence agents, and local government officials would then identify the Viet Cong members and isolate them from the rest of the inhabitants.

This type of operation had two primary purposes. First it allowed the GVN to attempt to destroy the local VC infrastructure that paralleled the legal political structure of the hamlets and villages, providing the leadership and support for the VC guerrilla operations conducted in the area. Second, the county fair operations provided a show of GVN strength, power, and concern for the welfare of its citizens. This last part was demonstrated by setting up within the target area medical clinics and government give-away programs, such as food, clothing, farming equipment, building materials, and other items locals needed. It also provided government political propaganda lectures and entertainment by government-trained singers, dancers, actors, actresses, and musicians who gave dramatic presentations extolling the virtues of the GVN.

Sergeant Wright added that when viewed from inside the village, these events looked just like small county fairs that you'd find back in the States out in the sticks.

I was informed that this was what the Third Battalion would be doing for the next few weeks, working with Lieutenant Colonel Bell's First Battalion of the First Marine Regiment, the 368th Regional Force Company from Hieu Nhon district and the Hieu Nhon district officials and advisors.

During the rest of the morning, Tony and Sergeant Wright used maps to acquaint me with the area in which we would be operating and the locations of known enemy positions and friendly troops. After lunch we returned to the ARVN Fifty-First Headquarters to meet the regimental commander and my new counterpart, Captain Van.

Major Haines took me into the office of his counterpart, Lieutenant Colonel Nguyen Tho Lap. The office was a plain room with an old, well-used, military-style wooden desk and some cabinets with an even older long conference table and chairs on the other side. The colonel invited us to sit down at the long table as a young Vietnamese soldier silently came in with a pot of hot tea and four cups. I knew Lieutenant Colonel Lap had been a Vietnamese officer for 20 years and was obviously a dedicated career soldier. But he didn't look like the commander of a combat regiment. He was a slight man with lean muscles, balding with thin gray hair, and he appeared to be somewhat stooped over with age. I guessed he was in his late 40s or early 50s. He reminded me more of a retired schoolteacher or an accountant than a military man.

Captain Van was tall for a Vietnamese, standing about five feet, eight or nine inches, and he moved in a loose, carefree manner. His close-cropped dark hair grew untamed in all directions with barely visible flecks of gray below his temples. He was very tan, indicating he had spent most of his time outdoors. His background suggested he was in his 40s, but he looked younger. He had a perpetual wide grin and smoked cigarettes from a short plastic holder.

After sipping the tea and exchanging awkward pleasantries in impeccable English, resembling a professor lecturing his students, the colonel briefed me on Quang Nam province.

Quang Nam had many problems, with 160,000 refugees from the war, more than 25 percent of the population of 600,000 people. The Viet Cong controlled 5 percent of these people and maybe only another 5 percent professed allegiance to the government of South Vietnam. That left 90 percent who could go either way.

At least 1,000 civilians every week were killed or wounded. The Quang Nam province chief, Nguyen Huu Chi, was a smart, educated man, with a doctor of philosophy degree from Michigan State University. Unfortunately, he was never in Hoi An but always away giving talks. From the north, he left Hanoi in 1954, and he had never been a soldier.

I was beginning to catch the drift. Lieutenant Colonel Lap, the military commander for Quang Nam, had to fight the war while Dr. Chi, who was responsible for the civil side of the province, was never here. The colonel was not hiding his disgust for Dr. Chi. Lap went on to describe the corruption in the province government and how hard it was for him to use his troops to pacify the countryside when Dr. Chi's civilians were totally unresponsive to the needs of the people whose lives and livelihoods had been disrupted by the war.

Colonel Lap pointed out that he did not believe Dr. Chi was corrupt or dishonest but too young at 31 and too intolerant of the Saigon government. Lieutenant Colonel Lap then discussed the upcoming county fair operation and working with the U.S. Marines. His attitude was both hot and cold toward the Marines. He praised their combat support and their fighting abilities, but he found fault with their attitude toward the ARVN units and their Vietnamese commanders. The Marines, with all their wonderful war technology, came to fight for only one year and then go home. They came and they went, but the Vietnamese were still here. They did not understand the situation. They had fast jets, many helicopters, skilled doctors. Each Marine had his own automatic rifle, and he did not have to find his own food.

Spreading his hands in front of him in a gesture of unanswerable questioning, he said softly that his soldiers were poor. They worried about their families. They did not have the strength or weapons of the Americans. This war was not over in a year. It was always a part of Vietnam. Even when his soldiers went home, they were still in the war. These things the Marines did not understand.

As abruptly as it had begun, the lecture was over. Lieutenant Colonel Lap, pushing his chair back, rose, as did the rest of us. He said we had to go to the briefing on tomorrow's operations as he led the way. We followed him down the hall toward a closed door guarded by a soldier armed with a carbine. As we approached, the soldier came to attention and remained so as we entered the room.

The windowless room had low benches in the back half of the room, while the front half was filled with well-worn straight-back wooden chairs.

Most of the seats were occupied. Covered map boards flanked a table at the front of the room. The Vietnamese saffron flag with red stripes hung on one wall as did a large plywood triangular replica of the regimental patch. This insignia was split diagonally in half with red on the top, blue on the bottom, and had a red "51" painted in the center of a large multi-pointed white star burst. The stale, humid air was slowly paddled by two ancient ceiling fans, weakly churning but providing no relief.

As Lieutenant Colonel Lap strode in, all talking ceased, and everyone rose. He went to the front row as did Major Haines. I followed Captain Van as he grabbed my hand and led me to two open seats in the second row. As soon as Colonel Lap and Major Haines sat down, the regimental sergeant major bellowed, "Be seated," and everyone else sat down.

Then the regimental executive officer, a sharp, trim young airborne ranger ARVN major, addressed the group, first in Vietnamese and then in flawless English. He introduced the commanders, staff officers, and advisors who would be running the operation. He began with Lieutenant Colonel Lap and Major Haines, then Captain Van and myself, then the Marine battalion commander, Lieutenant Colonel Bell, followed by the commander of the 368th RF Company, the Hieu Nhon District chief and his staff, and Army captain Dick Laskowski, the Hieu Nhon American district advisor. Lastly, he introduced the regiment staff who would present the operations plan.

Vietnamese sergeants quickly passed out copies of the operations order; copies in Vietnamese for the Vietnamese and English versions for the Americans. All the units were properly listed at the top under task organization. A Vietnamese lieutenant, the regiment S-2 (intelligence officer), began to describe the area of the operation as an assistant pointed out the references mentioned on one of the now-uncovered maps. The operation would take place in the village of Cam-An in Hieu Nhon district. Three different hamlets were the targets: Ha My Dong 2, Ha My Dong 3, and Ha My Tay 2, which lay across the Hiep River from Ha My Dong 3. The three hamlets, each home to approximately 500 Vietnamese, were between three and four miles northwest of Hoi An. The S-2 stated that the opposition would probably be one VC guerrilla squad, at the least, to one VC guerrilla platoon, at the most, in each hamlet. There was no intelligence indicating any VC main force units were in the area. The VC would be lightly armed, mostly with repeating rifles and grenades, and were not expected to offer much resistance. He described the terrain as lowland rice paddies with several meandering streams with heavy foliage around the hamlets and lining the stream banks.

The next briefer was a Vietnamese captain, the S-3 (operations staff officer). He explained the county fair, which was a clearing and securing operation. The three-day mission would be executed in three phases. In the first phase, the U.S. Marine battalion, using landing vehicles, tracked personnel

(LVTP-5) and amphibious tractors (AMTRACS), would move into blocking positions on the north and west sides of the hamlets. An AMTRAC is an armored vehicle which holds 34 combat Marines, originally designed to transport Marines from ships to beaches on amphibious assaults. In Vietnam it was used to cross inland water courses. The ARVN battalion would sweep from the south and southeast through the hamlets. The RF company would set up a blocking position on the north to catch anyone trying to escape the ARVN sweep. In the second phase, the Marines would remain on the perimeter, with the ARVN searching each hamlet for hidden weapons and underground tunnels and VC. The RF company would detain and question any VC or VC suspects. The third phase would involve district officials going into the hamlets, checking for ID cards, providing medical treatment, and issuing supplies and rations to the villagers during the three days of the operation.

The operation would begin at 5:00 the next morning with the U.S. Marines establishing their blocking positions by moving in from the north and the west. The RF company would follow the Marines and set up after the Marines were in position. Also, at 5:00 a.m., the ARVN Third Battalion would begin to sweep the countryside from the south. Different U.S. Marine liaison teams would be assigned to the ARVN Third Battalion, the RF company, and the district headquarters. Fire support would be provided by USMC artillery and/or USMC helicopter gunships and controlled by the USMC liaison teams or the USMC battalion. Medical evacuation would be handled by USMC helicopters on an on-call basis. Food rations for the estimated 1,500 villagers during the three-day operation would be provided by the civic action section of the First Marine Regiment and the district headquarters. The commander of the operation would be Lieutenant Colonel Lap.

Next, Colonel Lap made a speech about the value of this joint operation. He then asked Lieutenant Colonel Bell to take over.

Lieutenant Colonel Van D. Bell stood up and discussed how the liaison with the Vietnamese would work. In his mid–40s, he was a broad-chested, husky, muscular man with a thick neck and a blonde flat-top crew cut. His face, neck and hands were deeply tanned. He was a Marine's Marine. Tony's assessment of him was on the mark. Colonel Bell announced that each Marine liaison team consisted of an NCO and a radio man. He had each sergeant stand as he named which Vietnamese unit the NCO would accompany and then said he would like to see all the U.S. advisors after the briefing to discuss liaison matters.

After the group was dismissed, I went to the back of the room with the other advisors to meet with Lieutenant Colonel Bell. What occurred next was an eye-opener for me, even though it probably should not have surprised me. I had been forewarned. Colonel Bell told us he had a mission to search out and destroy the enemy, and to work with the Vietnamese military forces and civil government, and he would do that to the best of his ability, but he had no faith in our counterparts to do the same. He proclaimed that if he took his Marines out of here, back to Da Nang, the whole goddamn area would revert to the Viet Cong within two weeks.

Colonel Bell didn't care for the ARVN, nor did he seem to care for Army advisors. Before he left, I mentioned in passing that I used to be in the Marines in the late 1950s. For what it was worth, the fact that I was now in the Army seemed to reinforce his feeling that Army advisors weren't worth much. The advisors met with their Marine liaison teams and Colonel Bell explained how the liaison would work.

I later learned that Lieutenant Colonel Bell had been in the Hoi An area for about a month, having just completed combat operations along the northern border of I Corps near Khe Sanh. His battalion had conducted numerous operations with elements of the Fifty-First Regiment. By the end of the summer, Colonel Bell's Marines, fighting between Da Nang and Hoi An, had killed 307 VC guerrillas and captured another 307, while 42 Marines had been killed and 166 wounded.

Colonel Bell nodded to Captain Van and asked when Captain Van would be briefing the Vietnamese company commanders on the operation. Captain Van looked at his watch and held up five fingers, indicating five o'clock. Colonel Bell said he would have his S-3 at the briefing to make the final coordination, said good-bye to Lieutenant Colonel Lap and left. Staring at Bell's departing back, I was still absorbing what had been said and by whom. The lay of the land had been perfectly defined here. Bell certainly wasn't friendly toward us. Boy, did I have a lot to learn.

It felt like there was so much for me to do and so little time to get it all done. The next day I would be out on my first combat operation with the battalion, and I really didn't know anyone. In fact, I hadn't even met the other man on my advisory team, Staff Sergeant Curtis Bronson.

As I stood next to Captain Van, the sudden sound of my name, "Captain Worthington," shattered my concerns as a tall man, extending his hand, introduced himself as Sergeant Bronson. Standing before me was this slouching figure in his 30s, about six feet, three inches, and thin with a small paunch. Here was an NCO who physically represented the greatest antithesis of an infantry platoon sergeant I could ever imagine. Sergeant Bronson was wearing jungle fatigues that looked two sizes too big. Despite the disappointing visual effect, I was relieved to now have someone who could help me understand what I should be doing.

Captain Van briefly explained to Bronson the county fair operation. He then excused himself after saying he would meet us back here at five.

I explained to the sergeant that I had just arrived last night and tomorrow

I would be going out on my first operation with this unit. I said we needed to talk about what I was supposed to do. Sergeant Bronson said he had his Jeep outside, so we would go back to the BOQ and meet the guy I was replacing, Captain Calder. He explained that we could then talk about operation, implying it was no big deal because they had gone on this thing with "Ding Dong" Bell before.

Climbing into the Jeep, he explained he'd left early yesterday morning for Da Nang to pick up Calder, who had been hospitalized at Charlie Med, the Marine field hospital. They didn't get back until after lunch today. For the rest of the way to the MACV compound, we swapped brief histories and my initial impression of Sergeant Bronson began to change as I realized he knew his job well. We pulled up in front of the BOQ and went inside. Sitting on a bunk, shirtless, was Jason Calder, sorting his gear, packing a duffle bag. While Jason was skinny when I first knew him at Fort Bragg, DLI, and on our way to I Corps, he was now emaciated.

Greeting Jason, I said he didn't look too good and asked what happened. He explained that he just got some intestinal bug. He expected be okay now, showing me three small plastic pill containers. A steady diet of rice and fish heads for five months did him in.

I announced that I needed some help, asking what he could tell me about my job tomorrow. Jason explained that Captain Van and his officers, except for that son of a bitch Do, his XO, were all okay. They know what to do so I shouldn't try to tell them how to fight. I should take it easy with Colonel Bell. He was a damn good Marine battalion commander, but he didn't care for the ARVN or Army advisors very much.

I nodded, my first impressions confirmed. My primary job would be a liaison officer. I would coordinate with the Marines for their part of the ops, their artillery, gunships, tac air, medevac.

Calder said he asked questions, believing that was the best way to be an effective advisor, and said the battalion ops plan would be brief. Not like Fort Benning. No overlays with tons of annexes. Oh, someone would have something on paper, but the captain would just tell all his commanders what to do. Now, if Colonel Bell or one of his staff officers was at the briefing, he would probably get a copy of a written ops order. But it would be in Vietnamese, and Bell's interpreter would have to translate it.

At the briefing, Colonel Bell's operations officer would exchange radio call signs and frequencies and let you know what kind of support would be available. He would also work out with the Vietnamese exactly where the Marines would tie in with the ARVN. Jason explained that he kept the Marine liaison team with him and he stayed with Captain Van. Sergeant Bronson would go with the lead company that would link up with the Marines. That was the way to know exactly what was going on. Sergeant Bronson added

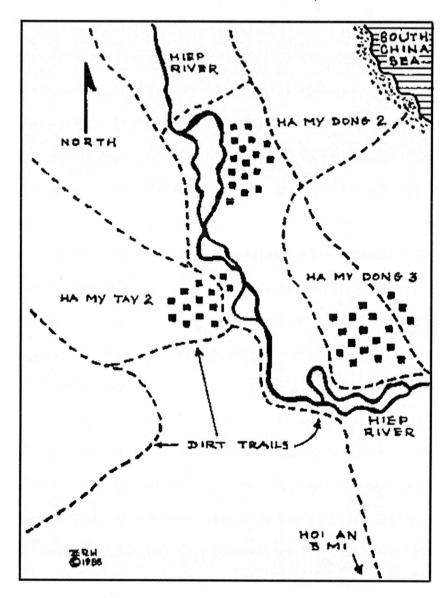

Hiep River

that because I would be with the captain, he could show me on the map where he thought all his troops were. With Sergeant Bronson with the lead company, he could tell me where he thought lead company was. The Marine liaison would keep me informed of where Bell's units were.

This way I should pretty much know where everyone was and what was happening. If one company ran into some VC, they usually had no problem. They were pretty good at fire and maneuver. If they got into some serious trouble, the captain would let me know, and he might ask for Marine support or tac air or medevacs or whatever. I just need to ask the Marine liaison team to call for help.

I asked if Jason ever left the captain to go out with a company. Jason explained that sometimes he did. During operations where the battalion was moving, Jason stayed with the captain, because he was the advisor's counterpart and that was expected. But if the battalion was in a defensive posture and the captain was not moving but a company was, the senior advisor might go with a company commander and leave the NCO with the battalion commander. I should check it out with Captain Van first.

I asked about Major Haines. What was he like? Jason responded that Major Haines was a soldier all the way but would leave the advisors alone in the field. A good man, Jason said, much better than those candy-assed advisors at province in that they were scared shitless about going into the field. Glancing at his watch, Bronson exclaimed that it was time for the captain's briefing.

The briefing went just as Calder predicted. Captain Van had a typed copy of the ops plan for the Marine S-3 captain. He explained which companies would go where and when. He very carefully showed the Marine captain and me, on the map, where each ARVN company would be and where the Third Battalion would tie in with Lieutenant Colonel Bell's units. I got the call signs and frequencies from the Marine S-3 and he left the two-man liaison team with Sergeant Bronson.

From the Fifty-First headquarters it would take the two-and-a-half-ton trucks 30 minutes to get to the line of departure (LD), that area on the ground where we would begin to deploy the troops. The trucks would leave at 4:15 a.m. and arrive at the LD at 4:45, giving the troops 15 minutes to move out. The captain told me to meet him at regiment tomorrow at 4:00. He said we would go in his Jeep so we could talk on the move to the operation. As he turned to go, he commented on how well I spoke Vietnamese. Sergeant Bronson and the two Marine liaison men looked at me as Sergeant Bronson echoed the captain, stating that I seemed to know Vietnamese pretty well.

That evening after supper I got back together with Sergeant Bronson and Jason. Sergeant Bronson said he would get me up at 3:00, and we'd have some C-rations together before leaving. When we got to the regiment he'd go with the lead unit, the Second Company, with First Lieutenant Phong, the CO. Lieutenant Phong would give him a radio man, a private who spoke English. I'd go with the captain and I would have with me the advisor radio man, Private Tuan, a Vietnamese soldier who spoke excellent English. The two Marines would spend the night with Sergeant Bronson and they would be in a three-quarter-ton truck with some of Captain Van's staff, right behind his Jeep.

I asked Jason what kind of gear he took in the field and how he carried it. Jason explained that he used a Vietnamese backpack, which Sergeant Bronson went to get for me, to carry his toilet articles, a change of clothes, and some C-rations. He also carried a nylon hammock, some nylon cord, and a rain jacket, which did double duty as a blanket at night.

Sergeant Bronson returned with a case of C-rations and a backpack, large enough to carry everything I needed. He broke open the box of C-rations with a bayonet and suggested I only take a few cans because I would probably be eating most of my meals with the captain, and they would be rice or soup. I could use the C-rations to spice up the rice. Then Sergeant Bronson asked if we needed anything else. He apologized for not having an extra hammock when I said I didn't have one, and after saying good-night, he left.

Rummaging through my duffle bag, I got out two clean sets of jungle fatigues (I only had four sets) and two sets of green T-shirts, jockey shorts, and socks. One set I'd wear and the other I'd put in the pack. I also put in a small toiletry kit, a couple of small towels, some nylon cord, my rain jacket, and a poncho. Sorting through the C-rations, I selected about eight cans and stowed them in the corners and pockets of the backpack. Next, I got my web gear ready. I had my USAF survival knife, a large first aid kit, a holster with my .45 pistol and a .45 magazine pouch, a couple of ammo pouches to hold extra magazines for my M1 carbine, a lensatic compass and its pouch, and two plastic canteens with aluminum cups and carriers (one canteen would be attached to the backpack). On a box next to my cot, I set aside a couple of ballpoint pens, a small pad of paper, my wallet in a plastic bag (to protect it from water and sweat), a Boy Scout–type pocket knife, and my rabbit's foot for luck. My dog tags with the Saint Christopher's medal were taped so they wouldn't jangle. I also got some plastic spoons and a couple cans of C-rations to go in the leg pockets of my jungle fatigues.

After a shower I went over the map of the operations area one more time. Finally, I figured I was as ready as I would ever be. I slipped the map with the Marine radio call signs and frequencies into a plastic bag that PRC-10 radio batteries came in, stowed it away, and then stretched out on the cot. After the two sessions with Captain Calder and Sergeant Bronson, I felt much more prepared and relaxed than I had been just after the regimental briefing. In fact, I thought, as I drifted off to sleep, I was very well prepared for whatever the next day might bring.

CHAPTER 10

The County Fair
in Hieu Nhon

At 4:00 a.m., we met as planned for the county fair operation in Hieu Nhon. The sky was pitch black, and the air was very still and warm. The soldiers were silently boarding trucks preparing to move out. In the darkness, I wasn't able to distinguish individual movements, but I got the impression that the battalion had done this many times before, since there was no confusion.

Sergeant Bronson went with me to the large porch at the front of the headquarters building. Lieutenant Colonel Lap, Major Haines, Captain Van, the American advisor for Hieu Nhon district, Captain Dick Laskowski, and the district chief were all there, talking in low tones. Sergeant Bronson found Lieutenant Phong, the Second Company commander, and left to join his unit.

After a round of greetings, Major Haines said he hoped I would have a good time and moved out with his counterpart, Lieutenant Colonel Lap. Captain Van grabbed my hand and took me to his Jeep. Hand-holding among Vietnamese males was an accepted custom in the country. It's sort of like a man putting his hand on another man's shoulder or slapping him on the back in our country. At first, when this happened in Da Nang, I had been embarrassed, but now I was used to it.

I motioned for the two Marine liaison team members who had come with Sergeant Bronson and me to get in the three-quarter-ton truck just behind Captain Van's Jeep. Two men were already in the captain's Jeep, a driver and a man holding a PRC-10.

A friendly Vietnamese man, speaking in Vietnamese, said good morning, introducing himself as Private First Class Tuan, my radio man. I returned the greeting, extending my hand, saying I was very pleased to meet him.

Passing my carbine to Tuan I climbed into the back of the open Jeep. Someone came running up to Captain Van, stopped, saluted, and told him the battalion was ready to go. The captain returned the salute, telling the man to move out, and he ran off into the murky night. Turning to me, Van said we would now go. One by one the vehicles came to life and slowly rolled out of the compound. At last we were on our way.

In Vietnamese I asked Private Tuan if he spoke English and repeated the question in French. He responded he spoke English and French, explaining that he also knew some Cambodian, Chinese, and Montagnard, specifically Rhade.

As we bounced along through the inky countryside, I learned that Private Tuan had been raised outside of Saigon and had gone to college one year before being drafted four years ago. He had studied French and English in high school and came from a middle-class urban home. His father was a civil servant and his mother worked in their home, taking care of the children. I was impressed with him.

PFC Thuan, the ARVN soldier assigned as my radio operator and interpreter. He grew up in Saigon and had some college. He was fluent in English, French, and some Rhade. He was very smart and thoroughly enjoyed working with the American advisors.

It was still dark when we stopped about 4:45 next to a small stream, the Song Hiep. The Second Company would move north, on the west side of the stream, surround Ha My Tay 2, and link up with the U.S. Marines. The other two ARVN companies would cross the stream and move north between the stream and the beach along the South China Sea, a distance just under one and a half miles. As the First and Third companies pushed north, the First Company would approach and surround Ha My Dong 3. The Third Company would continue forward and then surround Ha My Dong 2, at the same time establishing contact with the RF company. Hopefully, all three hamlets would be surrounded and secured by noon. Captain Van, his staff, elements of the battalion heavy weapons platoon, and a security platoon would follow the First Company and establish the battalion CP in Ha My Dong 3.

The captain and his group set up a perimeter by the stream to wait for the two companies to cross. Soldiers were setting up the two 81 mm mortars which would remain here until all three villages were secured as their 4,500-meter maximum range more than covered the operation area. The mortar men were also arranging range stakes, using the map and compasses, and working out various deflections and ranges for preplanned adjustment points located on the map. They unboxed high-explosive rounds, setting them up beside the two tubes. They already established radio contact with the forward observers of each company. The mortar section was ready for business.

The captain explained that his operations NCO was monitoring the progress of the three companies and maintaining a field log of what was transpiring. The Marine NCO was showing the battalion ops sergeant on the map where Lieutenant Colonel Bell's Marines and AMTRACS were. The mortars and security elements from the headquarters company would stay here as the battalion command group collected their gear to move out.

Soon the Marine sergeant told me one Marine company had made contact with the VC. Apparently, three VC had tried to sneak by the Marine forward line. When they had refused to halt after being warned, one had been shot and the other two had hidden in heavy bushes and had fired back. An M79 grenade launcher had stopped that. The Marines had three VC KIA and three French bolt-action rifles in their hands.

As we crossed the stream, the thigh-high water was cold, a real shock. We were about 50 yards behind the rear elements of the First Company when two shots rang out in the distance, spaced apart, sounding like sniper fire, then a semiautomatic carbine fired, seeming like a full eight-round magazine had been emptied. The voices coming over the Vietnamese radio were too fast and garbled for me to understand, so Private Tuan explained that the Third Company had been fired on by a sniper and a soldier shot back. Seconds later I heard more single shots from a rifle, followed by other single-shot weapons. It sounded like more than one VC was shooting. The ARVN fired their M1 Garands, .30 carbines, and some Thompson submachine guns. As each side brought more weapons into play, the other side escalated appropriately. Added to the sharp crack of the rifle bullets was the dull "whump-pow" of an M79 round crashing into the ground and exploding. This was followed by two more M79 rounds, but the rifle shooting did not even slow down. Finally, the high-pitched staccato sound of an air-cooled Browning .30-caliber machine gun signaled its entry into the fracas. As I listened, I silently praised the gunner, who had had set up a nice and slow sustained rate of fire of about 40 rounds per minute in short bursts. He sure wasn't going to burn out the barrel. As the machine gun chattered away, the single-shot fire dissipated. Then the machine gun stopped, and the ARVN rifles took over again. There were two more muffled "whump-pows" and then silence.

I looked at Private Tuan, asking what had happened. He replied that the machine gun probably killed most of the VC then the Vietnamese soldiers advanced, shooting with their rifles and throwing grenades. The two Marines came up beside me, asking what the hell was going on. While I was explaining that the Third Company encountered some snipers, Private Tuan turned toward me, his face lit up with a bright, white-toothed smile, exclaiming that the Vietnamese soldiers caught three VC, killed one and captured four rifles. The two Marines looked at me, smiling, giving Tuan a thumbs-up sign.

Status reports indicated that Lieutenant Colonel Bell's Marine companies were being slowed down by booby traps and that Lieutenant Phong's Second Company was just outside Ha My Tay 2. I could hear some scattered shooting from that direction and called Sergeant Bronson on the radio inquiring what happened. He replied that they got three VC who tried to run away, with no ARVN KIA or WIA (wounded in action).

Suddenly, about 60 yards in front of us an explosion ripped the air. I could hear several voices excitedly shouting. This time Captain Van told me one of the soldiers in front of us had tripped a booby trap and was wounded, but not seriously.

Then a barely audible explosion came from our left. Sergeant Bronson called on the radio to announce another booby trap with some minor wounds to an ARVN soldier. The man was treated and went back to his squad. The closer the ARVN troops got to the hamlets, the more careful they became.

By mid-morning Ha My Tay 2 and Ha My Dong 3 had been secured. Eight booby traps had been found, three of them set off by the ARVN troops, while five had been discovered intact and disarmed. The only dead VC were the three killed by the Marines and the one killed by our Third Company. The Third Battalion had thus far captured ten VC, three in the firefight where one VC had been killed and seven others outside the two hamlets.

Captain Van had taken over the hamlet chief's house after our arrival in Ha My Dong 3, designating it the battalion CP for the next three days. It was a large, sturdy structure with cement walls and a ceramic tile roof. The floor was concrete, and a large open porch spanned the entire front of the house. I asked the captain why he selected this house. He said it was centrally located in the middle of the hamlet and had thick cement walls and high windows, which provided more protection from small-arms fire. Also, there were no other houses or structures close by, and the jungle growth didn't come close to the dwelling. This allowed us open areas around the house so someone couldn't easily sneak up on it without being seen. And finally, the hamlet chief was used to spending his nights in houses other than his own to avoid being caught or killed by the VC, so he welcomed us to use his home.

With that, the captain grabbed my hand to take me for a walk around the hamlet. I noticed about half a dozen heavily armed soldiers were always around yet kept their distance. I later found out these were the captain's bodyguards, protecting both of us.

It was obvious that this hamlet had been the scene of extensive combat. We passed another concrete and tile house that artillery had left no longer habitable, with about 50 percent of the roof torn apart and the walls marred by jagged, gaping holes. Several grass-thatch and bamboo-frame houses had been burned; some had only four blackened corner posts remaining.

We watched the soldiers herding everyone into an open area surrounded by tall, swaying palm trees at one end of the hamlet. This was a temporary collection point we would use until the third hamlet was secured. When all was safe, an area between the three hamlets would be set up as a permanent holding area for the duration of the operation. Already district officials and their American advisors were checking ID cards.

A soldier came running up to Captain Van to give him a message. Turning to me, he explained that Company Three now had control of Ha My Dong 2 and captured five VC.

I met Captain Laskowski, and he showed me on the map where the holding area was to be set up. The estimate was that there would be close to 1,500 people in it. The 368th RF Company was already moving downstream to set up the area. After that the U.S. Marines would bring in rice and other food plus some corpsmen to hold a medical clinic for the villagers.

Captain Van met his First Company commander, Second Lieutenant Son, who reported his troops were going to begin searching for VC weapons, food caches, and underground tunnels. I knew that tunnel entrances or exits could be located in cooking fire pits and under large clay vats, bundles of hay, clumps of bushes, pig pens, or wells. These were all to be searched. Pitchforks, steel and wooden rods, bayonets, and rifle butts were used to poke, probe, scatter, or pound suspicious areas. It would take a couple of days to thoroughly search each hamlet. Sergeant Bronson, on the radio, reported the First Company was now searching the hamlet for evidence of VC and underground tunnels.

By mid-afternoon, the villagers were gone, temporarily quartered at the central collection point. One side of the holding area was cordoned off by the Marine AMTRACS. These huge armored amphibious vehicles were a lot bigger than the army's M113 personnel carrier, almost 12 feet tall and 30 feet long, reminding me of a beached whale. As we were walking around the holding area, we met up with Lieutenant Colonel Bell, followed by two radio men, each carrying a PRC-25. The standard U.S. infantry radio was much easier to use, had greater range and more channels than the old PRC-10 used by the ARVN and their American advisors. How I wished we had that radio instead of the PRICK 10. Every time I turned on the PRICK 10 or had to change frequencies, I had to recalibrate it by dialing in the desired frequency and getting the correct zero beat, a no-noise oscillation position that indicated the desired frequency was properly tuned in. The PRC-25, though, was tuned like a car radio, the frequency just dialed in.

Lieutenant Colonel Bell reminded me of a Hollywood version of a World War II Marine. He was fully dressed and equipped in Marine combat gear, from the helmet he wore to the .45 pistol and the K-bar (Marine issue combat knife) on his belt to the field utilities bloused into his boots. Captain Van also wore a helmet and had his jungle fatigues bloused in his boot tops. But Captain Van had the typical thin Vietnamese build, with his jungle fatigue shirt unbuttoned and hanging outside his belt, papers and maps stuffed in all his pockets, making him look most unlike a battalion commander. As Lieutenant Colonel Bell was leaving, I heard him make a comment to the effect that it was no wonder these people, the ARVN, couldn't fight, since they didn't even know how to dress like soldiers.

The RF company had the collection area well secured. U.S. Navy corpsmen with the Marines were holding a favorably received medical clinic, and food from two AMTRACS were being unloaded.

I told Captain Van I wanted to go back and see how the tunnel hunting was going. I hadn't seen any VC tunnel complexes before, but I was aware that they could be extensive and contain two, three, or four levels. My curiosity was about to be satisfied when an ARVN sergeant took me on a tour of one small section of tunnels that had been thoroughly searched and cleared of all booby traps.

We entered through a concrete bunker hidden in a thick cluster of bamboo trees and dense jungle brush. Climbing down the narrow shaft, I hit bottom eight feet below the surface. From this point, three tunnels branched out in different directions. The sergeant motioned for me to follow him into the largest tunnel which had a diameter about 24 inches. The small soldier had had no problem scooting through the tunnel, but I did, both physically and psychologically.

It was pitch black in there, smelling stale, damp and dirty, and feeling intensely claustrophobic. I could only faintly see the outline of the sergeant in front of me, holding his flashlight, as we moved on hands and knees. Because my back and shoulders were pressed up tightly against the top of the tunnel, I couldn't bring my head up to look ahead very easily. Very uncomfortable, I twisted my face sideways to keep the sergeant in sight, not wanting to lose him in this tunnel. To see ahead I had to stretch my elbows and arms out in front of me so I could lower my shoulders, and then turn my head sideways. My knees and elbows hurt, and I kept hitting my head on the top of the tunnel, knocking dirt in my hair and having it fall over my sweaty face and into my eyes.

My breaths were shallow, and constricted, providing only minimal air. Thoughts of getting stuck or running out of air or the tunnel caving in made me want to get above ground in a hurry. The tunnel bottom was packed hard as concrete, probably from the passage of the former VC inhabitants. Clumps of dirt dropped down from the ceiling and walls. Christ, how could anyone live down here? I wondered.

The deeper I went, the more pungent the musty smell of dust and dirt mingling with the rancid odor of unwashed bodies became. Ten feet into the tunnel it zigged in another direction, a structure intended to prevent an exploding grenade from sending shrapnel throughout the length of the tunnel.

Rivets of sweat began streaming down my forehead into my eyes, and I could not wipe them off effectively due to my cramped position. Instead, it seemed as if I was just rubbing mud all over my face. I really questioned my sanity about wanting to go into a VC tunnel. The deeper we went, the more my sense of time, space and direction vanished. Phobias had never bothered me before, but, in this situation, I could truly understand the fear of people who suffered from claustrophobia. I calmed my fear by believing that the sergeant in front of me knew what he was doing and sure as hell didn't want to lose his American advisor, so I put my trust in the sergeant and kept trying to push my fear into the far reaches of my mind. Besides, I decided, if things got really bad, I could always back out, exiting the way I came.

Just as I got to feeling better, the smell grew worse, with the stench of fetid urine and the repugnant aroma of rank sweat all around me. I contorted my body to see where the sergeant was, but all I could see ahead were the contours of the round tunnel and a lighted area. The light in the tunnel in front of me bounced and flickered as I scrambled forward to a place where the tunnel opened into a small square room. There I saw the sergeant against the wall of the room, which contained wooden boxes holding food, eating utensils, and clothing. First aid equipment was on a bench with straw mats scattered along one wall, some rolled up. An earthen crock held water, and a couple of bowls held moist rice and worn chopsticks.

The sergeant put his flashlight on the bench and pulled a wooden match from his pocket, striking it on the rough surface of the bench. Then he lit a small oil lamp on a dirt shelf cut into the wall. As the wick caught on fire, the room became brighter.

I couldn't stand upright because of the room's low ceiling. I did notice, though, that a small shaft angled out from a corner and was sucking the bad air out of the room. The sergeant pointed out moist patches of cloth behind the bench, stained a dark brown color indicating they were blood from a wounded VC. Looking around the room, I figured that two people had been interrupted while eating and had left in a hurry.

Over in a corner was another tunnel, the same size as the one we had entered. The sergeant motioned for me to look into that tunnel. It stopped dead in four feet, either boarded up or with a door. The sergeant handed me his flashlight, laid down on his back, and moved into the tunnel feet first, then kicked on the wooden barrier. I heard wood give way, and the tunnel filled with filtered light.

The sergeant then turned over on his belly, stuck his hand out for the flashlight, and called for me to follow him as he wiggled out into the tunnel and disappeared.

I braced my hands and knees on the floor and lifted my feet, one at a time, going into the tunnel backward. Pushing back with my hands, I slowly moved feet first through the short tunnel then backward to the doorway the sergeant had kicked in. I dropped to my belly and slid further backward, hoping my feet would touch ground, but they didn't. The sergeant's hand grabbed my boot heel and moved my toe into a groove that had been cut into the rock, where I was able to get a good toe hold.

Still holding on to the tunnel ledge and the sergeant, I dropped down next to him, ending up in three feet of cold water that came up to my crotch at the bottom of a rock-lined well. I recognized Captain Van's voice coming from above, calling down, chuckling, asking if I had a good trip.

A knotted rope was tossed down, and the sergeant motioned for me to climb up. Standing next to the well, I helped the sergeant out and thanked him.

There I stood, cold and wet from crotch to toes with my head, hair, and face streaked with mud, and my shirt soaked with sweat. A soldier handed me a bucket containing some of the water in which I had just stood. After taking off my shirt, I washed my face, pouring the rest of the bucket of water over my head and shoulders. I finished cleaning up by wiping my face with a large handkerchief, then shaking out my jungle fatigue shirt before putting it back on. That was my first and last experience exploring a VC tunnel system in depth.

By nightfall we had uncovered between 40 and 50 tunnels in our hamlet alone. The other two hamlets had about 20 each. The next morning the ARVN continued their search for more tunnels. In the afternoon, 64 tunnels, of which some had probably been here since the French occupation of Vietnam in the late 1940s, were blown up with C-4, a plastic explosive. It would be a long while before a similar tunnel complex would be rebuilt in this area.

On the third day, we packed up our gear and hiked a mile and a quarter to a hard-surface road where our trucks were waiting. By all accounts it had been a successful operation. We had discovered and destroyed more than 100 tunnels, captured eight VC weapons and a considerable quantity of military equipment. We had four VC KIA and 22 VC prisoners. Not a bad haul for two and a half days.

CHAPTER 11

Combat Operations
Around Hoi An

For the next three weeks, the Third Battalion participated in numerous one-, two-, and three-day operations, many of which were joint ARVN–USMC excursions. The Marines simply did not understand the role of the advisors or our command structure, so I had serious problems dealing with Marine battalion commanders. One thing that really bugged the battalion and regimental commanders was the fact that I looked very unmilitary in combat clothing. There were no army units in I Corps, so we had to go to Saigon to get replacement clothing and equipment. Sometimes we were forced to wait until we had almost no decent clothes or equipment left. The ARVN were even worse. It was not unusual to visit an ARVN platoon and find as many as ten or 20 different uniform combinations, from leather boots to canvas boots, shoes or sandals, jungle fatigues to regular fatigues, cammies (camouflaged fatigues) or tiger suits (like camouflaged fatigues except the pattern was green and black stripes rather than spots), and all kinds of headgear and weapons.

One afternoon I was working out coordination details with the major of a Marine battalion we'd be operating with the next day. It was cool and rainy, so I wore the rain jacket I had bought on the black market. Since it had been made from a poncho, it was at least OD in color. A poncho was impractical for combat, which necessitated freedom for quick movement, and a poncho was what MACV issued us for protection from the rain, so to get around this we bought our own rain jackets. As an advisor I wore no American rank or insignia, not wanting to be identified as a U.S. Army captain by the VC who put a premium on advisors who were officers.

As the Marine major and I were going over his maps and exchanging call signs and frequencies, a tall, sinewy Marine lieutenant colonel walked in. He didn't know who I was except that I was an American. Walking up to me, bellowing, he demanded to know who the hell I was.

The battalion mortar crew in action during a combat operation, firing at some fleeing Viet Cong.

He didn't write my officers efficiency report (OER) so I didn't have to jump through his hoops. I turned around slowly and replied softly that I was Captain Worthington, senior advisor to the Third Battalion, Fifty-First ARVN Regiment. My reluctance to jump when he yelled made him mad. The cords on the sides of his neck bulged and quivered, and the veins on his temples filled with blood.

He looked me over carefully, taking in my ripped and patched jungle fatigue pants, my jungle boots with the heels and toes scuffed white, my threadbare shirt, my lack of insignia, and my non-regulation rain jacket, then demanded to know where my U.S. rank was and why was I wearing those rags.

In a voice I'd use to lecture a petulant child, I explained that he had a battalion supply, a regimental supply, and a division supply to provide him with whatever he needed. My supply was in Saigon, and in the six months I had been here, I had only been able to go there once. I had to make do with whatever I could find. I didn't wear any rank because I was not with a battalion of Americans, I was in the jungle with the Vietnamese. Those who needed to know who or what I was, knew me. Those who didn't know didn't need to know, especially when I was in the jungle. As for my rain jacket, no, it wasn't Army issue. I bought it because the Army didn't issue advisors rain jackets, and I had nothing to keep me dry.

My answers only made him angrier, and he questioned why in hell I couldn't get my ARVN troops to look like soldiers, because they were the most raggedy-assed excuses for soldiers he had ever seen. I explained in a condescending voice that I knew pissed him off that I was not the ARVN battalion commander. I only commanded one Army staff sergeant. The ARVN supply was not as plentiful as his. They tried to do the best they could, but in most cases, they didn't have enough of anything for all troops. Most of the ARVN equipment and weapons were castoff U.S. World War II items. The Jeeps we used were early 1950s model civilian Jeeps. His privates were equipped with semiautomatic M14 rifles, while I was issued a World War II M1 .30-caliber semiautomatic carbine. I could have gone on, but I said but I hoped he got the picture. I was only an advisor trying my best to help an underequipped unit to do the best it could. I was aware of the deficiencies the Fifty-First Regiment. I just hoped their allies could be tolerant of these shortcomings.

Clenching his fists and glowering at me with anger building inside him, the lieutenant colonel turned sharply and left. This was a common scene played out time and time again with Marine colonels.

Another issue I faced at the time regarding my gear was how climate affected weapons. In the tropics, a big problem with metal objects such as pistols, rifles, machine guns and knives was rust due to the high humidity.

On operations I carried my .45 service pistol, which I had accurized, and my carbine. I left my .38 snub-nosed revolver in a duffle bag in a wall locker in Hoi An. Even though the .38 was heavily oiled, after only three days in the locker it would be totally brown with a light coating of rust.

In the gun magazine *American Rifleman*, I saw an article on a brand-new type of weapon Smith & Wesson had created: a stainless steel .38 special snub-nose, five-shot Model 60. This was just what I needed, so I would have no more rust. I asked my wife to buy one and mail it to me. It cost $95. To make sure she had enough money, I sold my .38 special revolver, for which I had paid $5 in early February, to a navy corpsman who worked at MILPHAP for $95. Anita wrote back saying that the Smith & Wesson Model 60 stainless steel revolver was not available for sale since every single one manufactured was going to the CIA, other federal agencies, or selected police departments.

When my wife told my father, a banker in New York City, about this situation, he tried to procure one of these guns. His chief of security was a retired New York City police officer who was best friends with the NYPD chief gunsmith. The retired cop talked to his friend the gunsmith about the pistol and learned that the NYPD was to receive two stainless steel Model 60s; one was to go to the NYPD chief of police, and the other was earmarked for the head of the New Hampshire State Police, who was going on assignment to Vietnam as a civilian police advisor.

Ultimately, one of the two pistols was sold to my father but the price was now $115. My mother packed it in a box of toys she sent me to give to the children of some ARVN soldiers. The weapon performed so well that I wrote a field test article for *American Rifleman* when I returned to the States.

I also discovered how difficult it was to carry submachine guns in the climate of Vietnam. The ARVN battalion had several .45-caliber Thompson submachine guns. Observing some of the soldiers carrying them, I recalled using the one we had in the Hanover PD, where I had worked as a cop while in college. I loved to shoot it on full auto, so I asked the battalion commander if I could sign one out, and he said yes. Most people's knowledge of submachine guns doesn't go much beyond how macho they look in World War II movies,

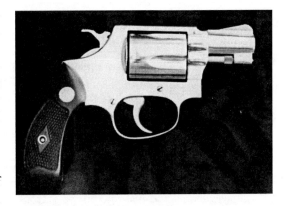

The Smith & Wesson .38 special new stainless-steel pistol, unavailable to the public, was obtained by my father from the New York City Police Department and mailed to me by my mother in a box of toys for VN children. Because it was the first stainless-steel pistol ever manufactured, it was very rust and corrosive resistant. Because of its size, I carried it for formal meetings, dinners, and the like with civilian leaders, where it was on my belt, concealed under my shirt. When I returned home I wrote an article for a gun magazine regarding the combat usage of the revolver and was paid more for the article than the gun cost me. I also used it during my second tour in Vietnam.

and they don't realize (nor did I) that they weigh a lot. With no bullets in one, it weighs ten and a half pounds, and each loaded magazine weighs more than one and a half pounds, so the gun and six magazines total 20 pounds. Carrying that sucker all day in the heat while slogging through muddy paddies and groping around in clinging jungles was challenging for me. What looked easy in the movies was very impractical; after about four or five operations, I returned it to the armory.

These problems with weapons, however, were not a real concern as the job of the combat advisor with the Vietnamese troops was not to shoot but to provide advice and to coordinate tactical support when engaged in combat. Therefore, we didn't need to carry carbines or other shoulder weapons. If it came to the point where an advisor needed to shoot to stay alive, there would be an abundance of weapons lying around the ground with no live owners, a scenario that didn't happen often, but it did. So unless I was going out with a small patrol or waiting in an ambush, customarily my only weapon was a .45 pistol.

There was disagreement among officers about the danger of the VC guerrillas in the area, which sometimes made it difficult to assess. One day, shortly before a joint ARVN–USMC combat operation, the Fifty-First Regiment put on a briefing. In attendance were the I Corps ARVN commander, General Lam, the I Corps senior advisor, and the senior USMC commander, General Walt. When the ARVN regimental S-2 completed his briefing on the enemy situation, which pointed out the many VC guerrilla units operating around Hoi An and the existence of a VC main force battalion, General Walt essentially called him a liar. General Walt stated that the ARVN estimates were typically inflated, and the situation presented was too pessimistic. To emphasize his position, the general called on some of his III MAF intelligence officers who acted just like puppets. Collectively, they downplayed the size and danger of the VC guerrillas in the area. Yet four months later, one of General Walt's Marine officers stated, "One local guerrilla is worth ten North Vietnamese regulars."

This was another frustrating example of the U.S. Marines belittling the ARVN troops. I felt embarrassed because I was an American like General Walt and his staff, and even though I had only been on operations in the area for less than three weeks, I knew General Walt's assessments were wrong. They presented too optimistic a picture of the VC activity in the Hoi An area. As I had been many times before, I was caught in a psychological bind with the American Marines on one side and the ARVN on the other.

The fact was that during nearly every operation we went on we encountered VC guerrillas. Mostly the engagements with them were limited to isolated sniper attacks but occasionally we came across a squad or a platoon that decided to fight it out. The biggest danger came from booby traps. I was really amazed at the ARVN's ability to detect them before they went off, yet even they missed some. During July, most of our casualties were due to mines and booby traps. One operation involving a booby trap dramatically emphasizes the differences in the resources available to the U.S. Marines and the ARVN.

The Vietnam War was a helicopter war. Food, supplies, ammunition, and troops were rapidly dispatched throughout the country via helicopters. American ground troops knew that if they got hit a medevac would be there in a few minutes (as I personally found out during my second tour). Helicopters were the links between the dangers of the bush and the safety of the rear. For the Vietnamese, though, helicopters were a luxury not always available to them. There were few ARVN helicopters and the pilots did not fly as often as American pilots. ARVN helicopters could not be counted on to support ground operations, especially if the area where helicopters were designated to land was hot—that is, fighting was occurring around the helicopter landing zone (LZ).

Once in mid–July we were on a search and destroy operation in a jungle area northwest of Hoi An. Based on intelligence information, we knew a VC guerrilla squad was operating out of Lai Nghe hamlet, part of Vinh Xuan village in Hieu Nhon district. Our mission was to surround the village, seek out the VC unit, and destroy it or capture the VC soldiers. The information indicated the area was heavily booby trapped and mined.

Before daylight we were trucked up a hard-surface road until we were a mile south of the village. The plan was for the battalion to move north along a trail through the jungle until the soldiers were three-quarters of a mile south of the village. At that point the First Company would continue to move north up the trail the remaining distance and then turn right, moving into position where it would be facing the hamlet from the west. The First Company would then set up blocking positions just east of the trail, hidden in the jungle, covering the east and north sides of the hamlet. The Second and Third companies would move off the trail to the east and then, in a line, move toward the hamlet from the south. The blocking forces would have the hamlet's north, east, and west sides, while the rest of the battalion would be advancing from the south.

After disembarking from the trucks at 7:00 a.m., we entered dense jungle with 20- to 30-foot trees, heavily laden with broad leaves, blocking the sun from the earth. This was not a jungle in the popular sense we know from books and movies about Tarzan in the wildest, deepest, most isolated land in equatorial Africa. Where I was in Vietnam was not the wildest, deepest, most isolated part of Vietnam but a very densely populated coastal plain next to the South China Sea, referred to as the Central Lowlands. Most of this area, due to its heavy annual rainfall and rich laterite soil, had been cleared for agricultural usage. But between the inhabited and farmed areas was a dense growth of thick rainforest-type vegetation. Pine forests, bamboo thickets, broad-leafed bushes, palm trees, and numerous varieties of vines grew unrestrained in this area, not conducive to farming and thus left untouched.

We moved along the trail through the heavy vegetation, the humid air very still. I began to perspire profusely, but the Vietnamese soldiers did not share my discomfort; they remained bone dry. In this type of dense foliage and with the lack of sunlight, we couldn't see very far ahead. The jungle was full of weird, loud, sharp sounds. Chirps, squeals, and squawks emanated from the different birds aggravated by our intrusion into their living space, effectively canceling out the noise of our troops moving along the trail. There was a strong smell of decaying matter, fungus, and mold.

Creepy, crawly things dropped off the leaves onto our bodies or climbed onto our boots from the soft soil. Bugs and ants feasted on our arms and necks, and the vines continually grabbed us tightly, forcing us to back up, disentangle ourselves, and hurry forward again to regain our position. As we

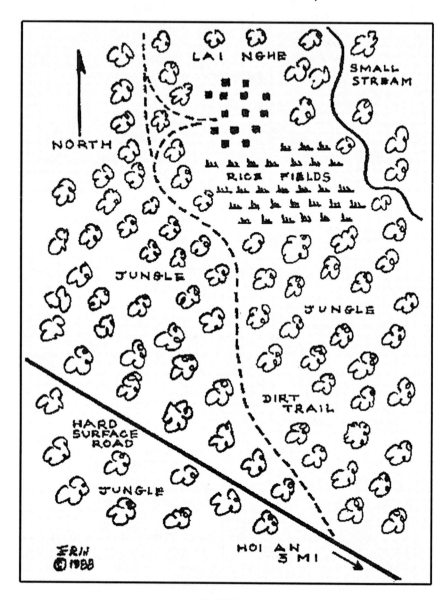

Lai Nghe

slowly moved toward our target, I silently cursed this tortuous journey through the jungle.

About an hour after we had off-loaded from the trucks, the march through the jungle ended. The three company commanders met with Captain Van. The First Company would continue up the trail and call the captain when it was in place as one blocking force. The battalion command group would remain with the Second Company which would approach Lai Nghe from the south. The Third Company would move further east and then north, surrounding the northern and eastern side of the hamlet.

Maneuvering into position to begin the assault on the small hamlet and, hopefully, its unaware residents, the captain moved up to the front line of the Second Company with its commander, Lieutenant Phong. I followed him as we crawled to the edge of the jungle. Looking across an open rice paddy area, we could see the cluster of grass huts about 100 yards away and barely make out some movement. A small group of people, both men and women, with hoes and baskets, moved out along a dike toward our position, stopping halfway to work in the rice field.

Lieutenant Phong excitedly motioned to the captain and pointed to the southeastern corner of the hamlet. Three men in black shirts and trousers, floppy hats, colorful neck scarves, web gear, and rifles were carefully moving along a bush line, toward that part of the jungle in which the Third Company was hiding.

A sergeant motioned to the captain, pointing to the radio. The captain talked softly for a moment and told me the First Company was ready. The Third Company was alerted to the three VC, which they had already noticed. The captain told the Third Company commander to let the three men get into the jungle and capture them, not shoot them.

Lieutenant Phong had instructed his weapons platoon where to set up one machine gun and the 60 mm mortar to provide fire support during the assault. As soon as the company moved into the hamlet, the machine gun crew, the mortar team, and the security element would move forward to join the company.

Ten, maybe 15 minutes went by. I laid on the ground as we waited to hear from Lieutenant Trung, the Third Company commander. Finally, the sergeant handed the PRICK 10 radio handset to Captain Van. As he listened, his mouth broke out into a broad grin as he gave me the thumbs-up sign. The Third Company had caught all three VC without any struggle. The prisoners said they all lived in Lai Nghi and that there were five more VC in their squad, but only two were in the hamlet now, as the other three had left an hour earlier to go to another hamlet.

The Second Company would now go inside the hamlet with one of the captured VC to identify the other two VC. But there was one slight problem: the entire area around the hamlet was booby trapped.

Two soldiers from the Third Company arrived with a very scared young VC. Lieutenant Phong and Captain Van asked him about the location of the booby traps, the best ways to avoid them, and the location of the two VC in the hamlet. The captive pointed out three ways we could enter the housing area and avoid the booby traps. Lieutenant Phong took the tied-up prisoner as Captain Van radioed the other companies, telling them that we were moving out.

As was always the case, I had mixed feelings of excitement and apprehension: excited about the prospect of possible contact and action, yet apprehensive about the outcome in which someone, maybe even me, might get wounded or killed. Ultimately my enhanced awareness due to the potential of combat overrode fears of injury or death. With my heart pounding and my adrenalin pumping, I was ready to go. Moving forward across the field, I ran next to Captain Van who was only ten to 15 yards behind the leading edge of the assault line. When the company was about 20 yards from the hamlet, several shots rang out, and we saw faint puffs of smoke dissipating between two grass huts.

One ARVN soldier had been hit. The group of people who had been working in the rice field had crouched down when we had begun the assault and now with the shooting had run into the jungle like the demons of hell were after them. Lieutenant Phong stood up, shouting at his advancing soldiers. A group of soldiers sprayed the area between two houses as well as the structures with rifle and submachine gun fire. Two more shots rang out from the hamlet, and then both houses were blown away by several ARVN M79 grenades.

Captain Van, bending down low but still moving, told his two radio men what to tell the other two company commanders. I was also bent low, looking for the soldier who had been shot, but I couldn't see anyone lying on the ground, so he had to be up and moving.

The first platoon to reach the hamlet went in with rifles blasting. Shooting into the two now-destroyed houses, they saw a man in black run away behind another grass hut. More rifle fire and another M79 grenade followed the path of the fleeing VC.

Captain Van, his command group, and I followed the route the platoon had just taken. By now the other two platoons were also entering the hamlet. Off to my left a sharp "whump" sounded, and I saw a cloud of dust falling to the ground. I could hear several voices yelling, "Booby trap, mine, explosive." Next a slight man wearing a helmet with red crosses on each side ran to the site of the explosion, where one of our men lay dead. The First and Third companies, surrounding the hamlet, reported that no one had run out, so the two VC had to still be inside.

Lieutenant Phong was getting angry. He had one dead and one wounded soldier, and at least two armed VC still loose in the village. He grabbed the prisoner with him, whose arms were tied behind his back, and asked several sharp questions about where the two VC could have gone. The captive just said over and over that he didn't know.

The lieutenant, tired of the lack of answers, slapped the man so hard he knocked him on his butt but to no avail. Why, I wondered, did the guy tell us so much when he had first been captured but now refused to talk? I asked Captain Van, who explained that when with us, alone in the jungle, he wasn't afraid to talk. But now, back in the village, he is afraid a villager, maybe a VC, can hear what he says and will kill him. He is more afraid of the VC, because he knows we will not shoot him.

Thirty minutes later all the people had been rounded up, but there were no VC. We also knew they hadn't left the area, so the only answer was that there must be a tunnel somewhere. Captain Van said something to his intelligence sergeant. The sergeant grabbed three troopers and they went to look for something, but I didn't understand what. The captain had said "con" something. Con, in Vietnamese, was used as a classifier word to denote animals. A cat, for example, in Vietnamese, was con meo. Apparently, the captain had sent his sergeant to find some kind of animal. I asked Private Tuan, my radio man, what kind of animal the sergeant was looking for, but neither he nor the captain knew how to say it in English. Finally, the captain said, "In French, it's la fourmi, fourmilier." I didn't understand that word and I told them. The captain, grinning with his plastic cigarette holder hanging out of his mouth, bent over next to me, and with a crab-like motion of his fingers, walked them across the ground, onto my boot, up my leg, then pinched my leg asking if I understood. I shook my head, but a shout from the sergeant brought the captain to his feet. He grabbed my hand and we ran off.

The sergeant and two of his men were standing in a clearing behind the houses, starring at a large pile of dirt. As we approached the three men, suddenly one jumped up and down, stamping his feet and slapping at one leg. Private Tuan pointed, and then I then saw what they had been looking for: an anthill. Here was a big one, full of juicy red ants. Some had apparently gotten on the soldier doing the Saint Vitus's dance. The captain yelled and Lieutenant Phong brought the VC with him to the anthill. As the prisoner was brought up to the anthill, the captain turned asked for my survival knife. Taking the knife from me, the captain grabbed the VC, knocked him to the ground, and ran the blade against his throat. Christ, I thought. He's gonna slit the guy's throat ... with my knife.

But that wasn't Captain Van's style. I had never seen him or any of his soldiers violently abuse any civilian or prisoner. He had simply been trying to scare the VC. He explained that he was going to have the VC sit down and rest a while, so he could think about where the other two VC might be in their tunnel. When the prisoner protested again that he didn't know, Captain Van told two husky soldiers to take the VC's pants off and sit him on the anthill and to keep him on it with his hands tied so he couldn't brush the ants off. Looking at the VC, the captain told him that if he remembered where the tunnel was, to let the soldiers know and they would get him. Screaming, the VC was stripped of his pants and pushed onto the anthill. The captain and I walked away.

Ten minutes later a soldier came up to the captain, reporting that the VC was ready to talk. We walked back to the anthill. Red ants and swollen splotches were all over the VC's thighs, buttocks, and groin. He was crying as he quietly told the captain where the tunnel was.

The two soldiers wiped the ants away, pulled the VC's pants back up, and he then led us to an area that looked like a woodpile, with odds and ends of wooden poles and logs strewn about. He said something to the soldiers, who began to clear away the pieces of wood, revealing a wooden trap door. The soldiers tore it apart, exposing a narrow tunnel that went down about six feet and then turned vertically, parallel with the ground.

A soldier was sent into a nearby house to get a small oil lamp. One of the sergeants took off all his web gear, got a .45-caliber pistol, and climbed down the hole, into the tunnel. Lighting the lamp, he pushed it into the tunnel in front of him, holding the cocked .45 in his other hand. He shouted into the tunnel, "Hey, raise your hands, come forward." There was no response. He yelled again. There was only silence. Pushing the hand holding the .45 deeper into the tunnel, he turned his head aside, and squeezed off three rounds. This time he got a response, two rifle shots. Dropping the lamp, he jumped back against the upright tunnel, reached up, and grabbed the hands of a couple of soldiers, who snapped him out of the hole like a cork popping out of a champagne bottle.

The next move was to get the young VC to go down into the hole and talk to his buddies. A long rope was tied around the VC's waist, neck, and wrists, which were still tied behind his back. Then he was put into the hole and told to tell his friends to surrender and they wouldn't be hurt, but if they didn't surrender, they would be buried alive. The prisoner could scoot about five feet into the tunnel before his forward progress was abruptly halted by the rope. We couldn't hear what he was saying but 15 minutes later he returned to say his friends would not surrender. Because of the angle of the tunnel, we couldn't toss a grenade into the hole. The VC was asked about other exits or entrances into the tunnel but he knew none.

Next, one of the intelligence sergeants who had considerable experience with VC tunnels made a wooden chute for rolling grenades into the vertical portion of the tunnel. Placing the chute at the proper angle, he motioned the rest of us away as he pulled the pin on an M26 fragmentation grenade. Filled with five and a half ounces of composition B, a high explosive, the fuse had a delay of four and a half seconds. Releasing the lever, and counting in Vietnamese, mot, hai, ba, he dropped it down the chute after three seconds. The three-second wait was to insure the enemy didn't have time to throw it back.

It rolled into the tunnel, and one and a half seconds later a whump shook the ground as dust, smoke, and pieces of the wooden chute came out of the hole.

The VC was dropped back into the hole, but his buddies still refused to come out. The next thought was to use a riot control tear-gas grenade (CS), but no one had any. Someone suggested using smoke grenades. The intelligence sergeant nixed that idea, because it would take too many grenades to produce any significant amount of smoke. The sergeant did think that a fire of straw, wood and coal oil, built at the bottom of the hole and then covered, might work. Consequently, soldiers began to gather the ingredients for the fire. Others were sent to find some canvas and buckets of water. A roaring fire was soon burning at the bottom of the hole, producing voluminous clouds of thick, billowing, dark smoke. The canvas, soaked in water, was spread over the hole and doused with buckets of water.

A few minutes later one soldier noted smoke rising out of a clump of bushes. The brush was cleared away, revealing a small pipe, about six inches in diameter, buried in the ground. The intelligence sergeant grabbed another grenade, pulled the pin, counted to three, dropped it down the pipe, and ran away. A muffled crump jarred the ground slightly, but we noticed nothing else. Two more grenades were dropped in the pipe as black smoke poured out of the air vent. After cooking the tunnel for half an hour, the sergeant decided it was time to put the fire out and check the tunnel again. The canvas was removed, the fire extinguished with water, and the prisoner pushed into the tunnel. This time he got no reply from his friends. He was brought back up, the ropes tying him were removed, and he was told to go into the tunnel and get his companions. Ten minutes later he returned, huffing and puffing. He had one body, a dead young man, close in age to our prisoner. A few minutes later the VC returned with another body, this one an older man with gunshot wounds, barely alive. The battalion medic tried to help the man, but he was pretty badly wounded. He had been shot in the thigh and the shoulder, grenade fragments had peppered his back and left side, and he appeared to have a concussion and was suffering from considerable blood loss. The intelligence sergeant now went into the tunnel and returned a few minutes later with two old French rifles and ammunition, documents, food, and medical supplies. It had taken five hours to get one dead VC and one dying VC.

Our count for the day, in addition to these VC, was three VC prisoners, several weapons, some documents, one ARVN KIA, and one ARVN WIA. A search of the village revealed no other VC supplies or weapons. Now all we had to do was pack up and boogie on home, I thought. Boy, was I wrong.

It was late afternoon. The two VC who had left the hamlet that morning had never returned. Captain Van ordered the battalion to prepare to move out. Now we had two VC KIA, as the old man had died. One might think it a waste of manpower to send a battalion of 300 soldiers (not everyone in the battalion went on this operation) to seek out a squad of VC, but it really wasn't. First, we weren't sure how many VC we'd encounter, if any, maybe the predicted squad, perhaps a platoon, possibly a company. Second, in addition to potential combat with the VC, other manpower was needed to cordon off the large geographical space of the hamlet and to search the area. Finally, soldiers were also needed to round up and control the 200 to 300 people living in the hamlet. Understanding the personnel requirements of an operation like this makes the manpower economics of guerrilla warfare clear. The guerrillas selected the time and place to fight while the counter-guerrillas had to respond to the guerrillas. One guerrilla could effectively tie up ten to 20 or more government soldiers.

As we were getting ready to leave, a firefight broke out on the northwestern edge of the hamlet. Several shots were fired from repeating rifles and immediately joined by ARVN semiautomatic weapons and exploding grenades. As quickly as the shooting started, it stopped. A soldier ran up to Captain Van, shouting that Sergeant Thom was wounded by a booby trap.

Captain Van and I ran over to an open area where the ARVN NCO lay inert on the ground, shaking and moaning softly. A Vietnamese medic was working on him, quickly scissoring his clothes apart while another ARVN medic was removing the cut-off clothing. Several soldiers pointed across the open field and gestured as they explained what had happened.

Captain Van returned to me, stating that two VC were returning to Ap Lai Nghe, saw our soldiers, and started shooting. No soldiers were hit so they shot back at the VC. Sergeant Thom, a platoon sergeant, had his platoon chase the VC, and then the sergeant stepped on a booby trap, a bouncing betty bomb. Pointing to his groin, Captain Van explained where it had exploded. A bouncing betty booby trap, when tripped and activated, pops straight up in the air 20 to 30 inches, exploding in front of the victim between the knees and waist.

The medic asked about a helicopter to get the sergeant to a hospital immediately. Grabbing my radio frequency code sheet, I changed frequencies and called the Marine operations section for the USMC battalion operating in this area. I explained we had a wounded soldier who needed a medevac ASAP. "Wait one," said the faceless voice with no trace of emotion.

Holding the handset of the PRC-10 radio, I looked down at the naked soldier, now turning an ashen gray color. The booby trap had apparently been some kind of canister filled with very small shards of metal and explosive. When it went off, it sprayed hundreds of sharp metal fragments all over the sergeant's legs, groin, stomach, chest, arms, and part of his face, making half- to one-inch slits all over his lower body.

Two things fascinated me, in a clinical sense. First, there was almost no blood. All the wounds just oozed moisture. Second, the victim's penis, which had received about a dozen shrapnel fragments, looked exactly like a hot dog that had been over-boiled in water and split in several places. Unconsciously I tightened my groin muscles as I empathized with the pain I knew the man was in. The medic had given him some morphine and was picking out pieces of metal that were exposed on the surface.

The radio came back to life, asking if the WIA was American. I replied that the WIA was ARVN and we needed an immediate medevac. "Wait one, out," came over the radio, and then it went dead again.

The medic looked up at me, asking when the helicopter would get here. The eyes of the medic told me he also felt badly for his fallen comrade and time was a critical factor, but I could only reply that I didn't know.

The Marines radioed back to say that no helicopters were available for medevac mission, suggesting my counterpart request medevac through his own ARVN channels. U.S. assets were for American purposes and sometimes the Vietnamese, but a dying ARVN was a very low priority. Getting an ARVN helicopter would be even more difficult because of the limited ARVN or VNAF air resources available in I Corps.

I called back again through my advisor radio net to try and get some action but was told to wait. Crouching in the boiling afternoon sun, sweat pouring off me like an open faucet, I took off my hat and fatigue shirt. Somehow, I didn't feel it would be quite right to move my radio into the shade and wait there for a response to my request.

Then, as if by magic, a U.S. Huey helicopter passed overhead at about 4,000 feet. The ARVN soldiers jumped and shouted, trying to attract the pilot's attention and thinking the helicopter was coming for their sergeant. This most precious vehicle, able to save a human being so easily, unaware of the man's losing battle for his life on the ground, just continued into the distance.

I had tried to contact the helicopter on some of the distress frequencies the Direct Air Support Center (DASC) in Da Nang had established for ground troops to use in emergency situations to contact aircraft passing overhead. A few minutes later we heard another helicopter. Again, I tried the DASC frequencies as it came into view, and this time a voice responded. I heard the background noise of a vibrating machine. The speaker's voice sounded like he was sitting on an electric paint can mixer, and I knew I was talking to a helicopter pilot. I identified myself, explaining I was in a hamlet to his ten o'clock position. I said I would pop smoke, saying that we needed a medevac assist for a dying soldier. I lifted a canister of green smoke off my web belt, pulled the pin, and tossed it to the edge of the field. As the fuse sizzled, billowing green smoke began to slowly rise in the still air.

The helicopter began a lazy bank and slow left turn overhead. The pilot asked what the problem was. He explained they were on a priority courier run to I Corps. He acknowledged seeing my green smoke. I replied that I had one ARVN WIA, serious from a booby trap. We needed to get him to Da Nang before he died. The pilot radioed that he had on board one Oh-Four (numerical designation for the rank of major) who would chew their butts for doing this, but they could take our soldier if we had a cold LZ, which we did.

I told the captain to get a platoon all around this field for security, and I told the medic to get the sergeant ready to go now, pointing to the helicopter that was making a final run from the southwest.

I grabbed my carbine and moved to the center of the open area, waving my hands over my head, then squatted down with both arms stretched forward in front of me, the ground-to-air signal telling the pilot where to land. The Huey stopped its forward motion ten feet in front of me, the nose pitching up. Flaring, it slowly settled down to earth resting on both skids. I turned my head sideways to avoid being directly pelted by the dirt whipped up by the rotor blades. From a distance, the only thing to identify me as an American advisor was my size.

The crew chief jumped out, his flight helmet radio cord still attached to the inside of the helicopter. He signaled me to get the wounded man loaded. Standing, humped over under the blades, I motioned for the medics to bring the sergeant to the helicopter. They had made a makeshift stretcher out of a couple of bamboo poles and two fatigue shirts, putting the poles through the sleeves of the buttoned shirts.

As the wounded man was being carefully transported to the helicopter, a man jumped out, brandishing a .45 pistol. The man, an American major of average build, lacked the dark tan of a field soldier. His fatigues were starched, and his jungle boots were spit-shined, as was his holster. He wore a MACV shoulder patch, so this had to be a U.S. Army advisor headquarters helicopter. He was so mad his face was bright red, and I was sure I saw blood shooting from his eyes. Facing me, he demanded to know who in the goddamn hell I thought I was to call his helicopter down.

I explained I was Captain Worthington, senior advisor to this ARVN unit, and that we just had a firefight, and this man had been blown up with a booby trap and that if he didn't get to a hospital immediately, he would die. The madman major shouted that the wounded sergeant was no goddamn American, he was a goddamn gook.

The whole time the major was ranting, he continued to wave his pistol all around, mostly in the vicinity of my face. At the same time, several ARVN soldiers realized the major wasn't very receptive about taking on any wounded ARVN passenger. They began to circle us with their rifles and carbines held loosely at their hips, pointed casually toward the major's legs.

I asked, politely, for the major to please put his pistol down, because no one was going to shoot him. As I said that, the major looked around at the soldiers, gulped a couple of times, and let his hand with the gun drop to his side. He explained that he was on a very important mission, and he had no time for my problems. He was not going to take my goddamn slope to any hospital, so I was to remove him from the major's goddamn chopper, now. I responded that I knew the major was not going to take him to the hospital, the pilots were. I pointed out that the man was dying, and he needed to get to the hospital.

Becoming more enraged, the major shouted that he was going to write me up for this, and without a hat or shirt, I was out of uniform, so he told me to get back in uniform. At this point I was ready to tell him to shove it, but the two medics and the crew chief were still working on getting the wounded sergeant set up in the helicopter. I wanted to keep the major occupied until the helicopter was ready to lift off. Running back a few feet to where my shirt and hat had been left, I put them on and ran back to the helicopter. He threatened to punish me by making a written report to my superior officer for being insubordinate and out of uniform.

Looking beyond the major into the open helicopter door, the crew chief looked my way and gave me a thumbs up. I then saw the senior ARVN medic jump out and knew the other medic would remain on board with the wounded sergeant for the trip to the hospital. I intoned sweetly, a smile of revenge crossing my face, that his chopper was leaving. Saluting, I jumped back out of the way.

I knew the major wanted to come after me and chew on my ass some more. But he abruptly turned, climbed into the helicopter, buckled himself into a canvas seat, perhaps realizing he'd be left out in the field if he chose to continue his haranguing. Stepping out from under the arc of the blade, I gave the pilots the thumbs-up sign. The authoritative Lycoming turbine engine revved up to its takeoff power of 6,600 RPMs. The tail began to lift as the big bird rose backward, looking like it could barely get off the ground. As the turbine whirled faster, the main rotor blade sliced through the air and the nose dropped. As the forward speed increased so did the lift, and the chopper very quickly rose up over the trees, banking over the field as it climbed higher and then took up its course heading toward Da Nang.

The sergeant's company commander and Captain Van both came over to thank me. Normally, when I would get reamed liked that, I'd feel bad about it. It's embarrassing to be talked down to like a shavetail. This time, though, I felt okay. I knew I had been able to get a dying man to a hospital. That counted for a lot. I felt sorry for the major who seemed so involved in his own self that he was totally unaware of what was really going on around him. The operation ended with no more incidents. We hiked back to the main road with our VC booty and prisoners to where our trucks were waiting.

A few days later I had a pleasant surprise when I received a copy of the endorsement added to my Form 1049 requesting assignment to Hawai'i after my Vietnam tour. The endorsement stated Captain Worthington would be assigned as commander, headquarters company at Fort Shafter, effective immediately upon reassignment from Vietnam. I thought there was no reason DA would not approve this. The CO's slot called for an infantry captain and it would be available the same time I would be.

I was also briefed on the new plans for the Third Battalion. On Friday, 22 July, the battalion was to be airlifted by USAF C-130s from Da Nang to Nha Trang. From there it would proceed, by trucks, north to the ARVN Lam Son National Training Center at Duc My. The battalion was to undergo six weeks of infantry refresher training. It would begin with squad and platoon tactics, then company training, culminating with a week-long battalion field training exercise (FTX). After some real screw-ups with the USAF which didn't have enough C-130s to move the entire battalion, we finally got the whole unit to Nha Trang.

I wasn't too happy to leave the field. I had found the combat operations stimulating and had learned much about myself and Vietnam through inter-action with the Vietnamese officers and soldiers. The battalion officers said I'd like Lam Son. I'd be able to go into Nha Trang on the weekends and could relax on the beach there.

CHAPTER 12

Lam Son Infantry Training Center

While I had initially regretted having to go to Lam Son, I ultimately found the time at Duc My to be a valuable and occasionally exciting experience. We made the 35-mile trip from the airport at Nha Trang to the Vietnamese Lam Son National Training Center at Duc My by two-and-a-half-ton truck convoy. Going north out of Nha Trang on Route 1 to Ninh Hoa, then northwest on Route 21, the trip took almost two hours.

Lam Son was located in the middle of a relatively level area surrounded on three sides by mountainous terrain. The training areas within Lam Son were mostly flat with occasional rolling hills and ridges. Much of the ground was covered with knee-high grasses and scattered twisted trees about 20 to 30 feet tall. The brush became very thick along the water courses with dense palmettos, heavy, broad-leafed foliage, and entangled treetops crowding out the sunlight. Lam Son was an ideal location for a training center with its wide-open spaces for weapons training and almost impenetrable jungle for combat maneuvers and patrols. The refresher course for the battalion would consist of classroom training for the officers and experiential training in basic infantry skills for the NCOs and soldiers. At the end of each week, everyone would be tested, the officers in their academic setting and the soldiers with practical examinations. Toward the end of the program, the officers would participate in a CPX, a practical exam of the battalion staff and commanders in the field without any troops, while the soldiers would be tested on the firing ranges with all the battalion's weapons. For the final phase of refresher training, the battalion would move out to the field to participate in a week-long FTX, during which the troops and leaders would be evaluated on their performance. The troops would begin their training with squad tactics and combat drills. Then the squads would join to participate in platoon training. Next the platoons would combine to undergo company training. The final exam would be the sixth week battalion FTX.

The advisors' role would be to provide input to the Lam Son staff on the battalion's strengths and weaknesses, to participate in and assist in the refresher training, and to act as a liaison between the battalion and the Lam Son advisors. We would also assist the Vietnamese Lam Son staff to evaluate the battalion.

After a couple of days of in-processing and getting settled in, the battalion began training. While the officers attended command and staff (personnel, intelligence, operations, logistics, and communications) training, Sergeant Bronson and I worked with the troops in their small unit combat training.

On one day, ambush and anti-ambush techniques were scheduled. This training began in the classroom and focused on how to select the ambush sites, how to conduct ambushes, and how to detect and initiate counter-ambush tactics in case of an ambush. After the classroom sessions, some of the squads practiced setting up an ambush while the rest performed counter-ambush drills. Sergeant Bronson worked with the squads setting up an ambush and I worked with the counter-ambush group. The squads worked in one site and then rotated to the other, about one-quarter mile away.

We worked with the ARVN soldiers who would be ambushing the squad. We selected a good site with excellent fields of fire and determined when the ambush would be executed. The soldiers were armed with M1 rifles loaded with blank ammo, and the plan was to attack the squad patrolling the jungle trail. My job was to stand off to one side, hidden, to observe the reaction of the squad moving up the trail as they approached the ambush zone. The squads had learned their classroom lessons well; most detected the ambushers early enough to effectively thwart the surprise attack.

At the end of the day after the last squad had completed their patrol, we decided to take a shortcut through the brush to get back to the main camp. Walking, talking, and joking, we weren't paying much attention to our surroundings. The ARVN soldiers still had blank ammo in their weapons and on their belts, and I had no weapon. We were following a four-foot-wide path along the edge of a wooded area, which curved out of sight ahead. As we rounded the bend we saw five or six farmers approaching us carrying what appeared to be hoes or sticks on their shoulders, apparently going home after working in the fields. We didn't pay much attention to them, nor did they to us. The sun was to our backs, so we weren't too clear to them. About 50 yards from each other, the black pajama-clad men realized we were soldiers and we realized they weren't farmers, but VC armed with repeating rifles slung over their shoulders.

What happened next occurred in a few seconds, though it seemed to take forever. The English-speaking squad leader walking next to me suddenly stopped, the VC stopped, the rest of the ARVN soldiers stopped, and I

An M29 81 mm mortar crew of the Third Battalion, ARVN Fifty-First Infantry Regiment training while at the Lam Son Infantry Training Center. This mortar was used by U.S. troops from 1952 until 1987.

An M18 single-shot 57 mm recoilless rifle crew of the Third Battalion, Fifty-First Regiment at the infantry training center. This U.S. weapon was used in World War II and Korea by U.S. troops and was now issued to ARVN troops.

stopped. "Oh, my goodness," the squad leader said in a hushed voice, "captain, Viet Cong."

I yelled to the soldiers to shoot their damn blanks—shoot—shoot. The VC didn't know we didn't have real bullets.

The men reacted like good soldiers and began to kneel or off-hand fire away with their blanks. Their Garands spit out empty clips when all eight blanks were expended, and the soldiers slammed in more clips of blanks. Our massive volume of fire must have scared the VC because –they only got off a couple of rounds, which were wild, before deciding to run off into the woods. I'm not sure who was most afraid, us or them. As soon as the VC left, we turned around and ran back to the ambush practice area and took the regular trail back to the base. No more shortcuts for us.

Afterward our little adventure provided everyone with a good laugh. From then on, though, we carried live ammo on all field exercises, I always wore my loaded .45, and we kept armed guards stationed around the training sites, their weapons loaded with live ammo, but we never saw any more VC in the training areas for the rest of our stay at Lam Son.

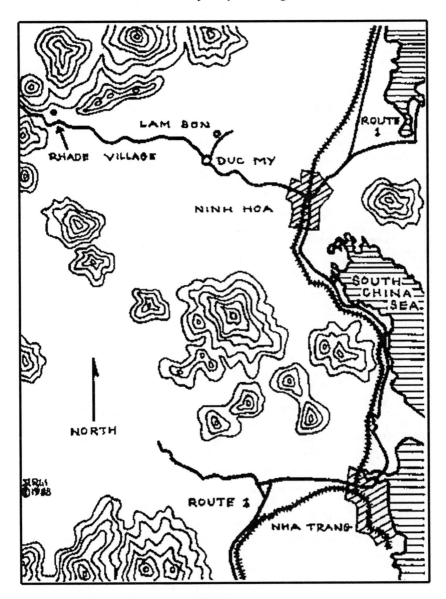

Nha Trang

During these training exercises, the battalion's morale was at an all-time high. For the past couple of months prior to going to Lam Son, it had been very successful in combat operations around Hoi An. Now the training was going very well, and the grades on the weekly tests revealed an exceptional degree of competence.

One day the battalion commander ordered all helmets be turned into the battalion supply NCO. The battalion sergeant major, Sergeant Sanh, had located a large, covered outdoor classroom area where all 450 helmets were lined up on the dirt floor. The supply sergeant painted the helmets with a base coat of forest green. Then came patterns of light green, dark green, and different shades of brown. When he was finished, every helmet sported a brand-new camouflaged look. Captain Van thought that having the entire battalion in custom-painted camouflaged helmets would create a unique look for the soldiers and foster even deeper esprit de corps. The new helmets were well received by all members of the battalion, including the advisors.

On the weekends I had the opportunity to visit the coastal cities of Ninh Hoa and Nha Trang, swimming and sunning on the beach during the day, visiting seafood restaurants and nightclubs in the evening.

On one of my trips to Nha Trang, passing through Ninh Hoa, a couple of battalion officers and I met Nguyen Dan, master knife smith. The Vietnamese officers in the battalion had told me about this local craftsman who made by hand quality combat knives described as strong, durable, and able to hold a sharp edge. Nguyen Dan greeted us as we approached his shop. He was dressed in the typical Vietnamese workman's garb, just black shorts. He stood about five feet, two inches tall, and he had the lean muscular build of a laborer. The business was a family undertaking with Nguyen Dan's children involved in various aspects of the manufacturing process. The method he used was out of the Middle Ages; hand-forging steel weapons, shaping blades by heating and hammering the metal. The crucial element during the tempering process was his ability to detect the temperature of the steel by its color. The basic components were simple. The blade was made from tempered scrap steel, usually Jeep springs; the crossguard was molded from melted scrap brass; and the handle was fashioned from water buffalo horns. He could produce eight to 12 knives simultaneously.

He was proud of his skills, keeping a logbook of customers and the number of knives purchased. Glancing through this book, I found that almost all the purchasers had been military men, American, Australian, Korean, or ARVN soldiers, and that customers usually purchased half a dozen or more to give to friends or resell. I bought two and returned three weeks later to buy three more. The total price per knife and sheath was three U.S. dollars. The knives proved to be as good as promised as they would cut all kinds of wood and still maintain a sharp edge.

Another day I was invited as Captain Van's guest to a special Vietnamese meal, an occasion that made an impression. A senior staff officer at Lam Son was an old friend of Captain Van. One weekend afternoon his friend hosted an outdoor sit-down meal served in the backyard of his house. Several tables had been set up close together, so they appeared to be one long table to seat

Me with Mr. Nguyen Dan, supreme custom knife maker in Vietnam. Even today, throughout the world, his knives are sought-after by collectors of custom knives.

the 15 guests. I was the only American. While Captain Van was helping his friend with the food, I mingled with the guests, some officers from the battalion and others from Lam Son. On the table was a hand-printed menu for each guest, a common feature with every dish listed as a separate course. In contrast to meals in the United States, where we serve first an appetizer, then a salad, then the main course followed by a dessert, the menu for the Vietnamese meal had ten items starting with two courses of dainty sausages, then chopped chicken necks, various fish and pork dishes, four different kinds of soup, fried rice, and finally a custard-like dessert. The beverages served were beer, root beer soda, and hot tea. I could understand most of the translations the Vietnamese gave me except for the chopped chicken necks, which apparently were some type of appetizer.

Captain Van's friend sat in the middle of the long table with Van beside him and me next to Van. The host and Van would help themselves to a course, then pass the food around the table. We'd eat and talk before another course would be passed around. The first two courses, the two different types of sausage, were excellent. Then the third course, the chopped chicken necks, was served. I watched as Captain Van filled my bowl with it. Just looking at what he was doing made me sick to my stomach. First with a large spoon he scooped away dozens of small brown ants that had crawled on top of the food. Then, digging down into the bowl, he ladled out several spoonfuls of chicken blood, containing raw chicken necks, bones, gristle, and skin. Captain Van looked at me askance and grinned as he continued to fill my bowl twice as full as everyone else's. After everyone had their dish of chopped chicken necks in front of them, we began to eat. Looking at Van I saw his bowl was empty. When I asked where his food was, he replied he didn't eat it as it was no good.

Some of the guests began to look at me to see what "Old Round Eyes" would do. Glancing around at them, I knew I would at least have to taste the dish, and placing my spoon in the liquid, I brushed aside a few stray ants and scooped up some blood. I forced myself to test it and found it tasted metallic, but not nearly as bad as the mental image I had of what I was eating. I took another spoonful, this time of the chopped neck parts, and chewed. It was like grinding cartilage and rubbery strands of muscle between my teeth. I put a few more small spoonfuls in my mouth and continued chewing. As hard as I tried, I couldn't swallow what I was chewing, my throat refusing to allow it to enter my stomach. One more bite, and I knew I'd throw up all over the table. Grabbing my napkin, I faked a cough and spit most of what I had in my mouth out into the napkin. Painfully I swallowed what little was left in my mouth and almost choked as it went down. The bile started up my throat, but I stopped it in my mouth and swallowed hard, forcing it back down into my stomach.

No more for me. Grabbing my beer, I gulped a mouthful and tried hard to wash the bits of gritty, crushed bone and gristle out of my mouth. For the rest of the meal, I ate as if I were on a highly restricted diet.

As we approached the halfway point in the six weeks training, the battalion began to set numerous training records at Lam Son. As a unit, ARVN and advisors, we worked long and hard to do the best we could, and our test scores confirmed our efforts.

At the beginning of our fourth week of training, a convoy from the U.S. Twentieth Engineer Battalion was moving from its base camp at Ninh Hoa west to Ban Me Thuot. About halfway on its journey, a short way into the mountains, the convoy was ambushed by a VC main force unit. The Twentieth Engineer Battalion was part of the Eighteenth Engineer Brigade which, in turn, was a unit of the Thirty-Fifth Engineer Group. The Eighteenth Engineer Brigade had arrived in Vietnam on January 1 this year.

The ARVN Third Battalion was ordered to execute a search and destroy operation against the VC unit that had attacked the Twentieth Engineer convoy. Mounting two-and-a-half-ton cargo trucks, we motored into the mountains. We set up our battalion CP in a Montagnard village along Route 21 near the ambush site. An ARVN artillery unit also set up their Howitzers next to our CP to provide fire support.

Montagnard, a French word for highlander or mountaineer, was the name given to inhabitants of South Vietnam's mountain region, which included some 40 distinct ethnic communities using 20 different languages and totaled more than 700,000 people. The Montagnards were an ethnic combination of Mongoloid (China) people and Indonesians. The various Montagnard groups were primarily identified by linguistic criteria. This was an oversimplification, though, because in addition to language differentiations, one had to consider cultural and economic differences. The popular South Vietnamese perception of the Montagnards was that they were inferior, non–Vietnamese-speaking mountain peoples, dark skinned, loincloth-clad, and living off the land by growing crops using rudimentary methods and stalking game with crossbows and governed by taboos, rituals, and malevolent spirits. These characteristics did not apply universally, as many Montagnards had been formally educated, spoke Vietnamese, French and English, had converted to Christianity, and occupied positions in the South Vietnamese military.

The tribe or group we stayed with was called the Rhade, one of the larger Montagnard groups. The Rhade were a matrilineal society in which the heads of the family and the property holders were

The ambush reaction operation took us into a Montagnard village. I saw a young mother stepping into an elevated grass house and had my interpreter call to her (while I was fluent in French and Vietnamese, I did not speak Rhade, the Montagnard language). We explained I wanted to take her picture with her children, so she happily posed for me.

females. Some of the females were bare breasted, but most wore a shirt or long cloth wrapped crossways across their chests and over their shoulders. They also wore ankle-length cloths wrapped around them like skirts, some with multicolored stripes. The men were more scantily clad, wearing shorts or loincloths with Western-style shirts. Their homes were long bamboo, wood, and grass-thatched houses placed side-by-side in rows, built six feet off the ground, on top of huge posts cut from tree trunks. In the center of each house was an open stone fire pit and a large earthen pot containing a home-brewed alcoholic beverage, rice beer.

One night during the operation some of the battalion officers and I were invited to participate in a Rhade ceremony hosted by the male leaders of the village. Part of the ceremony involved drinking their rice beer, which was made by filling a ten- to 20-gallon clay jug with water, rice, other grains, and any other handy flora or fauna which would then rot and ferment, becoming alcoholic. It was explained to me that all the rotten matter fell to the bottom of the jug, while maggots floated around the top feasting on the thick scum. The purest brew remained in the middle of the jug, between the bottom garbage and the surface residue.

During the ceremony, the beer was to be drunk through a long hollow piece of bamboo which served as a community straw passed to each man sitting in a large circle around the fire pit. The quantity of the beer consumed by each man was to increase as the ceremony progressed. The man holding the straw had to drink more than the person who had drunk just before him. Getting guests and visitors inebriated was seen by the Montagnards as one purpose of the ceremony. It was also necessary to keep the straw in the middle of the pot or ingest the rotting garbage or live maggots. Knowing beforehand that one purpose of the ceremony was to get guests inebriated, I made sure I stayed next to Captain Van, who sat near the beginning of the circle. When drinking I was also very careful to ensure that the end of the straw remained in the middle of the pot. Since there were about 12 of us in the circle, no one actually got drunk.

During our stay in the Rhade village, Lieutenant Colonel Lap, Major Haines, and some other Fifty-First Regiment staff paid us a visit. In a short ceremony in front of the battalion, I was awarded my Combat Infantryman Badge (CIB). I don't think I have ever been prouder of receiving any other award, even my PhD, which I earned several years later.

The day before we returned to Lam Son, the battalion sergeant major, Sergeant Sanh, came up to me and asked me to please follow him. He advised me to also bring my camera. Curious, I asked why. Sergeant Sanh responded by telling me to come and I would soon see why. Grabbing my camera, web gear, and weapon, I followed the NCO. We left the Rhade village and headed through the jungle. About twenty minutes later, we passed by some vegetable gardens and then pens holding cows and pigs. Entering another small Montagnard village, the sergeant major walked over to some men and asked several questions. After getting directions, we moved out of that village along another trail. Now the growth was much thicker with massive mahogany trees growing everywhere. Suddenly the sergeant stopped and turned to me and quietly told me to get my camera ready. He gestured for me to go through the trees to an opening in the jungle. Then he told me to hold my camera ready to take a picture.

Not knowing what to expect, I slowly moved toward the clearing. As I entered it, I saw a very large elephant. Around one of its legs was an iron cuff on the end of a chain, with the other end of the 30-foot chain attached to a large 20-foot log. Even though the elephant had the strength to pull the log along behind him, the trees growing close together prevented it from leaving the clearing. I held my camera chest-high, ready to shoot a photo as I approached it. I noticed it looking at me looking at it. As soon as I raised the camera to my eye, the elephant immediately went into a dancing pose with one front leg and the opposite rear leg held up, balancing on two feet.

The sergeant major explained that the elephant had previously been a circus elephant and had been taught to go into a dancing pose when someone pointed a camera at it. This elephant was another victim of the Vietnamese conflict. The circus had fewer and fewer shows as the war increased in intensity, until finally its animals had been sold with some elephants, like this one, now used in logging operations in the Central Highlands.

The next day we loaded the Lam Son trucks and returned to resume our training. The four-day operation yielded no VC. They had apparently made their ambush and then left immediately, but while the operation had not been a success from the viewpoint of catching any VC, it had been a welcome respite from the training.

When I returned to Lam Son, I found the army's official response to my request to be assigned to Hawai'i. It had been denied. The Department of the Army stated that I would attend the Infantry Officers' Career Course upon completion of my Vietnam tour and then be assigned to the U.S. Army Infantry Center at Fort Benning. Being selected to go to the infantry officer's career course was a boost to my ego, but not being able to go to Hawai'i was a letdown. I had just left Fort Benning before my assignment to Vietnam and I didn't want to return. However, I thought that maybe at Fort Benning I might be able to command a company, which would make the assignment palatable. While serving in Vietnam, it was always nice to dream of all the good things to look forward to after the tour of duty ended, not only the new assignment but civilian clothes, ice cream and hamburgers, friends and family.

A U.S. Army engineer unit had been ambushed, with serious casualties, on a major highway crossing the Central Highlands. The Third Battalion, Fifty-First Regiment was tasked as the ambush reaction force while we were in training at an ARVN infantry training center in the area. During this combat operation one afternoon, the battalion sergeant major told me to get my combat gear and camera and to follow him. He led me on a long jaunt through the jungle, then halted, told me to put my camera to my eye, and to step into a clearing in front of us and take a picture. I asked of what, but he just urged me forward. I stepped in the clearing and took this photograph of an elephant. But this was no ordinary elephant: it was a former circus elephant trained to perform. When anyone stood in front of the elephant, it would pose by lifting its front left foot and rear right foot. This is what the elephant did when I stepped into the clearing. Because of the war, the circus closed, and the elephant became a beast of burden for the Montagnard people.

The last three weeks of training passed quickly. I got a new member for my advisory team, USMC First Sergeant Hammerick. Sergeant Hammerick was my height but a little heavier. He wore his black hair Marine style, short and flat on top and shaved on the sides. He was an old Marine pistol shooter, so we had a lot in common and got along well. He had brought with him a Colt government model .45-caliber pistol slide with an oversized, match barrel and bushing and adjustable target rear sight. He also had a GI holster, which had been soaked in silicone and formed to fit a pistol with the match slide. I bought all these items from him for $75 and then accurized my .45 pistol. Testing it on the Lam Son pistol range, Top (nickname for a first sergeant) and I had no problem shooting three- to four-inch groups at 50 yards using standard military, jacketed ammo. At 75 yards, we could still consistently hit man-sized targets in the chest area.

As the weeks passed, more and more Third Battalion soldiers came down with malaria or other illnesses. While in Lam Son Sergeant Bronson got malaria and ended up in a U.S. military hospital in Nha Trang. First Sergeant Hammerick also got sick and never returned to Hoi An with us. I took my orange malaria tablet faithfully every week, a prophylactic pill containing 45 milligrams of primaquine and 300 milligrams of chloroquine. I had contracted malaria in the Middle East while in the Marines in 1958 and for several years afterward experienced reoccurring malaria attacks. A physician said that I had probably developed immunity to the strain of falciparum malaria mosquito in Vietnam. Whatever the reason, I never contacted malaria while in Vietnam, on either tour.

During our final battalion CPX, we were bivouacked in what had once been a hot springs resort area. The natural springs' water was hot enough to soft boil an egg in less than ten minutes. Among the former residents was Madam Nhu, who had built a vacation home there when her brother-in-law Diem had been in power in the late 1950s. The estate's buildings were in a state of disrepair, and the once beautiful and manicured grounds were now overgrown with weeds amid broken-down tiled outbuildings that had once housed hot tubs and sauna rooms.

During our stay the battalion XO, an opium addict who was usually only minimally functional, became sick. He had his orderly set up a tent for him where he just lay, moaning and groaning. I asked some of the battalion junior officers what was wrong.

"Dai-uy Do ban con khi," they said, snickering. This translated into "Captain Do would shoot a monkey." I knew that small monkeys lived in the trees around our CPX area, but I wondered what this had to do with Captain Do being sick. Then a lieutenant informed me that in Vietnamese, to shoot a monkey means to take opium, making the motion of a needle going into the arm. He explained that Captain Do was a heavy smoker of opium, but now, because the captain had no opium, he was very sick.

I asked what would happen to him and was told that he would go to a hospital in Saigon. He would not stay with the battalion, another lieutenant offered. I never saw the XO again.

During the last week at Lam Son there was a full-scale battalion FTX using all kinds of ARVN support. There were ARVN artillery units, VNAF FACS flying Cessna O-1 Bird Dogs, and close air support by VNAF single-engine Skyraiders, the Douglas A-1E attack aircraft. We attacked hilltops, established battalion defensive positions, launched counterattacks, and performed various other battalion combat operations. Lieutenant Colonel

Richard Bergstrum, the Lam Son senior advisor, praised us as the best battalion that had come through this camp.

The battalion completed its refresher training with honors. The stint at Lam Son had taken its toll on the battalion's troops, though, as several hundred men and officers had contracted malaria. By the time the training ended, we were no longer an effective combat force. Of the 450 men and officers of the Third Battalion carried on its roster, only 200 were now actually fit for duty, with 150 on quarters and 100 hospitalized. I was the only fit advisor to return with the unit. My two sergeants were in the hospital.

CHAPTER 13

Operations
in Thanh Quit

It was late September by the time we finally got what was left of the battalion back to Hoi An. The battalion commander, who had just been promoted to major, seemed to be okay as did his four company commanders. Many junior NCOs and enlisted men still had malaria.

Saigon replaced the 250 sick soldiers of the Third Battalion with a mixture of airborne and ranger troopers. The problem was these soldiers were not assigned to the battalion because of their battlefield prowess or fighting spirit.

They were airborne and ranger soldiers who had been AWOL (absent without leave) and were assigned to a leg unit (a military slang term for the infantry which depends on its legs for mobility) with a high probability of engaging in serious fighting. If these outcasts proved themselves again, they could then rejoin their former units.

By the last week in September, we had received both our replacements and our orders to resume combat operations near Thanh Quit. The VC guerrilla activity had picked up in this area, and the province chief wanted some ARVN troops to destroy the local VC.

Thanh Quit was a collection of five small hamlets located on the north side of the Thanh Quit River. It was on Route 1 about halfway between Hoi An and Da Nang air base. One hamlet was on the west side of Route 1 (Thanh Quit 1), while the other four were east of the highway. The farming of tobacco, an increasingly popular agricultural product in Vietnam, was the community's primary financial base.

The battalion moved to Thanh Quit 1, an area heavily populated with many houses built on the north bank of the river. The river, which flowed from west to east, served as the southern boundary to Thanh Quit 1. A large cemetery was located north of the hamlet, Route 1 to the east, and rice paddies and jungle to the west, the latter area the location of the VC. Many of the

A pretty 14-year-old girl in Tam Quit, one of two girls residing in this house who earned their living making (sewing) clothes. The village had quite a few young girls working by either making clothes or making tobacco products.

houses were elegant and sturdy, built of concrete with tile roofs. The battalion CP was set up in a beautiful two-story concrete house. From the windows of the major's headquarters on the second floor, we could look out over the tree-tops toward the west, where the VC were based. Our house also had a sun porch on the roof from which we could see the entire hamlet, the cemetery, the river, and the jungles to the west beyond the rice paddies. The Third Company was responsible for the hamlet's security. It set up its CP in another elegant two-story house. The other two companies were to be used for combat operations.

Before September ended, Staff Sergeant Bronson returned from Nha Trang, still feeling weak from malaria. We also received another team member, Army First Lieutenant Jack McRey, whom we called Mac. In his mid–20s, about an inch shorter than my five feet, ten inches, lank, with a short blond crew cut, he was an ROTC graduate. His first tour had been at Fort Knox, the Army's armor school. There he had been a platoon leader of a school demonstration platoon. He once told me his biggest thrill had been being in the James Bond movie *Goldfinger*. In one scene Goldfinger's girls, flying small planes, gassed Fort Knox and a platoon of soldiers all fell over. This was Lieutenant Mac and his platoon. He was well trained in infantry tactics and weapons, mature, had guts, was disciplined, and, most important, he knew he didn't know it all. He was the kind of lieutenant any commander would love to have.

When Lieutenant Mac in-processed through the Hoi An advisory team, the province advisors told him that being assigned to the Fifty-First Regiment would be an easy job; all the field advisors did was go to the field and sit around then return to Hoi An and tell phony war stories. Lieutenant Mac said he didn't believe what he had been told at Hoi An because at Koelper Compound in Saigon he had heard good things about the Fifty-First Regiment. Little did Lieutenant Mac know that in six weeks he would have earned his CIB and be recommended for a Bronze Star for valor and a Vietnamese Cross of Gallantry, certainly not earned by advisors who just "sat around" in the field telling war stories.

For the next three weeks we conducted search and destroy operations in the Thanh Quit area. Lieutenant Mac and Sergeant Bronson went with the companies on their daily operations against the VC, during which some type of VC-initiated action usually ensued. If the battalion commander went on any operations, then so did I. Many of the operations were joint ventures with a nearby USMC company commanded by Captain Ted Peters, a short, slim, balding career Marine who was a good field commander and an easy man to get along with.

On one operation during which we suspected we would find several tunnels, I was able to get a U.S. Marine K9 German shepherd to help us sniff out the VC. The young enlisted handler said his dog, Thor, was new at this. Boy, was he right; Thor couldn't find any tunnels or VC. Then Major Van, who was interrogating a VC suspect, had the idea to use the dog to get the VC to talk. He asked me if we could use the Marine dog to scare the VC, to jump and growl at the VC—but not for real. Calling the corporal over I asked if Thor could snarl and growl on command. We wanted to scare a VC by having the dog pretend to tear him apart.

"Sure," the corporal replied. Thor could do that.

I told Major Van we could have the dog play mean so how did he want to do this.

Major Van said he would tell VC if he didn't talk we would have dog eat him up. Van wanted to bring the dog next to the VC and have dog be mean but not touch the VC. If the VC didn't talk, we would have the dog attack him. The dog handler would make the dog jump on the VC. We would pull the dog off the VC and maybe the VC would talk. I told the corporal to first just take Thor next to the VC and have Thor snarl and growl at the VC. I asked if the dog could do that and the handler replied, yeah, he could.

Major Van and his two intelligence NCOs grabbed the man and told

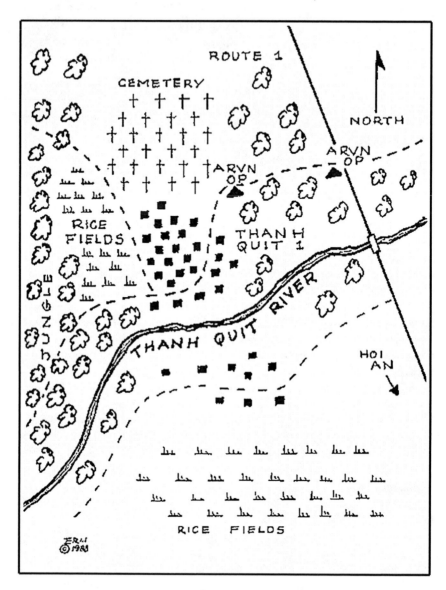

Thanh Quit

him if he didn't talk they would turn the Marine dog on him, and the dog loved to eat VC. I nudged the handler to have Thor growl. A movie star animal, Thor would never be. Thor jumped around, barking and baring his teeth, but anyone who had ever been around dogs could see that Thor expected to play games, not attack anyone.

On the other hand, the VC was a real actor. As Thor was doing his playful dance, the VC pretended to be scared out of his wits while maintaining he was just a poor farmer and not a VC. He was just an unfortunate, innocent bystander who had been mistakenly picked up by the soldiers. Major Van told the man that if he did not tell the truth, the Marine would turn the dog loose. The VC screamed as if in mortal fear for his life, protesting his innocence. Major Van cursed him in Vietnamese and said in English to let the dog go.

I told the corporal to make Thor attack the VC, now.

The large Marine, yelling, "Get 'em, sic 'em, go boy—attack!" and his playful dog charged the VC. Thor bounded to the crouching VC in one leap and playfully rubbed his back and sides against him, wagging his tail 90 miles an hour, yip-yip-yips emerging from his throat. Thor grinned and licked the man's face in a blatant display of affection, thinking he had met his new playmate. It was obvious to all that the playful pup only wanted the VC to befriend him. Thor's "tough dog" act was upstaged only by the VC's outrageous behavior

The Marine K-9 German Shepherd used in the operation where we tried to convince a Viet Cong to tell us where the underground tunnels were in his village. The dog's handler was asked if he could encourage the dog to act angry, growl and attack the VC. We tried, but the dog thought the request was to play, so the dog ran at the VC with his tail wagging. The VC, realizing there was no danger as the dog was friendly and playing, acted the part of a terrified man, responding like the dog was going to tear him apart. The situation was too comic to keep from laughing, as the dog was playing a game and the VC was playing scared to death. Our ploy didn't work.

of pretending to be scared shitless. He curled his legs up into a ball under him, threw his arms around his face to protect himself from the attack of the fierce Marine killer dog and rolled on the ground screaming. The whole scene was so ludicrous that most of us couldn't help but laugh.

The man I felt sorry for was the Marine dog handler. Here was this big tough Marine with his supposedly ferocious dog who had tried to get his animal to attack and all Thor would do was play. Finally, Major Van told the Marine to take his dog away, knowing we wouldn't get anything out of the VC. The Marine and his dog returned to their unit, hopefully to give Thor more training. The VC was turned over to the local district officials for further interrogation. We never again asked the Marines for K9 assistance.

As on similar operations in the past, our biggest problems were booby traps and snipers. In the evening, we would assemble on the rooftop sun porch of our CP. Without fail, as the sun descended, the VC in the tree line to our west would begin to shoot at us. We would respond, using our mortars or sometimes artillery fire to silence the shooters. We had preplanned targets selected around the village perimeter. When the sniper fire started, we would hide behind the parapet on the side of the sun porch and peer out over the top. The angle of incoming small-arms fire from the trees was too high to hit us. In a way it was like watching the war from the rooftops of Saigon except here we also had sound.

A typical evening would begin after our rice and C-ration supper. We'd be sitting around Major Van's room when we'd hear something hard hit the roof. Then, in the distance, we'd hear the crack of the rifle. We'd go up to the sun porch and, using binoculars, search for the source. If the shots came from one or two riflemen, we'd return fire using the battalion 81 mm mortars. Once we brought the 57 mm recoilless rifle to the roof. These activities became a nightly ritual, like an after-dinner game.

One evening the exchange began with two or three snipers shooting at the CP house. This night, however, the ante had been upped: the VC used a mortar. The exchange was getting serious. Luckily for us, the VC mortar crew was unable to see where their rounds were landing so they couldn't adjust their fire. We also had an ace up our sleeve: a USMC 155 Howitzer battery ready for some action. I tuned in the battery frequency on my PRICK 10, calling in a fire mission.

My call was promptly answered and I was told to send my request. I gave our pre-positioned request, concentration Tango Quebec, stating we wanted to shoot left 200 yards at a Victor Charlie mortar position. Calling for one round high explosive, danger close, I would adjust. Danger close informed the firing battery that friendly troops were within 600 yards of the target. My request implied that I would observe the first round and call in any required adjustments.

A few minutes later the voice on the radio told me it was on the way. We heard the whistle of the incoming round as it passed overhead on its way toward the tree line. We saw the dirt and debris flying all around. No fire was returned by the VC. I called the Howitzer battery back, saying cease fire. End of mission. I explained we didn't know if the firing battery got them or not, but their round was right on target and the Victor Charlie had quit firing. We would check it out in the morning and let the battery know.

A search of the tree line the next day produced no evidence of the Marine Howitzer hitting the VC mortar crew. We never knew if the 155 round got the mortar or just persuaded the VC to close shop for the night. Whatever, we received no more harassing fire or mortars that night.

Every day part of the battalion was out in the field on operations. Some days a few platoons were out on a sweep. At other times two rifle companies would be out on a three- or four-day operation. Almost every operation resulted in some kind of contact with the VC. Sometimes it was only in the form of a booby trap, other times sniper fire, and occasionally face-to-face confrontation with a VC unit. We never had any large-scale encounters with the enemy.

Operating in Thanh Quit proved valuable in allowing the new soldiers to get used to the battalion. Since 55 percent of our unit consisted of new people, we badly needed this shakedown period. Sergeant Bronson reported that our new lieutenant, Mac, was learning fast and doing a good job. The replacements were working out fine. They were behaving like soldiers should; they did not run away again, and they followed orders competently. Still, the battalion was nowhere near the level of proficiency it had at Lam Son. It would probably take several more weeks, maybe even months, to attain that level of functioning again.

During our activities, friendly casualties had been kept to a minimum. Mostly we had injuries caused by minor shrapnel lacerations or flesh wounds caused by bullets. Few of our soldiers were killed, and likewise, we had killed few VC. We had rounded up a lot of VC suspects but had captured few VC prisoners.

The VC were elusive and hard to catch. Seldom would they stand their ground and fight. Most of the face-to-face encounters had been sniper or ambush attacks or shootouts when we had surprised them. On the positive side, we had found quite a few weapons, military supplies, food caches, tunnels, and bunkers. Our constant patrolling denied the enemy the freedom of movement they had enjoyed before our arrival. As the weeks passed, we noticed a decrease in the booby traps and in our confrontations with the VC. Like a good trout stream that has been overfished, we soon found that our catches were few and far between.

After I returned from Vietnam, people always asked me how I felt about being with the ARVN, who were not known for being aggressive warriors. They felt I would have been safer with Americans. I didn't agree. For the most part, the Marines did not understand the local populace, and they did not always have the ability to communicate with the people. By contrast, the ARVN knew their countrymen and were able to learn much about VC activity which went completely unnoticed by the American units.

As an example, one time I was on patrol with an ARVN company. We passed through an area the U.S. Marines had just cleared. Coming upon an open, water-filled rice paddy, we avoided a direct path through the water and walked around the edge of the field. An old man who was working in the field said something to the point man. The ARVN soldier nodded, saying, "Thank you, sir." Before the point man reached the place where the trail crossed over one of the dikes into the next field, he halted. He broke off a branch from a nearby bush and stripped the leaves off. Moving ahead slightly, he stopped just before the top of the dike, got down on his hands and knees, and rummaged around. He then stood up, took a small white cloth out of his pocket, and tied it to the bare branch. Next, he pushed the stick with its little white flag into the ground and continued forward. The company first sergeant explained to me that the old man had told the point man about a booby trap. The soldier found it, disconnected the trip wire, and identified its location with the white flag. When the Marines had passed by less than 30 minutes earlier, no one had told them about the 81 mm mortar shell booby trap. Chance had been on the side of the Marines; no step had triggered the mortar.

Sometimes safety, however, seemed to be purely a matter of bad or good fortune. One afternoon I had to drive my Jeep into Hoi An. I took Private Tuan and two ARVN infantrymen for bodyguards. When the business was completed, we returned to Thanh Quit. The battalion had an outpost at the junction of the dirt road that led to the hamlet and Route 1. There was a second outpost just on the outside of the hamlet. Each outpost had five or six soldiers on guard. Upon our return, we dropped both bodyguards off at the first outpost. Private Tuan and I continued to the second outpost to talk to the soldiers since I had become acquainted with their young sergeant while at Lam Son. Sergeant Ton had studied English in high school and enjoyed talking to me in my language. He was an exceptionally fine young man, polite, eager, intelligent, and willing to defend his country for a cause that was not entirely clear to him. His wife was young and very pretty. Ton had shown me photographs of her but he was not able to see her often because she was living in Da Nang with her family. Sergeant Ton was also a respected NCO and leader. By any measure, he was an admirable young man.

Private Tuan and I sat in the Jeep, with the engine off, and talked to Sergeant Ton and his five men for a good ten minutes. Finally, I said we had to go. After starting the motor, we rolled down the dirt trail into Thanh Quit 1, only a few hundred yards away. As soon as I stopped the Jeep and shut off the engine, maybe two minutes after we left Sergeant Ton, we heard grenades, rockets and small-arms fire. The second outpost was under attack.

The platoon-sized reaction force of the Third Company, the security unit for Thanh Quit, grabbed their weapons and moved out on foot toward the outpost. I grabbed my carbine out of the Jeep and ran with the platoon. In less than two minutes, all noises from the fight had ceased. The security force soldiers fanned out from the outpost to find the attackers. The platoon leader, a medic, Private Tuan, and I stayed there. All six men who had been manning the outpost were dead. Their bodies were crumpled on the ground, in almost the same place where Private Tuan and I had left them standing six minutes before. Their weapons were still on the ground near the torn-apart sandbags, which had surrounded their king-size foxhole. Three soldiers had been killed by multiple bullet holes in their upper bodies and heads. Two soldiers had been killed by rocket or grenade shrapnel, which had penetrated their bodies in dozens of places. Sergeant Ton had been next to the sandbags when a round from a Russian RPG 2 grenade launcher had slammed into the sandbags and exploded. The right side of Sergeant Ton was nothing but shredded meat, bones, and gristle; his intestines were splattered all over.

Looking at the remains of Sergeant Ton, I thought of his wife. My God, she was so young, Sergeant Ton was so good. Why him? Who would tell her about her husband and when? Here he was, lying mutilated at my feet, his blood coursing out of his body and fading darkly into the sand while she was probably home with her family, happy, only 20 miles away. Curiously, I did not think about my own mortality or my own family.

Upon inspecting the evidence the VC had left behind, including the mashed down grass and empty rifle shell casings, it was apparent what had happened. About six to ten VC had snuck through the trees to within 30 yards of the outpost. As soon as Private Tuan and I had driven off, they had attacked the outpost soldiers with RPG rockets, rifle fire, and grenades. It appeared that the ARVN soldiers had only gotten off a few rounds before being slaughtered. The VC had killed all six ARVN soldiers and had then run away, not even coming to the outpost to collect the weapons.

The unanswered question was why had the VC waited for Private Tuan and me to leave since killing an American advisor would have been a special coup. An RPG round could penetrate six to seven inches of armor. One round would have blasted the Jeep with Private Tuan and me in it to smithereens. I knew a good gunner could fire five or six RPG rockets in less than a minute. From the evidence, we knew they had been lying in the grass for a long time, so it wasn't as if they had not been ready while Private Tuan and I had been there. I'll never know why we were spared, but I felt fortunate to be alive.

Standing amid the carnage of the brutal attack, I could only reflect on the effects of war. I felt horrible about the six young men whose lives had been snuffed out in seconds. In war it often seemed it was primarily the good and the young who were killed or wounded, but I also knew these soldiers had died for their country and that I had chosen to become a military man as had these soldiers. Yet if the situation had been reversed, if the dead had been VC, I would have had no regrets; in fact, I would have been elated.

The battalion had flak jackets for most soldiers and advisors. Theoretically, the flak jackets were for our safety, but normally we did not wear them unless we expected to be in fierce firefights because they were too hot and heavy. I do not recall a single instance where a flak jacket saved any of our soldiers' lives, so they were not seen that often on operations. Even if the outpost soldiers had been wearing flak jackets, they still would have been killed.

Life in the hamlet went on despite the war. The seemingly tranquil life of these people often belied the fact that a war was being fought on their front steps. I enjoyed being around the villagers. During the day, when we had spare time, the S 2, Lieutenant Lam, or the commo officer, Warrant Officer Diep, and I would wander about visiting. The older men and women worked in the fields tending to tobacco or rice crops. Inside the houses, attractive teenaged girls rolled tobacco or operated foot pedal-powered sewing machines, making clothes to be sold in Hoi An or Da Nang. The smaller children spent the days attending one of the two local schools, either the private Buddhist school or the public school. The private school was housed in a large concrete and tile building with wooden doors left open for ventilation when classes were being conducted. The public school was constructed of bamboo logs with a grass thatched roof and a dirt floor and was open on all sides.

Many families had pet pigs, like American families had pet dogs. The pigs were just as friendly as pet dogs, played in the front yards just like dogs. If a family ate outdoors or on the porch, the pigs would be beside them, begging for table scraps.

On 10 October, I received my reassignment orders. I would get 30 days' leave and then go to Fort Knox, Kentucky, to attend the Armor Officers' Career Course. This course was a career progression education program that all Army officers attended for their branch, designed to give junior captains the education and training necessary to function as field-grade officers. It concentrated on command responsibilities, tactics, staff functions, weapons, and current Army policies and procedures. I was on my way as a career officer, at any rate. Upon completion of that in mid–1967, I would go to Fort Benning for duty at the U.S. Army Infantry Center. At this point, my actual Fort Benning assignment was not known.

In response, I sent a letter to the Infantry Branch, Captain's Division, inquiring why I, an infantry officer, was scheduled to go to the Armor Branch Officers' Career Course. The Infantry Branch replied that outstanding infantry officers who had experienced a wide variety of duties and assignments were being selected to be cross-trained in another combat branch school. I did know for a fact that the combat arms did select a few of their officers to obtain their career training in a branch other than their own, but I accepted my branch's statement that I was an outstanding young officer being honored by attending the armor school.

By mid–October, we were experiencing few enemy contacts and the Third Battalion was ordered to return to Hoi An. The unit had done okay during the past three weeks. If our operations continued to go like this, it wouldn't be too long before the battalion would be back in shape for some major combat operations.

Sergeant Bronson had recovered nicely from his malaria attack. Lieutenant Mac and Sergeant Bronson were able to stay with the maneuvering companies, so I could focus my attention on the battalion staff and my liaison duties with the U.S. Marines. The move back to Hoi An on 16 October was welcomed by the troops as it would allow time to visit family or friends before our next assignment.

CHAPTER 14

The Battle for Nong Son: Day 1

Monday, 17 October 1966, was a damp, gloomy day, typical of the beginning of the monsoon season in the northern part of South Vietnam. Dark clouds hung all around the horizon, threatening rain. Over the weekend, the battalion had moved out of its field CP at Tham Quit into a temporary staging area just north of Hoi An, which is where the Fifty-First Regiment headquarters was located.

As the day progressed, I became aware that something was amiss. The troops were usually upbeat when they had a couple of day off to visit family and friends, but they were somber. The battalion commander, with whom I had an excellent relationship, appeared to be preoccupied with some concerns I didn't understand. I picked up bits and pieces of some fighting going on outside of An Hoa in a place Vietnamese soldiers referred to as Nong Son, an area where the only operating coal mine in South Vietnam was located.

In the afternoon, the commander and his staff huddled over maps and conferred about something that bothered them. I told Sergeant Bronson to monitor the advisory radio nets and Lieutenant McRey to find out what the hell was going on. I contacted Major Haines, the regimental advisor, who he said he'd get back to me. From what I could make out, the Trung Phuoc outpost (OP) near Nong Son, manned by some local Vietnamese PF troops, had been overrun during the night. The Second Battalion, Fifty-First Regiment from An Hoa had left about 4:00 a.m., on foot, to serve as a rescue force. So far this didn't seem too ominous.

An Hoa was just north of the Que Son Valley, the home of the VC First Regiment and also north of the operating area of the R 20 Battalion, a VC main force unit called the Doc Lap Battalion. In the back of my mind, I knew that the Que Son Valley was also used by the Thirty-Sixth NVA Regiment, a hard-core unit from North Vietnam. The problem, as I understood it, was that the Second Battalion, Fifty-

In October 1966 two battalions of the Fifty-First Regiment fought for more than a week in one of the biggest and bloodiest battles the ARVN had ever fought against the North Vietnamese Army up to that point in the war. There were about 1,500 casualties on both sides (out of about 1,900 men on both sides; each ARVN battalion had a little more than 300 men and the NVA had 1200). The fight was over the Nong Son coal mine in South Vietnam, the only producing coal mine in the country, which the NVA were trying to destroy (but did not do). This photograph shows the part of the coal mine complex where the administrative offices were and living quarters for the staff and engineers with the actual coal mine at the right. When the Third Battalion crossed the river into safer ground, it was bivouacked on the slopes just above the buildings in the center. The black spots in the photograph are debris in the chemicals used to develop the film in Vietnam.

First Regiment had moved into a smaller outpost, just east of the Trung Phuoc OP that had been overrun. Both outposts were across the river from the Nong Son coal mine. The battalion was now pinned down and couldn't move, so the Third Battalion, Fifty-First Regiment would go there to rescue the Second Battalion. Major Haines and his NCO, Master Sergeant Wright, arrived by Jeep to explain the Fifty-First Regiment's plan. Major Van, the Third Battalion commander, Lieutenant Colonel Lap, the Fifty-First regimental commander, and their staffs surrounded the hood of a Jeep to finalize their plans. Glancing at the conference, I could see only one emotion … fear.

Finally, Major Haines and Master Sergeant Wright briefed me, First Lieutenant Mac and Sergeant Bronson. The Second Battalion was pinned down and taking heavy casualties. They had USAF air support and USMC artillery support, but they were fighting a numerically superior force and losing.

The Vietnamese were not yet sure exactly who the attackers were, but they did know this: they fought like regular NVA troops, they were dressed like regular NVA troops, and they were heavily armed with NVA weapons.

When I asked Major Haines about their strength, he said that we didn't know, there were at least several hundred, maybe a thousand or more. The plan was that this would be totally an ARVN effort except for the transportation going in, air support, and USMC artillery. The Third Battalion, loaded into USMC CH 46A Sea Knight troop assault helicopters, twin rotor cargo/troop carriers with a rear loading ramp, would attack Trung Phuoc OP, now held by the enemy. The helicopters were on their way in from the Marine airbase at Marble Mountain, which was on the South China Sea southeast of Da Nang and the headquarters for some of the USMC medium helicopter squadrons. I commented, incredulously, that it was almost dark, and we were to land in the middle of hundreds or thousands of NVA regulars. Were we to commit suicide?

The major explained that we had no choice because Captain Vince Popps, Sergeant Harry Cousins, and Sergeant Randy Sessions (the U.S. advisors to the Second Battalion) would not be able to last the night, and if we didn't get some troops in now they would all be dead. He continued by pointing out that he tried to get the Marines to help, but no troops were available, so Lieutenant Colonel Lap decided the Third Battalion would go to the rescue.

Now I understood the fear on my counterpart's face. A helicopter assault at dusk on a regular NVA unit of unknown strength, using a battalion that had been together less than a month was a very risky operation. Jesus Christ, I wondered, why had I ever volunteered to be an advisor?

Major Haines briefed us on the operation. Because the insertion of the Third Battalion, Fifty-First Regiment would commit a second battalion of the regiment, command and control of the operation would pass to the regimental commander, Lieutenant Colonel Lap. Major Haines's call sign would be Tiger Six and Master Sergeant Wright's Tiger Six Alpha. I would be Tiger Three, Lieutenant Mac Three Alpha, and Sergeant Bronson Three Bravo. Captain Popps was Tiger Two with Sergeants Cousins and Sessions being Two Alpha and Two Bravo.

The battalion would make the assault in three lifts. The battalion command group (the commander and his staff) would be spread out over the three lifts. Each lift would involve five or six helicopters and the normal combat load for a CH 46A was 15 to 17 American combat soldiers or 20 to 25 Vietnamese soldiers.

Each lift would have one of the ARVN infantry companies plus its share of the battalion support, about 120 to 130 combat troops for each lift. The First Company, heavy weapons of headquarters company, the battalion commander, myself, Lieutenant Mac, Sergeant Bronson, and elements of the battalion command group would go in the first lift. The Second Company and the rest of headquarters company would be in the second lift. The Third Company, some battalion staff, and the regimental command group with its advisors, Major Haines and Master Sergeant Wright would be in the third lift. ARVN artillery would provide fire support when on the ground; USMC Bell UH 1E (Huey) gunships would provide air support during the insertion. Master Sergeant Wright was coordinating the helicopter support with the Marines and Major Haines would take care of our air and artillery support.

With no artillery forward observers and landing at night in an unknown area, I had no faith in any worthwhile artillery support, be it USMC or ARVN. What we did have on call, though, was an AC-47 gunship, a World War II twin-engine cargo plane that had been converted into an airborne artillery battery. Because of its ability to fire its three 7.62 mm Gatling type mini-guns at the rate of 6,000 rounds per minute, it was called "Puff the Magic Dragon," in reference to the popular 1963 folk song sung by Peter, Paul and Mary. An asset of the USAF Air Commando Squadron from the Da Nang air base, Puff also carried 56 parachute flares. The short distance from Da Nang to Nong Son would allow Puff, whose call sign was "Spooky," to remain on station above us for six to eight hours.

The task for the battalion advisors would be to assist in the coordination and use of U.S. air and fire support and to provide tactical advice as needed.

I walked over to my counterpart, Major Van, to get his version of the operation. Looking at the man, I saw a person I didn't recognize. Today he wore a heavy field jacket and green wool scarf wrapped around his neck. Pale, drawn, and stooped over, looking more like 60 than 40, he moved slowly and weakly. Instead of slowly enjoying his cigarettes through a cigarette holder as he habitually did, he chain-smoked in short puffs, quickly crushing the half-smoked stick only to begin smoking a new one. What's wrong with him? I wondered. One of the younger battalion officers sidled up to me and said that the major was very sick with malaria.

Approaching the major, I could see he didn't look well. What bothered me, though, was that he had had no signs of malaria before now; in fact, he had constantly bragged that he didn't get malaria.

Major Van called me over to plan the operation. Moving next to his Jeep, I looked at the map he was spreading out on the hood as he explained that this operation would be very bad for his unit. There were too many North Vietnamese soldiers, and this time we would lose. In a joking manner, I replied that it couldn't be that bad.

My friendly banter did not elicit the typical amiable response I was used to. His shaking finger pointed out where we were, the Thu Bon River, An Hoa, and then Nong Son. Our helicopter route would be a straight line to

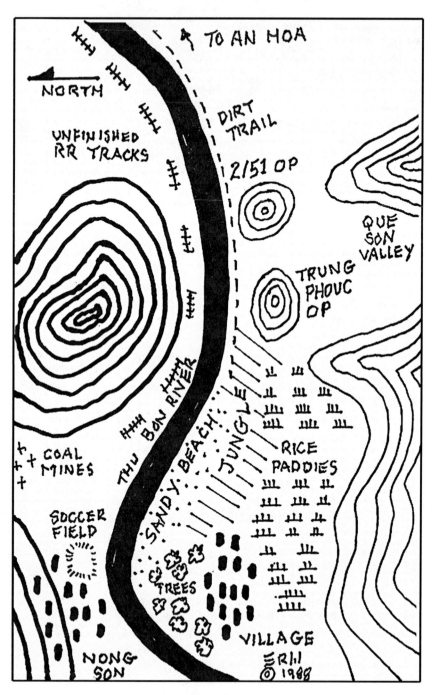

Nong Son

An Hoa, about 20 miles to the southwest, and then up river to Nong Son, southwest, about ten miles, from An Hoa.

In the Nong Son area, while quite curvy, the river generally flowed northeast from the southwest to An Hoa then east, emptying into the South China Sea. On the north bank at Nong Son, on a bend of the river, was a canyon leading into foothills next to a small mountain, where the mining operation was located, as well as several elegant concrete and tile homes for the engineers and their families. On the south bank, just before reaching Nong Son, was a large hill where the Trung Phuoc OP was situated, and just east of that was a smaller hill, the second outpost and where the Second Battalion was presently getting decimated. West of Trung Phuoc, on the same side of the river but across the river from the coal mine was a small grass-hut village at the bend of the river. Just to the south of the small village and Trung Phuoc the land rose rapidly, giving way to the northern edge of the rugged Que Son Valley Viet Cong and North Vietnamese stronghold.

The major pointed on the map to a small sandy bar on the south side of the river next to the village. This was where the Marine CH-46As would land the troops, just west of Trung Phuoc OP, which the NVA now occupied.

Master Sergeant Wright announced that the Marine helicopters were inbound, and I should get the troops lined up. The first lift would have six 46As. I told Major Van that the First Company commander should get the first lift into six groups of about 20 to 22 men each, and he, part of his staff and I would get in the last chopper. Lieutenant Mac and Sergeant Bronson would go with the First Company commander. The major nodded, saying that he would meet on the last helicopter, and off he went, not the alert, sprightly man I thought I had recently known but an older, scared, broken version.

The loading of the troops didn't take long, and soon we were airborne. Moving toward our objective, I could see it was lighter at 3,000 feet than on the ground, and darkness would soon be on us. Scanning the troops in the helicopter, I realized Major Van was not with us. Other than troopers of the First Company, Private Tuan, my Vietnamese radio carrier and I were the only ones of the battalion command group. I wondered where the major was.

Upon landing, without taking any fire, the First Company immediately formed a perimeter around the sandy LZ to secure our assault area. The company commander, Second Lieutenant Son, would establish his CP on the riverbank, as would Major Van with the battalion CP.

Probably the last thing the NVA had considered was a twilight helicopter assault on the river's edge. I was glad they had no doubt ruled out that suicidal possibility, because it allowed us to get the entire battalion on the ground and organized before the NVA became aware of what had happened. Their immediate attention was still focused on trying to overcome the Second Battalion

Troung Phuoc outpost as viewed from the Nong Son coal mine across the Thu Bon River.

on the smaller hill. Throughout the day, the Second Battalion advisors had managed to keep the outpost they occupied intact using close air support. USAF Douglas A-1E Skyraiders (single-engine propeller World War II fighters) had inundated both the Trung Phuoc OP and the surrounding area with 20 mm cannon fire and tons of high-explosive bombs. USMC 155 mm artillery batteries provided additional direct support via radio relay to the firing batteries back near An Hoa.

The Second Battalion advisor, Captain Popps, had been slightly wounded, but the advisors were okay and in good spirits. As long as they had air and artillery support, they thought they could hold on. Their problems were food, water, medical supplies, ammo and adverse weather such as rain or lower ceilings that would inhibit close air support. Now that the Third Battalion was in the battle, Captain Popps felt the tide would turn. Over the radio I could sense his relief when we landed.

First Lieutenant Phong, the CO of the Second Company and the ranking battalion officer next to the major, immediately took charge upon landing in the second lift. The tall young man could be very arrogant at times, speaking only Vietnamese when he wanted to avoid contact with the advisors, even though he could speak English.

He was typical of the many proud, educated young Vietnamese men caught in the war, fighting for a cause in which they believed, placed in leadership positions they did not foresee ending in the near future. The intensity of the fighting had forced them to become dependent on U.S. aid, U.S. troops, U.S. weapons, U.S. support, and U.S. officers and NCOs telling them how to fight the battles. Obligated to be tolerant of Americans because they held the power to battlefield success, these young officers constantly endured inner conflict because of the subservient role fate compelled them to play amidst the stress of battle.

Lieutenant Phong was never disrespectful to the advisors, but at times he would withdraw within himself and totally ignore their presence. Tonight, it was obvious that's what he wanted to do, but the situation he had been thrust into dictated otherwise.

I asked Lieutenant Phong where Major Van was. My first clue to Lieutenant Phong's attitude was his curt reply in Vietnamese that the major was sick, with malaria, so he went to the hospital. He emphasized that he was in charge of this operation, he commanded the Third Battalion, so if I would excuse him now, he would get back to work.

I told Lieutenant Mac and Sergeant Bronson to check the perimeters, make sure they got listening posts out. Check the machine gun positions. Get down and personally check their fields of fire. Report back to me at the battalion CP.

Lieutenant Phong had moved over to Lieutenant Colonel Lap to get his next orders. I went to Major Haines and Master Sergeant Wright, asking if they knew who wasn't here. Major Haines stated that my counterpart got sick, so the colonel told him to go to the hospital. I questioned if the major believed that. The major replied that it wasn't up to us to believe or disbelieve, and Major Van sure as hell looked bad back at Hoi An, and because he wasn't here, I just needed to carry on with my new battalion commander.

I pleaded with the major that he didn't know Lieutenant Phong. Sometimes he got a hair up his ass about advisors and wouldn't even acknowledge our existence. It was impossible to advise a guy like that.

Major Haines bluntly told me that we all had our little problems. Right now, we had a war to fight, so he was sure I could work it out some way. Okay, I would talk to Lieutenant Colonel Lap, and ask him how I could best help the new battalion commander. If I would do it when Lieutenant Phong was present, at least both of us would then know what is expected.

By now, it was dark. Trung Phuoc OP was about half a mile east of us. Captain Popps was still calling in Marine fire missions, but the Air Force Skyraiders had gone back to Da Nang. Shortly, Puff, the AC-47 gunship, would be on station. The war was right next to us and the sounds of small-arms fire and artillery explosions were clearly audible.

Lieutenant Colonel Lap explained about Major Van and Lieutenant Phong taking over. Looking at both of us, he stressed the necessity of sending out a force to relieve the pressure on the trapped Second Battalion immediately.

Discussing our options now, it was decided to send the Third Company, with Lieutenant Mac and Sergeant Bronson, out to contact the enemy. The Second Company would establish a defensive perimeter around the village next to us on the riverbank. The First Company would revert to battalion reserve and prepare for a dawn attack against the Trung Phuoc OP.

So far things seemed to be going okay. We had met no resistance on the ground, and we had a plan that made sense. Lieutenant Mac and Sergeant Bronson returned, giving our defensive setup high marks. I briefed them on the plan for the evening, making sure that they had the frequency and call sign for Puff.

I had no doubts about the straight-standing young officer or the slump-shouldered, laconic NCO. While none of us knew what the night would bring, I knew they could hold their own in any situation. With nothing else to say, I whispered good luck to them as they walked away.

The night turned out to be one of the longest of my life. Major Haines, Lieutenant Colonel Lap, Lieutenant Phong, Master Sergeant Wright, and myself, with our radio operators, spent the night sitting or lying on the dirt floor of one of the grass huts in the village. The battalion intelligence NCO had his men talking to the villagers about what had happened to Trung Phuoc. Evidently, during that night, hundreds of soldiers from the north, with many weapons, had moved through the rice fields next to the village and had attacked Trung Phuoc from three sides. The fighting had continued into the early morning when the soldiers had finally overcome the PF defenders. By that time, though, a South Vietnamese battalion (the 2/51st) had moved into the smaller outpost, reinforcing it so the enemy could not take it. All day long American airplanes had bombed the rice fields, Trung Phuoc, and the jungle area around the outpost.

When questioned about specifics, such as the number of soldiers, kinds of weapons, or number wounded or killed, the villagers didn't know. Descriptions such as "many" soldiers, "big" guns, and "many" hurt were as accurate as we got. We also learned that several young men and women villagers had been conscripted by the North Vietnamese as human bearers to carry wounded, weapons, and ammunition around the battlefield. From what we could piece together, we were up against at least a Regular North Vietnamese Army Regiment which would have no less than 1,000 troops. Between the two ARVN battalions, we had less than 700 soldiers.

About a quarter of a mile out of the village, the Second Company stopped. The unit was about halfway between the village and Trung Phuoc OP, establishing a night defensive position. The acting company commander, who had taken over from Lieutenant Phong, called back to report he was encountering heavy resistance and could go no further. Sergeant Bronson called back to report the patrol in front of the company had met an enemy patrol, made contact, and withdrawn. No amount of urging on the advisor's part had been able to get the unit moving again. I whispered in the mike for Sergeant Bronson to dig in tight, because Spooky was on the way.

Unfortunately for the Second Company, the NVA was not going to let them rest. Shortly after Spooky came on station, the company began to receive random incoming small-arms fire. Over the next hour as the NVA continued to probe by fire, the returned fire by the Second Company began to define the limits of the defensive lines. Very slowly, the AK-47 rounds became mixed with fire from DP and RPK 7.62 (.30-caliber) light machine guns and the DSH K-38 12.7 mm heavy machine gun (like the U.S. .50-caliber MG). As the NVA soldiers moved in closer, the Second Company began to receive rocket fire from Russian RPG-7 shoulder-fired rocket-grenade launchers. Sergeant Bronson crawled around the defensive position giving advice, adjusting automatic weapons fire, and encouraging the gunners.

Lieutenant Mac began to talk to Spooky, the AC-47 which had been orbiting over the Second Battalion's outpost on the hill, dropping flares and using mini-guns to repel assaults from the slopes to the south. With the enlarged battle picking up in the Second Company area, Spooky moved its orbit to cover both the 2/51 OP and the Second Company. Looking down into the darkness, the pilot said he had no trouble identifying Lieutenant Mac's position. He could make out a circular area from which came red-orange tracers, radiating like spokes on a wheel. From two sides, he could also see where the NVA's green tracers were coming from, all going into the Second Company's position.

Sergeant Bronson called back to me that the unit was now taking incoming 60 mm mortar rounds. Several soldiers had been killed or wounded, and casualties were beginning to mount. Lieutenant Mac asked Spooky to drop parachute flares. From our position, jungle trees precluded us from seeing most of the ground fire except for occasional orange and green bursts arcing through the sky above the trees. Because of the darkness, the lack of knowledge about the enemy's location and numbers, and the fact that the reserve soldiers might be reluctant to make a night attack to aid the Second Company, Lieutenant Colonel Lap decided not to commit the battalion reserve, the First Company.

Feelings of complete helplessness and fear for the safety of Lieutenant Mac, Sergeant Bronson and the Second Company clashed with my building anger at my counterpart for deserting his unit. There was nothing I could do or say that could help anyone, so I just lay there, listened to the battle and prayed to God that the unit would last through the night. Another fear was also smoldering in my stomach. The ARVN regiment had two units already tied down by the NVA. We knew from the intensity of the fire power we were engaging more than one battalion. What we didn't know was who they were or what else they might have. Further, they could tell by counting the Marine helicopters that a battalion had landed by the village. But we didn't know if they had part or all the battalion pinned down in the jungle. If the NVA brought more reinforcements further west to make a flanking movement on the Second Company position, they would have to move next to the village, and then the rest of the battalion would be in the fight.

I told Major Haines my concerns and we suggested to Lieutenant Colonel Lap that it was necessary to get some patrols out in the rice fields around the village to make sure the NVA wouldn't overrun us. He agreed and spoke to Lieutenant Phong who said the headquarters company commander could take care of that. I said I'd help and moved off with the commander, Lieutenant Tham.

Lieutenant Tham was an average-sized young Vietnamese man who spoke excellent English and was friendly with all the advisors. Once, while in Saigon for a few days, I had met Lieutenant Tham and spent some time with his family. He was also very well educated and would constantly ask questions about the world outside Vietnam. I enjoyed him as a friend and respected his ability and dedication as an infantry officer. Helping him with the patrol would take my mind off the problems with the Second Company.

With the jungle lit up by the flares, the Second Company could better see enemy movements and guide Spooky's mini-guns to push the NVA back. Each time the probes increased and the pressure tightened, Lieutenant Mac would command Spooky to fire up to the edge of the company's defensive line and repel another potential breakthrough. Throughout the night Lieutenant Mac and Sergeant Bronson took turns directing Spooky and moving among the soldiers, letting them know they'd live to see the morning. In the village, I felt better because at least Lieutenant Mac and Sergeant Bronson were hanging in there, and we had two patrols out to warn us of any flank assault. Major Haines, Lieutenant Colonel Lap, Lieutenant Phong, and I began to plan the morning's activities.

The First Company would move out at dawn to attack Trung Phuoc OP. By daylight the USAF promised to have both Skyraiders and Martin B-57 Canberra bombers support the attack. The B-57s with a 500-pound bomb under each wing would initiate the attack by bombing Trung Phuoc OP. This would continue until the First Company moved within a hundred yards of the bottom of the hill. The outpost would then be strafed by the Spads and Douglas A-1E Skyraiders, and we would overrun the hill. Neat, clean, simple, no problem, we thought. But during the following days the battle turned out to be anything but neat, clean and simple.

During the night, some Vietnamese soldiers explained the significance of Nong Son. It had been the only producing coal mine in South Vietnam, part of the An Hoa industrial complex to be constructed in the early 1960s.

The actual Nong Son coal mine complex (the only producing coal mine in South Vietnam) which was fought over by almost 2,000 soldiers on both sides, resulting in about 1,500 KIA and WIA on both sides. The South Vietnamese prevailed, and the coal mine was not destroyed.

The war prevented most of this from happening, and Viet Cong ambushes made it impossible to move any coal away from the mine. From a military perspective, the defense of the mine was too costly. But from a psychological point of view, the coal mine represented independence from the many coal mines of the industrial North Vietnam, and a promise for the future. It could not be destroyed by the NVA.

CHAPTER 15

Nong Son,
Losing the Battle:
Days 2 and 3

The Second Day

As the night slowly wore on, the NVA began to lighten up on the Second Company, breaking off contact and pulling back before dawn. Lieutenant Mac said close to half the company had been hit during the night. The advisors were okay, not even scratched, but there were about ten to 15 KIA and about 30 to 35 WIA. As soon as it was light, the company would pull back into the village and assess the situation.

The B-57s screamed in on their designated targets on time. The First Company jumped off. I was the only advisor with the company. Lieutenant Mac and Sergeant Bronson needed some food and rest, so they went back with their company. Moving east out of the village, single file, we passed through a small grove of banana trees and moved along the south edge of the trees on a rice field dike. The day was cool and overcast, but the clouds were high enough to allow good air support. Major Haines radioed to tell me he also had Marine UH-1E gunships standing by to support us when the Skyraiders left.

Walking on the dike, we couldn't see Trung Phuoc because of the trees, but we could see the Canberra B-57s dropping their 500-pound bombs with the impacts followed by crushing explosions we could feel as well as hear. NVA bodies were tossed 30 to 40 feet high with all the rest of the debris blown about by the bombs.

In spite of this visual display proving that Charlie was getting his collective ass kicked in grand style, the soldiers began to have second thoughts. Looking at the carnage on the hill somehow riveted the soldiers to the dike on the edge of the paddy. Many even began to sit down when we were about

146

200 yards away. I couldn't see the observation post top of the hill, but we were close enough to hear the NVA automatic weapons firing at the Canberras and smell the pervasive, acrid cordite of the high explosives. Each time a bomb landed, the thundering impact shook the ground like an earthquake, taking our breath away.

As the B-57s departed, the Skyraiders swooped in, blasting away with their wing-mounted 40 mm cannons. Another wave of the Spads (originally a name given to the Skyraiders by the navy in World War II but now used sarcastically by jet pilots to reflect their ancient heritage) dropped napalm on the hilltop, and black smoke billowed over the treetops, bringing with it the pungent odor of burning oil and human flesh. We could even sense the heat at this distance. Now was the time for the company to move out to prepare for a frontal assault.

I screamed for the lieutenant to move his troops out. Running from the middle of the line, with Private Tuan, my radio man, staying by my side, I screamed at the soldiers to stand up, to hurry up and get going. As I passed the company commander, crouched down, I grabbed him and pulled him, yelled for him to move forward, to advance, to come with me. The lieutenant was torn between his duties as a leader and his mounting fear, which was quickly becoming reinforced by his soldiers' reluctance to move.

Pointing to the attacking Skyraiders, I urged the soldiers on. Running back down to the end of the line of them, I moved forward again but with little luck—the soldiers didn't want to move. Standing at the head of the line with the lieutenant, I glared at the approximately 100 soldiers stopped at the beginning of an assault, some standing, some sitting, all scared. I wondered what the hell I should do now.

Crack—crack—crack—a sheet of AK-47 fire erupted from our right, from across the open rice field. A dozen soldiers crumpled to the ground as I threw myself into the mud behind the dike. On our right flank, to the east, about 400 yards away, the rice paddy gave way to a gentle sloping hill covered with elephant grass. The whole side of the hill was alive with a million (or so I thought) NVA soldiers, slowly moving toward us.

Fuck Trung Phuoc, I mused, now we've got a real problem. I screamed into the radio, calling for Major Haines, Tiger Six. I explained that we were 200 meters south of Trung Phuoc. We had just been hit on our right flank by at least a company of NVA. They had automatic weapons and mortars. We had at least 12 KIA. We needed those Marine gunships here, now.

Dropping the radio headset, I turned my attention to my front, where I could see an NVA machine gun on a rocky outcropping on the hillside, shooting at us. I pointed it out to the two-man .30-caliber machine gun crew to my right about six feet away. I yelled to them, pointing to the rock, telling them it was a VC machine gun and the gunner was shooting too high, over their heads. In the confusion the gunner didn't understand and continued to over-shoot.

Rolling over, I grabbed for the gun to move the trajectory lower. As I did, Private Tuan told me that the American advisor, the major, was calling me. I rolled back to grab the radio. Major Haines said the gunships couldn't get in yet, but Marine artillery was available instead, on the Bravo Net.

Before switching to the Marine artillery radio relay frequency, I glanced at our machine gunners. Holy shit, both had been shot, right between the eyes. I now knew the NVA had sniper teams on the hillside. That hadn't been done by random shooting. About ten feet away was our 60 mm mortar team, pumping out rounds as fast as they could drop them down the tube. Their aim, though, was inferior to their enthusiasm; all they were doing was blasting away on the far side of the rice paddy, short of the NVA soldiers on the hillside. Jumping to a crouch, I moved next to the tube and, kicking the base plate, tried to drop the angle of the tube so the trajectory would not be so high and short but longer, allowing the rounds to land on the hillside.

Private Tuan called me again. Crawling back to him, behind the dike, I heard Sergeant Wright tell me the Marine artillery fire was on the way and I could call adjustments to them, on their frequency. Christ, was it confusing. We were really pinned down. The sharp crack of the incoming AK-47 bullets tearing through the leaves over our heads, smashing into the tree trunks, and thudding into the soldiers on the ground was frightening. The never-ending, staccato grinding of the machine gun on the hill raked the low dike protecting my head, spraying me all over with bits of rocks, dirt, and mud.

Whump! Suddenly a body-crushing explosion slammed into the ground covering us with more mud and debris. Looking to my right, I realized an incoming mortar round had just hit the two-man mortar crew, tearing their bodies apart like an invisible meat grinder. I was lying in the mud facing south, looking across the rice paddies to the rising hill. Trung Phuoc OP was to my left (east), and another 400 yards away, further east, was the outpost where Captain Popps and the Second Battalion were. Behind me was the dense banana grove and jungle foliage, and west of that was the village from which we had just come, south of our present position. The southeast corner of the rice paddy in front of me was bounded by a small ridge, a finger that jutted out from the hill to my front.

The first volley of the Marine artillery landed far west of that ridge, to the west even of the NVA positions on the hillside to our front. It landed beyond the swarm of NVA soldiers, who were slowly moving toward us. I knew the firing battery was northeast of us at An Hoa, shooting southwest, so the volley, from the battery's position, was landing long by about 300 yards.

The NVA's incoming fire was increasing, and the company wasn't doing very well. We were pinned down behind the dike. Machine gun fire chewed up the thick foliage over our heads, and sniper bullets continued to systematically hit soldiers who weren't protected. Shouting into the radio to the Marine artillery relay team, I called out corrections to drop 300 and fire for effect, I would adjust.

Another volley smashed into the hillside but in the same place. What the hell was going on? I wondered. I had just given them corrections. I called that the rounds were landing too long. Drop 300, I said again.

I recognized Captain Popps' voice as he cut in on the frequency telling Charlie Bravo, the Marine artillery, to disregard my adjustments. He said they were on target and to keep firing. Confused, I called Major Haines to get the Marine gunships in, but he said they wouldn't fly in with the artillery firing, they'd be flying into the Howitzer trajectories.

The company commander, Lieutenant Son, crawled next to me, and with tears in his eyes, said his company couldn't last much longer. They had to pull back. I would try to get the artillery straightened out and provide cover for the withdrawal.

Charlie Bravo was no longer on my frequency. Major Haines had called to say that the artillery rounds I had seen landing too far to the right (which I thought were the Marine shells) had actually been from ARVN artillery. I then gave him the corrections based on where the ARVN artillery was positioned, but by now the NVA were massed along the far edge of the rice paddy, lined up for the attack. I could clearly see their tan uniforms, silver belt buckles, and tan pith helmets.

I didn't know what had happened to the Marine artillery. I couldn't adjust the ARVN artillery. The gunships couldn't move in. The Skyraiders were gone … so I thought, why wait? I told Private Tuan it was time to go.

Pushing back into the underbrush, we got out of sight of the advancing NVA. Looking around we saw we were the only live soldiers left, so we quickly moved back toward the village as AK-47 rounds cracked all around us as we ran through the dense jungle.

I called Major Haines and told him the company was coming back in and right on our tail was an NVA company. We would pass through our lines, but the perimeter around the village had better be ready to counter the NVA attack. I could no longer see the NVA soldiers due to the heavy jungle. Bullets continued to crack all around us, with an occasional muffled whump as another 60 mm mortar round exploded in the soft soil, tearing apart the trees and thick, jungle growth. The smell of death and fear was all around us.

Moving through a small clearing, I passed by an ARVN soldier, on my left, between me and the NVA. As I passed the man, a sharp crack whipped by my chest and I felt an impact on my left elbow. It was covered with blood, tissue, and bone fragments. Instantaneously I realized, though, that I felt no pain, and I wondered how that could be. When the man next to me groaned,

I saw it was his elbow that had been shot with his bone, flesh, and blood splattered all over mine. At that moment one thought flashed through my mind: what could I be doing in civilian life now instead of being here?

Soon the company reached the battalion perimeter and passed through into the village. Lieutenant Mac and Sergeant Bronson were on the perimeter with the Second Company and most of headquarters company.

The NVA stopped short of attacking our lines. Firefights broke out up and down the line, but the ARVN held fast and didn't give in. By noon the NVA pulled back, and we regrouped to plan our next move.

The ARVN dead and wounded were moved to the river, where a barge would take them across the river to a gymnasium, next to a soccer field, being converted into a field hospital. Ammunition was redistributed, and platoons rearranged around the perimeter.

Lieutenant Colonel Lap said a company-size force would move forward again to retrieve the bodies left during the morning attack. Some of the conscripted villagers who had escaped from the NVA returned to their homes, told tales of how badly the NVA had suffered from the air strikes and artillery shelling. They explained that behind the hill, leading into Que Son Valley, from which the First Company had just been attacked, was an NVA regimental field hospital complete with female nurses and full of NVA wounded.

Lieutenant Colonel Lap was convinced that the NVA were on the run, and he wanted to exploit the perceived rout, so in addition to bringing back the dead, the troops would pursue the NVA. The attack force, led by my friend Lieutenant Tham, headquarters company commander, moved out about 2:00 p.m., heading straight for the hillside where the NVA had been that morning. Lieutenant Mac and Sergeant Bronson were with the platoon on the left recovering the bodies, while I was with the middle platoon and Lieutenant Tham was with the third platoon on the right flank.

Skyraiders swept the hillside to the south with bombs, napalm, and cannon fire. ARVN artillery was being controlled by the regimental command group. Two platoons moved southeast across the first set of rice paddies to the bottom of the hillside and then east toward the ridge line where the NVA had initiated the attack in the morning. The platoon on the left flank with Mac and Bronson moved directly to where we had been hit on the dike that morning.

Crossing a low bushy area between the rice paddies, the middle and right platoons were hit. Halting the line, we waited for the ARVN artillery to plow up the hillside so we could move forward again. The artillery fire lifted, and we ground our way through the thick grass. Again, we were hit with small-arms fire, automatic weapons, machine guns, and mortars, which hit several soldiers. Moving out this afternoon with only my .45 pistol, I now had my choice of M1 Garands, one which I immediately snatched up. In this violent battle, an advisor was no longer needed, but a rifleman was.

Every time one of the two platoons gained a little ground, the other was pushed back. The left platoon had reached the bodies from the morning fiasco.

Lieutenant Tham attempted to push his platoon further up the hill and get on top of the NVA. The advance slowed as we continued to trade bullets. Before Lieutenant Tham could get into position his platoon got hit hard and pinned down.

Part of the platoon Lieutenant Mac and Sergeant Bronson were with had moved back with the dead to return to the village. The rest of the platoon, which they were with, was now moving up on our left. Lieutenant Tham had tried to maneuver to our right. I was pinned down with the middle platoon and we couldn't go forward. All three platoons were now taking heavy casualties and going nowhere. Regiment was massing the artillery in front of us, but the NVA were dug in too well to be forced out. I knew they were taking a lot of punishment and wondered how they could continue to fight like they did. Then the NVA moved toward us again. I wasn't sure what had happened to Lieutenant Tham and his platoon, still stalled to my right. Up until now our force had fought hard and well, under the command of Lieutenant Tham, in spite of the superior force they had faced. The platoon leader was lying on the ground next to me, jabbering rapidly to Lieutenant Tham, to the platoon leader with Sergeant Bronson, and to Lieutenant Phong back with Lieutenant Colonel Lap in the village.

The firing continued on all sides without letup. Confusion and arguing began to consume the Vietnamese platoon leader who was on the radio. As he looked up at me, I immediately recognized stark terror. "Trung-uy Tham bi chet," he cried, tears streaming down his cheeks. "Lieutenant Tham is dead."

Apparently in his last attempt to maneuver around the NVA, Lieutenant Tham stood up, raising his left arm to motion the troops on, and although he was wearing a flak jacket and helmet, a single bullet struck just under his left armpit, puncturing his heart, killing him instantly. With him dead, the platoons weren't motivated to go anywhere. A sergeant moved over, talking on the radio to regiment. Lieutenant Colonel Lap ordered the unit to gather the weapons, the dead and the wounded, and make an orderly withdrawal back to the village. Major Haines confirmed the order and told us to make sure it wasn't a rout.

The lieutenant beside me and I planned the withdrawal. The wounded, dead, and the loose weapons would go first. The rest of us would hold the line. I told Sergeant Bronson to go with the first group. The platoon with which Lieutenant Tham had been was having trouble, carrying all the wounded and dead, so the platoon leader next to me took a group of soldiers with him to help this platoon, but mortar rounds and machine gun fire cut them down. Now we were really in a bind.

Sergeant Bronson helped a platoon sergeant organize the first group to pull back. Lieutenant Mac worked with the remaining Vietnamese officers to bring in artillery fire and get our machine guns to the front. I grabbed some soldiers, and we crawled our way over to what was left of Lieutenant Tham's platoon. Grabbing the dead, the wounded, and weapons, we scrambled back toward the center of the line, half running, half crawling. I cradled Lieutenant Tham's body, distraught over losing a good friend, like I was carrying a sleeping baby. He did not seem heavy.

But, ultimately, we couldn't get back with all of our dead, wounded, and weapons. Lieutenant Phong sent another platoon to help us. The new troops grabbed what we couldn't carry. I carried Lieutenant Tham back to the village while Lieutenant Mac and the platoon moved back slowly, covering our retreat. Night would be on us again soon. In less than 24 hours, 30 of our soldiers had been killed and around 70 wounded—about 30 percent of our force.

Lieutenant Colonel Lap had decided to move the regimental CP across the river to the hillside overlooking the jungle and rice paddies over which we had spent the past 24 hours fighting. The battalion would remain in the village. Colonel Lap would take the dead and seriously wounded back with him. The clouds had lowered to the point where we would have no air support that night; no resupply of water, food, ammo, or medical provisions; and no medevac of the wounded.

In the midst of contemplating these conditions, Major Haines explained why Captain Popps had countermanded my Marine fire mission that morning. Because I had mistakenly thought the ARVN artillery was the Marine artillery, I had called in corrections to the Marines based on the impact of the ARVN artillery. What had actually happened that was the Marine volley had been falling short and landing east of the ridge to my left front. From my place on the ground I couldn't see that. However, Captain Popps had been able to observe from his OP on the hill where the volley was landing, and he had also seen an NVA company running toward the ridge from the back of the hill to hit us on our flank. The Marine artillery had landed right in the middle of the NVA unit and that was why Captain Popps had wanted the Marines to continue firing in the same place. That firing had disrupted an attack that surely would have killed us all. I thanked God for whomever looks out for wretched soldiers as I fingered my Saint Christopher's medal and my rabbit's foot, figuring it really didn't hurt to be a little superstitious now and then.

The dead, the wounded, Major Haines, Sergeant Wright, and the regimental command group crossed the river in large boats from the coal mine as darkness and relative quiet descended over our diminished battalion. The river was about 200 feet wide, very swift, and 20 feet deep—not a fordable water course. The Second Company remained on the perimeter of the village. Lieutenant Phong designated the First Company as the battalion reserve. The Third Company would augment the Second Company on the line.

Captain Popps and his advisors would coordinate Marine harassing and interdicting (H & I) artillery missions with random firing at preselected suspected enemy positions throughout the night, while Lieutenant Colonel Lap's staff would do the same with the ARVN artillery.

Lieutenant Mac, Sergeant Bronson, Private Tuan, the battalion medic, and I selected a grass hut to be our night CP. In the hut next to us was Lieutenant Phong and his battalion staff. We were all bone tired, hungry and scared. At one point, a small chicken snuck under one of the sides of the grass hut, slowly moving about and pecking at the floor, skinny with very few feathers—it looked like a miniature refugee from a cockfight. We all froze, looking at one another.

Then Bronson, Tuan and the medic simultaneously pounced on the bird. Pooling our resources, we got two canteen cups, some rancid water, a couple handfuls of rice, and a pinch of C-4, a form of putty-like high-explosive, dangerous when exploded but safe when ignited with a match, used to generate

One of the grass huts used as our battalion CP during the Nong Son combat operation.

tremendous heat for cooking or boiling water rapidly. Private Tuan and the medic dressed the chicken, cut it up, and with the rice made chicken soup, the first food most of us had had since early morning.

Looking around our new quarters, the medic screamed with delight. Apparently, we had unknowingly selected the village store for our shelter. Almost invisible in a corner was a glass enclosed store cabinet–type display case. Inside were three to four dozen spanking new, clean Kotex pads. The medic grinned broadly as he stuffed his medical kit with his newfound bandages.

As Lieutenant Mac took his last cigarette out of its crumpled pack, Sergeant Bronson reminded him of the words on the package stating that cigarette smoking could be hazardous to one's health. Looking at the smoke curling up from the white cylinder, then looking at the sergeant, Lieutenant Mac, grinning, guessed that the warning really didn't bother him much right now.

We decided that we would spend the night in two-hour shifts. One of us would man the radio; one would stay outside, checking our defensive positions to make sure everyone who was on the line was awake; the third advisor would sleep (if he could). I made one other decision I explained to my team. Our job was to advise this unit and provide liaison with U.S. air and artillery support. I did not envision that our job included dying for this unit as clearly dead advisors could not perform their assigned tasks. Therefore, I briefed Lieutenant Mac and Sergeant Bronson on operation "Bug-Out," my own personal plan to get us out of here alive if the unit was overrun and became ineffective. One of my prime responsibilities was to keep my team members living. If the unit reached the point where it was no longer able to fight, a possibility that was conceivable at this point, and if our role as advisors was negated by the lack of a unit to advise, we would then execute the plan. Our potential escape route was to go to the river and move downstream toward An Hoa during darkness.

Throughout the night we were probed by the NVA, but nothing like the previous 24 hours. Probably the artillery H & I firing kept the NVA from making a major attack. Still, it took a long, long time for morning to arrive.

The Third Day

As the darkness slowly receded, I thought about the past 36 hours. We had met an obviously superior force, yet we were still intact as a unit. The Third Battalion advisors really were lucky because none of us had even been scratched. Why, I wondered again, hadn't the NVA shot me the morning before when I had been walking up and down the dike when the ARVN refused to move forward? Surely the NVA had seen that I was an American advisor, the crucial link to the Air Force and Marine air support. Call it fate, luck, or whatever, we advisors sure must have been living right to have escaped any injury thus far. Well, I thought with irony, reminiscing about some of the things I'd done in my life, I guess there must be some truth to the saying "Only the good die young."

As dawn approached, it became evident that an aerial resupply would not be possible due to low clouds. Regiment had not yet decided what our next move would be. What soon happened, though, decided for us.

Sergeant Bronson was on the perimeter line, Mac was asleep, and I was musing about the misfortunes of war when, suddenly, incoming mortar rounds and small-arms and machine gun fire announced that the NVA hadn't left; in fact, it seemed that they seriously wanted the village we were in. The action began on the southern edge of the village, which gave way to water-soaked rice paddies. About 150 to 200 yards further on, the rice fields ended and the elephant grass began on the slopes, intermingled with low, thick, broad-leafed jungle trees.

This was mostly the Second Company's portion of the perimeter; the hut we were in was next to this defensive line. Sergeant Bronson was on the east side of the village with the Third Company. The battalion had spent the night digging in; from a defensive viewpoint, we were in pretty good shape. The village was bounded on the west and north sides by the river, while to the east and south, it was bordered by rice paddies anywhere from 150 to 300 yards across. The water in the rice paddies varied in depth from six to 12 inches, which made running fast across the fields very difficult. The terrain surrounding the north and northeast corner of the village was covered with dense jungle, thick enough to impede fast movement and render the firing of mortars from within it impossible, but not spacious enough to hide a lot of troops. From a tactical point of view, though, we clearly had the advantage. High earthen dikes running around the village edge on the east and south held back the water in the rice paddies. These served as excellent revetments behind which we could hide and shoot.

I didn't expect any frontal assault across the rice paddies since we could mow down any ground attack coming from this direction. The trees and huts in the village allowed us to move about without being seen by the enemy and, if we stayed low, would keep us from being hit by bullets.

The activity from the southeast increased and we called in artillery as well as using our own 60 mm mortars. Lieutenant Mac began working with the Second Company, and Sergeant Bronson remained with the Third Company. I stayed in the middle with Lieutenant Phong, talking on the radio to Major Haines. Regiment said to just hang in there.

At least our presence took a lot of pressure off the Second Battalion.

According to Captain Popps, since our arrival the NVA had seemed satisfied to maintain the status quo with the ARVN troops in the outpost. While the besieged battalion was in no position to mount any counterattack, it was also not in any danger of being overrun.

Major Haines said some of the regiment staff was scrounging around the mining facilities and engineers' homes for food, water, and medical supplies for the Third Battalion. But what we really needed they couldn't find—more ammunition.

As the morning progressed, Sergeant Bronson radioed to say the fighting in his sector was picking up. It appeared that we were probably facing an NVA battalion, and it became obvious the situation would not get better. We were taking casualties from mortars, and more NVA soldiers were joining the battalion opposing us. Our mortar and ARVN artillery did not seem to slow down our adversary. In fact, the more high explosives we dumped on the enemy, the stronger the enemy seemed to become.

Then a new element of weaponry was introduced to the battle. RPG rounds began to slam into the village, blowing away the huts and splattering shrapnel around the inside of our position. Then what I thought wouldn't happen, actually did. The NVA began a frontal assault on our south sector across the rice paddies. The mortar and rocket attacks increased, and accurately placed machine gun fire began to rake the top of the dikes. Bayonets extended, firing their AK-47s from the waist, two waves of khaki-clad soldiers moved slowly across the rice paddies, their forward movement only slowed down by the water in the rice paddies. Earlier in the morning I had worked out some preplanned Marine artillery targets in the open areas around the village.

I radioed for the fire mission, assaulting NVA troops in the open, requesting white phosphorus rounds and to fire for effect, stating I would adjust any corrections. The Marine artillery responded, on the way.

Before the soldiers could completely cross the rice paddies, the piercing whistle of incoming artillery rose above the clattering of machine guns and cracking of automatic weapons. Crashing into the water-logged fields, the volley of white phosphorus spewed clouds of white smoke, mud, water, shrapnel, and bodies. The advancing soldiers were stopped just short of reaching our lines, and our soldiers were able to shoot the NVA troops the artillery barrage hadn't hit.

It was then that it began to sink in that these NVA soldiers were not just run-of-the-mill regulars. The punishment they had taken for two days and the suicidal attack we had just witnessed suggested that the NVA presence here and refusal to retreat, despite sustaining tremendous casualties, meant they had some special military objective we didn't realize. I wondered what their true objective was and who they really were.

As casualties continued to mount, Lieutenant Phong pleaded with Lieutenant Colonel Lap to allow the battalion to move across the river. During daylight, enemy troop movements across the open fields could be seen, but at night, without Spooky because of the low clouds, the enemy could not be detected. We didn't have enough mortar flares to last through the night. Artillery flares would help some, but it was uncertain whether the artillery units could keep the battlefield illuminated. Additionally, Lieutenant Phong told Lieutenant Colonel Lap he didn't believe the battalion could hold out all night against the constant pressure as we were low on ammo, out of food, and the water around the village was contaminated.

Lieutenant Colonel Lap asked Major Haines to talk to me about what was going on. I told Major Haines that it seemed that we were getting weaker and the NVA was getting stronger. I agreed with Lieutenant Phong; I didn't think the battalion could hold out another night. My belief was that if we moved across the river and set up defensive positions on the ridge above the coal mining community, we would effectively be out of small-arms and RPG range. The mortars would still be able to reach out to the ridge, but the NVA would not be in position to observe or control where the rounds landed. I told Major Haines that moving across the river would be a help. We could take care of the wounded, feed the troops, get some rest, and, if we could get resupplied, we could better prepare for a counterattack.

A few minutes later Lieutenant Phong looked at me and smiled for the first time since the operation began. He said we would move across the river now and asked if I could help plan the move. Things were looking up. Phong was talking to me again in English. Lieutenant Phong, his staff, the company commanders, Lieutenant Mac, Sergeant Bronson, and I discussed how to move across the river. I explained that we needed to do it so the North Vietnamese don't know that we were leaving. This meant we would have to keep our defensive perimeter until the last soldiers left. We would have to keep the NVA away from the village.

We decided that we would move the battalion across the river a company at a time. There was a large coal barge tied up on the opposite riverbank at Nong Son that could hold a company. There were two or three motorboats that could also be used. We could move the entire battalion in three trips. I wasn't sure that the NVA wouldn't know what we were up to as the barge and boats did make noise, but we had crossed the river several times in the past 24 hours, and apparently the NVA had not been in a good position to see what was in the boats, so maybe it would work.

Waiting until dark would provide concealment but that increased the risk of being overrun, so daylight movement, if done carefully, would be best. The reserve company, the First Company, would lead off with our dead and wounded. Half of each of the two companies on line would go on the second

This large coal barge belonging to the Nong Son coal mine transported coal down the river to Hoi An for further distribution in South Vietnam. The barges were no longer used as the VC would attack them on the river, destroying them and killing the barge operators. These barges were used to transport the ARVN troops across the river to safety during the fight for Nong Son.

trip. Next would be the hard part, holding onto the perimeter with only the strength of one company until the barge returned for the last load.

During the retrograde movement of the First Company, the toll of the past two days became evident. Many of the soldiers had been so terrified they moved like zombies, responding automatically to the order to move out. Dejection was etched into their faces, their eyes lifeless, sunken and glazed. Weary, clad in dirty, tattered, smelly uniforms, the First Company carried the dead and wounded past me toward the river. As I watched them move out of the village through the trees, I wondered how much longer we could last and how could we ever get this group to mount a counterattack.

Lieutenant Phong, his two remaining company commanders, myself, and the other two advisors had worked out a fire plan to try and keep the NVA away. When the barge returned for the second load, we would use both ARVN and USMC artillery to cover the sound and movement. Preplanned fire missions would hit the jungle area immediately east of the Third Company positions and also the thick, grassy areas southeast and south of the rice paddies in front of the Second Company. Hopefully, these barrages would keep the NVA pinned down and maybe even make them think we were preparing for a counterattack.

The First Company left without incident, and about 45 minutes later, the barge returned for the second load and our artillery symphony began. The strategy must have worked because we were able to move half of each of the two remaining companies without any problems. Sergeant Bronson went with the second load to help establish defensive positions at Nong Son.

We continued with the artillery barrages and increased our rifle and machine gun fire to our respective fronts. All we could do was wait for the barge to return for its last trip and hope we weren't attacked in the meantime. Lieutenant Mac would meet the barge and then move back toward the village to help coordinate the withdrawal of the troops to the river. Lieutenant Phong and I would remain on line with the two company commanders. Rather than leave the line by entire sectors, we would reduce by half each time the number of soldiers on line across the entire perimeter, every other soldier, would move to the river into the barge. Finally, the remaining quarter of the soldiers would withdraw. Lieutenant Mac would cross over in the barge. Lieutenant Phong, the remainder of his staff, and I would be the last to leave, crossing in the motorboats. Even so, we would still beat the barge to the other side.

Most of the villagers had left; some had crossed the river in small dugouts to Nong Son, some had gone downriver to neighboring villages, and some had disappeared into the jungle. A few, though, had refused to leave their huts and retreated into makeshift artillery shelters next to their homes. These were small, man-made caves dug into the ground, reinforced with bamboo poles and scraps of wood and covered with mounds of dirt, providing effective protection from small-arms fire, and, except for a direct hit, from a mortar, rocket or artillery shrapnel.

As we moved more soldiers off the line, our small-arms fire decreased, but the artillery barrages picked up. Hopefully the NVA would assume we were setting up for a counterattack. Whatever they thought, they never attacked the village, so we were able to successfully complete our last trip to Nong Son. Before nightfall the entire battalion was repositioned on the hillside, looking across the river, down into the village where we had lost so many lives.

I met the major and asked what our next move would be. He said that there was a good chance the weather would break tomorrow. A resupply and medevac mission has been planned for the morning. He said to grab some food and then see how the battalion looked.

Mac and Bronson were already beginning to eat. The local Vietnamese at Nong Son had prepared a real feast for the regimental and battalion command groups and the advisors. Other food had been distributed to the soldiers. As we ate we discussed our plans for the night.

While stuffing my mouth with rice and fish, I told Sergeant Bronson to go down to the gymnasium after supper with Sergeant Wright and get a count on all our dead and wounded. I wanted to know our exact KIA and WIA status and how many wounded needed to be medevaced out and how many could stay with the battalion. I told the lieutenant to work out the details with the major on what kind of choppers would be coming in tomorrow, where they would land and when. I said I would check the perimeters of the companies and see what Lieutenant Phong's next move was. I told Lieutenant Mac to also check on the battalion's status on weapons, munitions, food, and medical supplies. "We'll all meet back here in about an hour, hour and a half."

I asked Major Haines how he thought Captain Popps and the other advisors would do in their OP tonight. He replied that he didn't think the NVA even realized the battalion had moved. He and Sergeant Wright were still using Marine artillery and Colonel Lap's staff was coordinating the ARVN artillery. Since the NVA didn't know what had happened, he was hoping they wouldn't attack the Second Battalion tonight. He thought they would be okay.

With my belly full, I walked over to the small house where Lieutenant Phong had set up his CP with his staff and commanders. Their disheveled appearance, haggard faces, and fearful eyes told me all of them were on the edge. Doubts started to rise in my mind. Could these men still lead? What kind of motivation and courage would they instill in their soldiers? Would the soldiers stay here during the night, or would they run away? What could be done to reverse the lack of leadership being displayed here?

Softly I told the lieutenant that I needed someone to show me where the company positions were. Slowly, dejectedly, Lieutenant Phong responded by saying that because so many soldiers were dead and wounded, the battalion would not be able to attack tomorrow. Looking at the commander of the First Company, Lieutenant Phong told him to go with me check the company perimeter.

As we moved across the crest of the hill I saw a sight I had never encountered in my military career: pure panic—soldiers in a state of mortal terror. They were clustered together in small groups, their rifles scattered on the ground. Squatting, staring at the ground, they were shaking, even crying, all immobilized. The fear of each individual soldier unwittingly reinforced the terror in his buddies. Something had to be done, immediately, to stamp out this spreading hysteria. I shouted, in Vietnamese, at the poor officer escorting me to get these soldiers and weapons in defensive positions.

Reinforcing my words, like a demon possessed, I immediately started grabbing the frightened soldiers by their belts, waists, arms, legs, or necks and physically lifting them off the ground and then throwing them down in a line around the crest of the hill. Christ, I was furious. I wondered how much longer was I going to have to tell these people what to do, when to do it, and how to do it. Why the hell didn't their officers and NCOs take charge? And why the hell couldn't these damn cowards fight their own war? Angry, tired, and totally frustrated at the lack of leadership on the part of the Vietnamese, I took it out on the scared soldiers. Fear of the enemy quickly turned into fear for the big American advisor who seemed hell-bent on picking up and throwing the small soldiers around the hillside like bags of rice. Apparently, the company commander with me decided it was better to become a part of the wrath than become another target of my anger, so he too began to shout and cajole the soldiers into moving into a resemblance of a defensive line. Soon the soldiers began scraping out shallow shooting positions facing the river. NCOs and platoon leaders began making appearances.

By the time Lieutenant Son and I had completed our tour of the battalion line, much of my pent-up anger had been released. Looking the poor second lieutenant in his eyes, I spoke slowly, clearly and deliberately, telling him I was just as tired as he and Lieutenant Phong. I had fought just as hard as he and the rest of the soldiers, but I would not quit, and my advisors would not quit. I extolled how he, Lieutenant Phong, and the other officers must not quit. All of us must show the soldiers how to fight. We must act like officers and leaders. I told him to tell Lieutenant Phong what we did. Tell him to act like a battalion commander and get the soldiers on the line. I would be back in an hour to check the battalion again. Tell Lieutenant Phong. Acknowledging me, the young man scrambled off toward the Battalion CP, and I began to return to the regimental CP.

At the CP I went to Major Haines who remarked quietly that he had spoken to the colonel, who would have a pep talk with Lieutenant Phong and the battalion staff. The major thought that I stirred things up enough, so the leaders should regain control and act like leaders again. Sergeant Bronson reported that there were 41 KIA and 94 WIA. Sixty-eight of the wounded needed to be hospitalized, with 32 so bad they probably wouldn't last the night. About 40 percent of our battalion was combat ineffective.

Lieutenant Mac explained that we would get them out in the morning because we would have six Marine UH-34Ds coming in as soon as the clouds lifted which should be about mid-morning. The 34Ds were Sikorsky HUS-1 Marine helicopters; each one could carry up to eight litters plus some additional walking wounded. The ARVN at I Corps had the supplies waiting at Marble Mountain to be loaded. The choppers would bring in food, radio batteries, medical supplies, and ammo. Three choppers would kick their loads out over Captain Popps and the rest would come in to a soccer field, next to the gym, off-load supplies, load up all the wounded and as many dead as the Marines would take, and finally return to Da Nang air base and drop off the dead and wounded.

Colonel Lap returned from his chat with the battalion officers. Whatever he said must have done some good because we could hear digging activity and commanding sounds all around us.

The evening artillery H & I firing was still aimed at the preplanned targets around the village. I was sure by now the NVA must know we had left. We also were firing into the wooded area between the village and the river, not wanting the NVA to set up there. Like McArthur, we did plan on returning. No fires had been laid on the village—not yet, anyway.

Colonel Lap sat in a chair next to the small concrete house he had chosen for his CP. Built into the hillside, the roofless front porch, where all of us were congregated, offered an excellent view of the river, the village, and the rice paddies where we had fought. ARVN artillery forward observers, by climbing up on the roof of the house, had a perfect spot for seeing the entire battlefield and being able to adjust Marine or ARVN artillery. I suggested the advisors check the lines one more time. Feeling a hundred years old, I wearily pushed off a small wooden chair, straining to rise to a standing position, telling the major that we would return in about 30 minutes.

Making the rounds of the perimeter revealed vast differences from my first tour about two hours before. Foxholes were being dug, machine guns were properly placed to fire down the slopes and to provide interlocking fields of fire across our front. Satisfied the defensive setup was okay, I told Mac and Bronson to check with each company commander regarding their plans for security during the night. Going back to the regimental CP, I hesitated, thinking I should go to the battalion CP, which was in another small concrete house about 30 yards away from regiment and about 20 to 30 feet further down the hill, but I decided not to bother Lieutenant Phong again tonight.

On the cement porch, I started to collapse in a chair when Sergeant Macbeth said the Vietnamese had some hot tea and soup in the house on a little bed of coals. I grabbed a tin can, went inside, filled it with some noodle soup, and returned to the porch. Major Haines and Colonel Lap were discussing the past events and what was to be done tomorrow. Sipping soup, and looking out beyond the river, I felt the intensity of the past two days had lessened. The danger of being attacked tonight was fairly remote. I didn't see how the NVA would be able to cross the river. All the boats were on our side, and to the best of my knowledge, the NVA had no boats. Besides, the ARVN artillery kept dropping flares on the river, keeping it well lit, so we would be able to see if anyone tried to cross.

Colonel Lap made Lieutenant Phong put a company by the dock where the barge and boats were tied up. Another part of this same company was in and around the soccer field next to the gymnasium. The other two companies were up with us on the hillside.

Across the river to my front, the H & I shells were landing in the jungle, in between the village and the river, and throughout the rice fields and the hills beyond that. Looking to my left, I could see the Marine artillery flares lighting up the rice paddies surrounding the outpost occupied by the Second Battalion.

Major Haines's three radios, stacked on the sill of an open window, softly disclosed their presence. One was tuned to the Da Nang DASC to communicate with and coordinate our air support. The second was monitoring the Marine artillery radio relay net. On this one I could hear Captain Popps or one of the other advisors with the Second Battalion calling in fire missions, adjusting fire, and telling the marines how much their efforts were appreciated. The third was on the Tiger Net, our advisory frequency, now still.

A quiet, light breeze swept over us and the smell of cooking scented the air, coming from the dozen or so houses which dotted the hillside. The night battle noises seemed distant, as if the war were now in another world—like in Saigon where at night it is possible to be on the rooftop of the Rex BOQ watching the war outside Saigon, but physically and mentally removed from the danger of battle.

Colonel Lap called to me, saying he would like to talk to me about Major Van. I sat in a chair next to the colonel, whose fuzzy outline I could barely make out in the darkness. Even so I could clearly visualize him as I listened. His voice tonight was low, calming and soothing. His English was impeccable. Listening to him was very calming. I could understand how he was able to turn the battalion officers around.

He began in his perfect English, explaining how he could understand why I had become disenchanted with Major Van. He emphasized that the major was a sick man. The colonel allowed him to remain in Hoi An because he would not have been able to be an effective leader at Nong Son because he was too sick. Perhaps he was also fearful in addition to having malaria. The colonel admonished me to please remember we did not shoot a winning race horse because it had lost one race. He told me to give Major Van a second chance to prove himself. He had fought the Viet Minh and the Viet Cong all his life. He had proven himself to be a brave soldier and a good leader many times over. Colonel Lap warned me to not let what happened spoil the good relationship I had with Major Van. He was a good man and he would need me when he returns. I should not abandon him. With that said, the colonel bid a good evening.

My two advisors had returned, both reporting that the battalion looked like they had the situation well in hand. Sergeant Wright came over, showing us where some straw sleeping pallets were rolled up in a corner, also producing some blankets that the Vietnamese had found.

Checking our radio gear, ammunition and weapons, we made sure everything was clean, in working condition, and ready to go. Rolling out my straw pad, I told Mac and Bronson good night. I loosened the laces on my boots, folded up my rain jacket as a pillow, and laid on the mat, scrunched up into the fetal position, the blanket drawn tightly around my head. Before I could even think about falling asleep, I was asleep, proving that a good infantryman can sleep anywhere, anytime.

CHAPTER 16

Nong Son,
Regaining Lost Ground:
Days 4 and 5

The Fourth Day

The scurrying of soldiers woke me in the predawn darkness. Glancing at my Seiko, I realized I had slept almost seven hours. Although I felt rested, sleeping in the cold, damp air had left me sore. Looking through the open doorway I saw the sky lighten behind the hills to the east down the river. I struggled to a sitting position, my body creaking and groaning. My eyes were crusted with sleep, and my face was raw from three days of beard. Even I recoiled from the smell emanating from my armpits. My crotch was itchy and sore, and my muscles rebelled every time I moved. When the water on the fire warmed up a little, I'd take a bath using my helmet. Fumbling in a small pack on my pistol belt, I located my toothbrush and some toothpaste. Grabbing one of my canteens, I painfully rose to a semi-upright position and, still wrapped in the blanket, moved outside to a small clump of bushes where I emptied my bladder. Returning to the house I filled my steel helmet with warm water, stepped outside, poured some water into my hand, and wiped the scum from my eyes. Using a smelly, soiled bandanna as a towel, I dried my face. I put a little toothpaste on my toothbrush, took a swig of water, and scrubbed my teeth.

Back in the house I rolled up the straw pad, folded the blanket, tied my boots, tucked in my T-shirt, and hitched up my pants. After buckling on my pistol belt, weighed down with a first aid kit, my small overnight pack, air force survival knife, holster with my accurized .45, ammo pouches, and two canteens, I struggled into my rain jacket. Now dressed for work, I was ready to begin the day. Colonel Lap's batman (servant) had hot soup and coffee ready. Ordinarily I didn't drink coffee, but these were not ordinary times. I would take any help possible to get me going. Taking a tin can of each, I moved onto the porch to greet the day.

Dense fog rimmed the surface of the river, spilling over onto the banks on each side. Despite the fog, the sky overhead and to the east was relatively clear of low clouds. Maybe today the tide would turn after all, I hoped.

The NVA had not left. Captain Popps and the rest of the Second Battalion were still exchanging shots. During the night the NVA had moved through the village, where we had not shot artillery, and were positioned across the river from the boat docks in the lightly wooded area. Using rockets and machine guns they shot across the river intermittently, firing a few rounds, moving to another position, then shooting again and moving again. The NVA couldn't attack across the river, and with our artillery capability they didn't want to mass any troops in the woods. It was a stalemate; they couldn't get us, and we were not yet able to go after them. Still, I couldn't figure out why they remained here constantly suffering our air and artillery strikes.

By mid-morning we had been told by radio the Marine helicopters were getting ready to depart Marble Mountain and would arrive in about 40 minutes. We already had the dead and wounded lined up next to the gymnasium beside the soccer field. The people who had built the soccer field, using the coal mining earth moving equipment, had no idea how their design would turn out to be a blessing for us. About the size of a small high school football field, it had been built on a rise next to the river and had a flat playing surface scrapped out of a rounded hillock. The extra dirt had been pushed to the sides forming an eight- to 12-foot-high sloped wall for the spectators to sit on. For us this wall shielded anyone on the field from any rocket or gunfire from across the river, so it would be the LZ for the helicopters.

Standing on the side of the field with my PRICK 10 and a couple of colored-smoke grenades, I waited for the helicopters' arrival. They radioed inbound for landing with supplies, and when I had them in sight, I pulled the pin to release the handle of a smoke grenade. I tossed the grenade into the center of the soccer field because the smoke, moving by the wind, indicates the direction of the wind, and aircraft always land facing the wind.

I could hear the armed Huey Marine gunships preceding the arrival of the 34-Ds. We had told them about the NVA across the river and the need for suppressing fire as the slicks (unarmed helicopters) came in. The Hueys came in high above Nong Son, out of small-arms range, and dropped rapidly, wheeling around to hit the area between the river and the village. The M-60 machine guns and the 2.75-inch rockets tore into the ground grinding up the trees and tearing apart the underbrush. The Hueys came in by twos; as soon as one pass was complete, another pair would replicate the barrage. Other gunships were doing the same thing around the Second Battalion area. Now the deep whup-whup-whup of the large, single-engine 34-Ds became audible as their blades slashed through the air.

Three huge, lumbering transport helicopters swung into view as the pilot radioed he had three ships with three more coming in 20 minutes. Hovering momentarily over the soccer field, they dropped rapidly, flaring over the half of the field closest to the gymnasium, then crashed the last few feet, engines revving full pitch, bouncing on the ground. Dozens of ARVN troops swarmed out to help off-load the supplies we needed so badly. They quickly tossed boxes, canisters, bags, and other containers to the ground. Like a well-choreographed musical, the Vietnamese soldiers began carrying the wounded to the helicopters which were straining against rising into the sky again.

Since we didn't have any military stretchers, the wounded were carried or put on makeshift stretchers, then placed on the medical stretchers inside the helicopters. Observing the wounded soldiers being loaded, I noticed most were bandaged with the Kotex pads we had taken from the village. I wondered what the corpsmen at Charlie Med would say with all our wounded being bound in sanitary napkins. Such is war.

The last three helicopters arrived, hovering overhead, maneuvering for a landing in the open half of the field. As they were descending I could hear a heavy machine gun firing at them from across the river. After the choppers, the Vietnamese swarmed around them to unload supplies and replace them with our wounded and dead.

I saw three Marines dressed in tan flight suits and white helmets rapidly exit the 34-D closest to the river. One was swinging his arms around wildly, arguing with the Vietnamese loading the wounded on board. Two of the Marines each ran to a separate helicopter. Shaking his head and flapping his arms, the third man grabbed some gear off the helicopter and then he too ran to another helicopter.

I called on the radio, asking what was going on with the helicopter the crew left.

A pilot replied that it just been shot out of the sky by a machine gun across the river and it wasn't going anywhere. To redirect the loading, I ran to the Vietnamese sergeant loading some wounded into the pilotless helicopter. The rotor blades were now slowing down, the engine dead. I yelled over the noise of the other five helicopter engines, telling the sergeant the helicopter had been shot and couldn't fly. I yelled, pointing to another helicopter, telling him to move his wounded to that helicopter.

By now I realized we had too few helicopters and too many passengers. In addition, some of the soldiers who were unloading supplies and loading the wounded were also climbing on the helicopters, hoping to leave Nong Son. One of the Marine pilots radioed that there were too many soldiers on board and they weren't wounded. Either I had to get them off or the Marines would kick them off. I had two minutes.

Running over to Mac and Bronson who were also confused about what was happening, I shouted that the last helicopter had been shot down. I said to tell the NCOs to get all the soldiers off who were not wounded badly. No dead would go back. The helicopters had too many people on board, so each of them had to take two choppers and kick off those men who weren't wounded.

I dashed to the closest chopper and told the ARVN sergeant only the badly wounded would go—if he didn't do that the Marines would not take anyone. As if to reinforce my statement the Marine crew chief drew his revolver and pushed one solder away, then turned the gun toward another soldier; he didn't have to do any more. The unwounded soldiers jumped out. Lieutenant Mac and Sergeant Bronson cleared the other four helicopters of the dead and able soldiers.

The five birds rose as one and hopped over the soccer field west wall. Making a hard-climbing 180-degree turn to the east, away from the river and the NVA guns, the slicks and gunships departed. I radioed our thanks for their efforts and taking our wounded to the hospital.

Walking over to Mac and Bronson, I suggested we see what kind of goodies we got.

The arrival of food, medical supplies, munitions, and other items of equipment the ARVN had requested rekindled their spirits. The rest of the day was spent doling out the supplies, rearming, and reorganizing. The next day at dawn we would cross the river again and retake the village.

By evening the NVA had moved into the wooded area by the river. The Second Battalion, invigorated with the new supplies, remained secure in the outpost. The night would be clear enough to use Spooky, the AC-47 gunship. As soon as the sun set, the enemy across the river began to open fire on our positions. Rockets, heavy machine guns, and mortars were employed against us but without much success. The line of sight weapons were no danger because we were high on the hill, behind its crest. With our foxholes and troop dispersal, the mortars also were not that effective. As the night wore on, the NVA increased the firing.

Major Haines and Colonel Lap were discussing the situation when the major told the colonel that we should just wipe the NVA right off the face of the earth. We could blow those woods and the near part of the village to hell and gone and kill every bastard over there.

Plans were made to have Spooky orbit above the Howitzers' trajectories, both Marine and ARVN. DASC out of Da Nang would help coordinate Spooky's position with that of the artillery firing batteries. The idea was to illuminate the entire area from Captain Popps' OP to the village and bring in massive barrages of white phosphorus and high-explosive shells. As the

NVA would pull back through the rice paddies to get back to the sanctuary of the hills, Spooky would drop them with its mini-guns. Major Haines, Sergeant Wright, Colonel Lap's artillery FOs and I would be on the roof of the CP monitoring the devastation.

About 11:00 the barrage began. With the flares from Spooky we could see the battlefield with no problem. I don't know how many thousands of tons of explosives were delivered in the next three hours, but it sure ended the firing from across the river.

Watching the massive gunship slowly banking with the left wing pointed down, pivoting around an invisible point on the ground, we could see multiple streams of red lines coming from mid-ship. After the tracers stopped, the sound would then reach us, a high-pitched "bruuupppttt." The Gatling guns spewed the 7.62 mm lead out so fast that the explosion of each cartridge blended together as one single noisy burst, like an out-of-control electric drill. The AC-47 pilot radioed Major Haines to let him know that they fired upon a group of soldiers exiting the jungle and crossing a rice paddy, killing about 20 of them. Throughout the night the artillery and Spooky kept up the pressure across the river.

The Fifth Day

Before dawn two companies moved quietly to the riverbank next to the dock to cross the river. The First Company crossed and set up a beachhead to secure the area to receive the Second Company. Lieutenant Mac and Sergeant Bronson went with the First Company. Lieutenant Phong, the battalion staff, and I went with the Second Company. By first light we were across and moving in two lines toward the village.

God, I couldn't believe the extent of the destruction. Trees were shredded like kindling wood and were tossed about as if a giant had pulled them out of the ground and haphazardly thrown them all over. It reminded me of a World War II beach scene where the Marines had made an amphibious assault on an island after the pre-invasion naval gunfire and airplane strafing had destroyed all vegetation.

Closing on the village, the Second Company held back while one platoon from the First Company moved around its left side, another platoon to the right, and a third platoon swept through the village. We had Marine Huey gunships overhead to provide aerial fire support if we needed it.

Watching the troops, I felt good. They were once again performing as they should. The fear that had been pervasive throughout the battalion when we left here two days before was no longer evident. The officers and NCOs were in command, and the soldiers were responding accordingly.

The village was clear, so we moved back inside again. While the village itself was not torn up as much as the surrounding countryside, it had not escaped unscathed. Huts had been blown apart and Howitzer craters were scattered around. The bulk of the destruction remained outside the village. Some grass huts were missing part of their roofs, others were missing walls, with many burnt or collapsed. All in all, though, probably less than 10 to 15 percent of the homes were beyond repair, and more than half appeared to be untouched. Taking two platoons we made a second and very thorough detailed sweep of the wooded area the NVA had inhabited the night before. Despite the constant artillery barrages and Spooky's mini-guns, the battlefield had been cleaned up perfectly. The only clues we found that indicated the NVA had been there were part of an NVA soldier's pith helmet, covered with blood, the wrappings of a North Vietnamese bandage, and a single 7.62 mm empty cartridge from an AK-47 rifle.

We did find about a dozen paths of beaten down grass, about six to eight feet wide, that led into the village and then out across the rice paddies, making us wonder what could have been dragged from this area back to the hills. The intelligence NCO had found some scared villagers coming in from the jungle, and they explained the paths by reporting that several villagers had been conscripted by the NVA the day before to help haul weapons, munitions and other supplies from the hills into the village. They had been forced by armed guards to stay with the NVA unit. Throughout the day the NVA soldiers continued to dig defensive positions in the wooded area and set up weapon positions to fire on Nong Son. Every NVA soldier had a short rope made of vines tied around one leg. At the end of the rope was a small loop, big enough to put a fist through or to hold with two hands. The villagers were also given these ropes to put on their own legs. As we listened, one man produced the rope that had been on his leg. As the NVA soldiers had been killed or wounded the villagers were told to grab the vines and drag them off the battlefield. Other villagers were required to pick up anything the soldiers had dropped. It was not difficult to see because of the flares dropped by Spooky. Several villagers who had been killed or severely wounded were also dragged back behind the hill.

According to the villagers, several hundred North Vietnamese soldiers had been killed or wounded, and on the backside of the hill across from Trung Phuoc was a big headquarters, a rear supply area, and, in an immense cave in the hillside, a large field hospital with several physicians and nurses. The NVA unit had had plenty of food and a considerable quantity of weapons and munitions. The field hospital had been adequately stocked with medical equipment, supplies and personnel. From the descriptions provided by these villagers we estimated the original force we had been up against was at least a regiment, 1,000 to 1,200 soldiers. Because no attempts had been made to overrun the Second Battalion since our arrival, we guessed the regiment probably had not been reinforced. If the villagers' estimate of the dead and wounded was accurate, the enemy strength was now probably no more than 600 to 800 soldiers. We now had about 200 functioning men in the Third Battalion and the Second Battalion had less than 300 on their hill.

One of the older men volunteered some information that helped explain why the NVA had been especially focused on this area. He said that several North Vietnamese soldiers had come from the same place around the North Vietnamese city of Lang Son on the China border northeast of Hanoi and that the entire unit had been recruited and trained on the China border specifically to attack the coal mine. This was the first information we had on the NVA unit and its purpose here. It made sense from a propaganda standpoint for North Vietnam to want to destroy Nong Son. If the destruction was to be permanent then it would take a large, specially trained force, including people with knowledge of mining operations, to seize the area and hold it long enough to demolish the mining complex. Things were looking up. The troops were in much better spirits, and we had our first good information on whom we were fighting and why.

Lieutenant Phong had made arrangements for the villagers we interrogated to cross the river by motorboat and talk to Colonel Lap. Major Haines was contacted about the villagers so he could be in on their meeting with the colonel.

After talking to the villagers, Colonel Lap ordered Lieutenant Phong to prepare to move out again. He would take two companies, one to the east toward Trung Phuoc and the other southeast to the ridge just south of Trung Phuoc OP. The Third Company was preparing to cross the river and join us. Lieutenant Phong, his commanders and battalion staff, Lieutenant Mac, Sergeant Bronson and I planned the operation. By midday we were dug in around the village. We had two patrols out, one southeast of us against the bottom of the hill and the other east of the village in the dense area between us and Trung Phuoc OP.

Both patrols reported no active signs of the enemy. The patrol to our east said that there was no evidence that the NVA had even been in the area since our big fight on our second day of this battle. The patrol to our southeast reported that the paths made by the dragged soldiers continued alongside the bottom slope of the hill and crossed over the ridge to their front. While the NVA had left nothing on the battlefield next to the village, the patrol reported that numerous bodies, killed by Spooky, badly shot or blown up and their weapons destroyed, were lying in the rice paddies. The only items found on the bodies were personal documents, like letters, family photographs, poems, or short stories.

The patrol did, however, glean some other important information by searching the soldiers such as the status of their health, uniforms and equipment. The patrol discovered that the soldiers were in their late teens and early 20s and were not lacking for clothing, headgear or footwear. Their uniforms were regular NVA-issued in good condition. The weapons and webbed gear were also in excellent condition. The soldiers were armed with Chinese Communist copies of Russian AK-47 7.62 mm automatic assault rifles. Some rifles were the newer model with the permanently attached, folding, triangular-type bayonets while the older model used the detachable bayonet carried in a belt sheath. The rifles, bayonets, canteens, and rifle cleaning kits were all marked with Chinese inscriptions. We could only conclude that this unit was a well-trained, well-equipped fighting force, highly disciplined and dedicated for their mission. With this information from the patrols, we planned the next phase of our operation.

The First Company with the battalion command group and myself would move east toward Trung Phuoc and take up defensive positions on the forward edge of the tree line. This was about the same location where we had gotten whacked the first morning. The Second Company, with Lieutenant Mac and Sergeant Bronson, would move southeast and set up a night defensive position on the ridge line. The Third Company would remain in the village as the battalion reserve.

Major Haines radioed that when we arrived at our positions, the Marine helicopters would drop off night kits, consisting of Vietnamese combat rations for the evening and morning meals, water, ammunition, claymore mines, and concertina wire to string around our night perimeter. Spooky would be on station and overhead throughout the night. The next morning the U.S. Air Force would again bomb Trung Phuoc, and the First Company would then take the hill. The Second Company would remain on the ridge to repel any counterattack or ambush any NVA escaping from Trung Phuoc toward Que Son Valley.

We made the movement to our night positions without incident. The helicopters arrived with the night kits, but, because of some last-minute confusion, no water was put on board. We dug in, wrapped concertina wire around the perimeter, and set up the claymore mines—plastic enclosed, slightly curved, 3.5-pound anti-personnel mines, command detonated to spray 700 steel pellets to the front. Named after the ancient Scottish broadsword, they were placed a few inches off the ground on their own short, spiked legs, and when detonated would cut a swath as high as a man out to 50 meters. Interlocking bands of machine gun fire were laid out to our front. As I watched the activity of the troops preparing for night, I thought I felt secure. Now this was the way a combat unit should operate.

As dusk approached, I was very thirsty and needed water, but the only source was the rice paddy water which, unfortunately, contained several dead

NVA soldiers, lying on their bellies, face down in the muck. When it comes right down to it, man can do some amazing things to survive. In front of me was plenty of water so crouching on the edge of the dike I shoved a body aside with my foot and pushed my canteen down below the surface of the water, then slowly turned it over so the air inside burbled out and the plastic container filled with the brown, brackish, foul-smelling water. With one canteen filled, I repeated the process with the other one. Then, taking my small bottle of halazone tablets from my belt pack, I shook out four into my hand. The normal dosage was one tablet per canteen of clear water and two if the water was cloudy. I tossed in two more for the dead NVA. Four more tablets went into the second canteen. In 30 minutes, after the water had been purified by the tables, I could quench my thirst.

Lieutenant Mac radioed that the Second Company was dug in and secure for the night. As dark descended on us once again, Puff, the AC-47, checked in, stating they would be on station in 20 minutes. I explained that when Puff passed overhead, I would flash my light, and our sister unit would be about 400 yards south of us. The pilot said he had flown over here a couple of nights ago, so he knew the area. Flying over us, he acknowledged he had identified both our positions.

Well, now all we do is wait, I thought. I told Private Tuan that one of us would sleep an hour and the other monitor the radio, then we'd switch. If a call came in on his shift, he would wake me.

Private Tuan took the first shift from ten to 11, then came my turn. During my 11 to midnight shift all was quiet, nothing happened. The next two shifts were same, nothing moving.

At 3:00 I turned the radio over to Tuan, thinking that this night would be a piece of cake and that maybe the NVA had left. Then, just as I dozed off, I heard the muffled explosion of a claymore mine from the Second Company position. Next came more muffled explosions—these were hand grenades.

I heard Lieutenant Mac quietly call the orbiting aircraft. He needed flares on his east edge; he had company. The large plane made a 45-degree bank and swung over the rice paddies to Lieutenant Mac's east, dropping a flare. Almost simultaneously we also came under fire as did the Second Battalion on the hill. The intensity of the attacks on all three positions increased as NVA small-arms fire was joined by machine guns, rockets, and mortars. I radioed Major Haines and asked him to get another AC-47 out here if he could—we needed more help.

With Spooky overhead, we couldn't use any artillery. Because I was in direct contact with Spooky I preferred the plane stay here instead of using artillery. Captain Popps, though, was able to use the Marine artillery as long as Spooky's orbit remained west of the Trung Phuoc OP.

The Second Company was on the exposed ridge. While it held the high ground, they were still in the open. The battle's focus appeared to be on the Second Company position. The First Company would probably be harder for the NVA to overrun. Since it had cover and concealment from the rice paddy dikes, the overhead trees, and the dense jungle growth behind. If the NVA could overrun the Second Company, the NVA would be in a good position to dump on the First Company from above. Due to the illumination of the flares, the pilots in the aircraft could see more of what was going on than we could from our positions on the ground.

Spooky radioed Lieutenant Mac to tell him it looked like troops were massing on the hillside to his southeast and beginning to move fast toward their position. The pilot told Mac to get their heads down, as he would bring his fire up to Lieutenant Mac's lines. Spooky brought its flaming, red death right into the concertina wire around Second Company's position. Mac told him to do it again. Spooky spun on the left wing- tip and put another burst of 7.62 mm rounds around Lieutenant Mac's position.

We seemed to be holding our own okay and the same with Captain Popps. The brunt of the NVA attack was clearly on the Second Company. From our foxholes, we could see the action around the Second Company. The NVA were attacking both the First Company and the Second Company from the east. The Second Company was also being hit from the southeast. With the brightness of the flares and only 400 yards separating us, I could clearly see the concertina wire and the movement outside of the wire. Spooky was ringing the Second's position with every burst.

What happened next had to be seen to be believed. Some of the forms moving to the wire suddenly burst into flames—people on fire, screaming and running into the concertina wire, falling on it or getting hung up in it. Then even more flaming people rose up and ran over the backs of their comrades who had been shot down in the wire.

Lieutenant Mac screamed in the radio that his position was being overrun by burning bodies, telling Spooky to bring its fire into the perimeter wire, now. The plane banked sharply on top of Mac's position and fired over the Second Company's heads into the wire.

By now about a dozen burning bodies were charging across the wire, using the backs of their downed companions as stepping stones, and then the firing from in front of Lieutenant Mac's position slacked off, probably so the NVA would avoid hitting their wire-hopping, blazing soldiers. This allowed the soldiers of the Second Company to shoot down the attackers crossing the barbed wire. The horrendous firepower directed to the front and sides by the Second Company quickly turned the attack back.

Spooky continued to rake the outside edge of the Second Company's perimeter with its mini-guns as the ARVN soldiers kept firing into the wire.

Finally, as quickly as the battle had begun, it ended. Spooky followed the retreating soldiers as they melted into the thick grass and jungle on the other side of the hill, back into the valley.

When the attack on the Second Company broke off, so did the attack on us and the Second Battalion. It was 4:15 a.m. The fight had only lasted about an hour. Spooky called to say the replacement Spooky would arrive in ten minutes. While he missed the action, his arrival was timely because the first Spooky was almost out of flares, ammunition and fuel.

As the new gunship passed over I flashed my light and the pilot acknowledged spotting us. Dropping a flare over the paddies to our southeast, he quickly identified the Second Company without Lieutenant Mac's help.

As the first Spooky turned back toward Da Nang, Lieutenant Mac promised the pilot that the next time Mac was in Da Nang, drinks were on him at the DOOM Club (Da Nang Officers' Open Mess, the Air Force Officers' Club), because they really pulled their bacon out of the fire.

Everyone was wide awake, anxious, and praying for morning to come quickly. No one slept for the rest of the night.

CHAPTER 17

Nong Son,
Winning the Battle:
Days 6 to 8

The Sixth Day

Slowly the sky in the east turned from inky black to various shades of gray; dawn was finally on its way. Major Haines said air support was to begin just after first light. He had arranged for sorties with maximum ordnance loads. We would have F-4B Phantoms, which could carry up to 16,000 pounds of external bombs to blast again at the NVA-occupied Trung Phuoc OP. Phantoms were a 1,500-mph, two-seater carrier fighter based at Da Nang, flown by the U.S. Navy, USMC and USAF. Their initial primary role had been as U.S. Navy carrier–based, long-range, high-altitude interceptors, but they also soon became used for reconnaissance, electronic warfare and close air-ground support missions.

At dawn, we could hear the low roar of the twin GE jet engines as the Phantoms screamed in from the east. Lining up on Trung Phuoc, they aimed right at the outpost. Dropping their loads of 500-pound, high-explosive bombs and napalm, they quickly transformed the hill into a flaming pyre of death and destruction.

After a few passes, both the pilots and Captain Popps reported a mass exodus of troops moving quickly into the valley just east of the Second Company's position. Because of the heavy growth leading into the valley, the company was not able to see the retreat. Due to the dispersal of the running NVA troops, the Marine Phantoms were not able to successfully bomb the departing soldiers.

Colonel Lap told Lieutenant Phong to keep the Third Company in place in the village, have the Second Company retain its position on the ridge line, and have the First Company assault the smoking hilltop. By early morning,

The trenches at the Trung Phuoc outpost.

the First Company had packed up everything from the night defensive position and was ready to take the hill. Lined up about 200 yards from the bottom
of the hill, two platoons up front and one in the rear as the reserve, we moved
out. What a difference from the last time we had tried to do this four days
ago. Slowly moving forward, the unit had positioned machine guns and mortars to our rear to provide covering fire from behind and over our heads as
we maneuvered toward the hill.

As we approached the blackened mound of earth we could smell charred
bodies burned to crispy masses by napalm. The pervasive, sickening odor
underscored the power of death by flaming gasoline. When first encountered,
the stench of scorched flesh creates instant nausea as the brain involuntarily
conjures up images of the horror and pain associated with being burnt alive.
The smell and the mental images create within most individuals such a repul-
sion that retching is not uncommon. Wars do not stop for such human
responses, so we continued our advance on the hill. This time we encountered
no opposition so there was nothing to stop us from moving to the top—or
so we thought. As we arrived at the bottom of the hill we saw battered wooden
signs which stated, "Dung lai, min." The "Stop, Mine" sign announced to the
local Vietnamese that the area around the base of the OP had been mined.

Oh Christ, I thought as I read a barely perceptible sign that somehow
had survived the battle. Lieutenant Phong had the company surround the
base of the hill while he called Colonel Lap for further instructions.

The intelligence NCO called back to the village for the Third Company
to see if any local residents could provide information on the minefield. We
knew the local PF unit had a map of the minefield, but it was likely inside
one of the bunkers on top of the hill.

While Lieutenant Phong discussed the problem with the regimental
commander, Lieutenant Son (the company commander) and I walked around
the perimeter of the outpost. We could make out, by the tracks in the bombed
earth, where the NVA had crossed the minefield to exit the hill. Lieutenant
Son had his men mark this area off. On the side facing the river, we could
recognize what we believed to be the original entrance to the outpost, also
marked off. An unexploded 500-pound HE bomb, found lying at the bottom
of the hill near the dirt road passing by the outpost, was marked for later dis-
posal. As we completed our circle around the hill, it was evident that most
of the destruction had been caused by the Phantoms. Between the outpost
and the river were the remains of several houses, mostly straw huts but some
constructed of concrete blocks, all severely damaged by the week-long
artillery and aircraft bombing attacks. Most had been at least 50 percent
destroyed, missing roofs and walls.

As we approached Lieutenant Phong and the battalion staff officers, I
told him in English that we found the entrance into the outpost and the path

the NVA used to escape this morning. I suggested we try to get in one of those ways. Lieutenant Phong agreed, stating that some villagers who had been located could show us the way, and we could get soldiers from Second Company who knew how to do this.

Lieutenant Mac radioed to say he would be coming over with the soldiers from the Second Company. While waiting for the various people to arrive I radioed Major Haines to report our situation. He informed me that the Second Battalion would remain in their outpost overnight. The commanding officer, Captain Popps and the other advisors would be picked up by motorboat and taken across the river to talk to Colonel Lap and Major Haines.

I approached Warrant Officer Diep, the battalion communications officer, and asked him to walk around with me. Short but compact, he had always been a favorite of mine. Friendly and outgoing with an excellent command of English, he had also been a good friend of the late Lieutenant Tham, killed a few days ago. Warrant Officer Diep called to three soldiers and we told Lieutenant Phong the five of us were going to scout around the area to assess the damage.

The area we walked through around the outpost consisted of a cluster of severely damaged grass huts with a few concrete structures. It was a rural, agricultural-based, isolated area. The death and destruction were overwhelming. Dead, decomposed bodies, both North Vietnamese and PF, were scattered all over.

The landscape, which typically was green and lush, was now denuded and blackened, resembling garbage carelessly strewn about. Craters, large and small, pocketed the ground in all directions, most half-filled with stagnant rainwater, containing dead animals or the remains of soldiers. The once neat rows of barbed wire fences were scattered over the hillside, some totally buried by bombs or artillery shells. Metal fence posts were twisted and bent. Formerly tall, luscious, statuesque trees had been reduced to fire-scarred caricatures without leaves or limbs, like features in a scene from Dante's purgatory.

The destruction, the stench of the dead, and the awareness that it would be years before either the people or the land would be able to fully recover, highlighted the severity of the damage caused by the war. Thus far in Vietnam my encounters with the effects of the war had pretty much been limited to small-scale fighting. Death and dying were swiftly overlooked in the heat of battle. The dead were quickly removed, and the injured were sent to the rear for care. In most cases there was very little evidence afterward of what had occurred or the long-term consequences of battle.

Nong Son was different. So far, the prolonged contact had resulted in the death or wounding of more than 40 percent of our unit as well as the destruction of the homes of dozens of poor farmers who probably had no idea why the war was even being waged. I had been exposed to a depth of human brutality I would never again experience. No, "exposed to" was not the proper way to put it; I had been an active participant in this brutality.

My rational being, though, reminded me that the annihilation I saw had not been the result of something I had started. Rather, my role had simply been to assist one of the contenders to learn the art of battlefield survival. As I contemplated the destruction, I was sure of one thing—my side had learned their lessons well, and I had played a role in those lessons.

When we returned to the battalion CP, Lieutenant Mac was listening to Lieutenant Phong talk to some villagers who claimed they could show the soldiers where the pathway into the outpost used to be. Lieutenant Mac would go with the villagers and some soldiers to try and clear the entrance path to the mine, while I would go with some other soldiers to try to clear another path where the NVA had exited the outpost. Our goal was to get at least one safe way into the OP, but two would be better.

Clearing a minefield by hand is a very slow, laborious, anxiety-producing endeavor. A quicker way is to use a metal mine detector, but we did not have one. The person doing the clearing gets on his hands and knees and very carefully probes the earth with a sharp object, such as a long-bladed knife, a bayonet, or a sharp stick.

First, a section of ground 24 inches wide by 24 inches deep is tested to see if any mines are buried beneath the surface. If none is found, the prober moves forward two feet and repeats the process. Locating the mines is the easy part. Removing them is dangerous. Once a prober locates a mine, the earth is carefully scraped away so the type of mine can be determined. The mine can then be disarmed or exploded in place. If an area is not heavily mined it is possible to establish, by probing, a safe path through the minefield.

With the team I accompanied were two soldiers trained in disarming mines, but all their training applied to the detection and disarming of mines in a "normal" minefield, not one torn apart by bombs. Because of the days of bombing we could not tell how disturbed this minefield might be. One or more mines could have been dislodged or so damaged by explosions that they could now be set off by a minor movement of the ground. Not one of the soldiers or officers, including myself or the two soldiers who knew how to disarm mines, had probed a real minefield before. To gain the confidence of the men who would do the probing, I demonstrated how to do it.

Using stones as my corner guides, I marked off a two-foot square. Gently probing from my knees outward, with a soldier's bayonet, I cleared the small piece of ground. Moving forward, I slowly cleared a second two-foot square, marking off the cleared area with ropes. A sergeant replaced me and moved forward another two feet and then two more.

Our intended path was to be in the tracks left by the NVA. The minefield originally was only about 12 feet across, bounded on both sides by barbed wire. We could still see parts of the fence indicating approximately where the field began and ended. What we didn't know was if any live mines had been tossed over the fence in one of the bombardments and reburied by the blown-up dirt.

As the afternoon progressed and the clouds threatened rain, two Vietnamese soldiers and I alternated probing. Upon breaching the mined strip of land, we still had to probe through that portion of the ground beyond the minefield to the OP that had been torn up by the bombs to ensure no mines were there. By late afternoon, we had reached the hilltop. Lieutenant Mac and his crew had just gotten through their path and were inside the old fort. The sergeant who had replaced me doing the probing was the one to finish the job and the first one in our group to reach the top. We never found a mine.

We made the trip one at a time so if an explosion occurred only the one on the path would be injured. I waited until the sergeant had climbed over the top of the outpost earthen wall, unscathed, before I carefully picked my way along the footpath to the top. I breathed a sigh of relief as I hopped over the parapet. With my back to the path through the minefield, I was looking into the destroyed outpost when I heard a loud explosion, right behind me, below the OP berm. Quickly turning around, I saw a cloud of dust mixed with the arid smoke of an explosive device, and the twisted, lifeless, ripped-up body of the Vietnamese private who had tried to follow me up the hill. Then another soldier unwisely moved up the path, shouldered the dead man, and moved back down to safety. A sergeant said the soldier had stepped in every one of my footprints and after going ten feet blew up. Why, I wondered, had he died when I hadn't, especially since he stepped only in my tracks, and I was so much heavier than him? Realizing our probing had been for naught, we blocked off the path so no one else would use it.

Looking around the hill the OP was on, I couldn't believe the pounding the OP took. Before the battle, the hilltop had consisted of a large rectangular dirt wall, reinforced by wood, about 30 yards across on each side. Behind the walls was a trench system, zigzagging in a different direction every ten to 12 feet to prevent shrapnel from hitting everyone in the trench. Each corner had a large bunker with gun ports built in, so machine guns could set up interlocking fields of fire across each wall. There had been several small wooden buildings inside the compound as well as more underground bunkers, but now the entire fortress was nothing but mud and rubble.

While some of us were occupied with breaching the minefield, Colonel Lap's staff had rounded up several people from the mining complex. They were sent over with digging tools to extricate and remove the dead. The gray,

The ground in the top half of this photograph shows the mine field area surrounding the Trung Phuoc outpost through which the ARVN soldiers and I cleared a path to gain access to the OP, only to have one soldier blown up while on the cleared path.

cloudy afternoon had turned misty as a very soft, gentle rain fell. Lieutenant Mac and I walked around helping to clear the larger debris from the bunkers. All the civilians and most of the ARVN soldiers wore handkerchiefs or cloths tied over their mouths and noses since the whole hilltop reeked of death and the putrid smell of decaying bodies.

As we cleared the top away from the first bunker, we couldn't believe what we found. It was a room about ten feet square that apparently had become the hospital. The room was lined with bunks on all four walls, four high, each occupied by a body. The first one we looked at was what appeared to be a large black soldier, not a Vietnamese, with swollen and grotesque skin, his facial features—nose, mouth, eyes, and ears—minuscule compared to the bloated cheeks, neck and other parts of the body. I asked Mac how in hell could a black soldier end up here, and he replied he didn't know.

We asked one of the sergeants how a black soldier got in this PF outpost and he explained that what we saw was not a black man but a very badly bloated dead Vietnamese. Six days of post-mortem decay resulted in the body almost doubling in size due to expanding internal gases and his skin turning black.

As more bunkers were cleared, we found more dead PF soldiers. Some had died slowly like the ones we had found in the first bunker. Others had apparently died quickly, as they were still clutching their weapons. We also found women who had fought alongside their husbands and died with them.

It was decided the First Company would spend the night on the hilltop along with the battalion command group and the advisors. The Second Company would pull back from the ridge line and set up a defensive perimeter around the eastern half of the hill. Sergeant Bronson would come in with them and rejoin us. The Third Company would move in from the village and take the western half of the hill.

Before it got dark Lieutenant Mac and I decided to dig a hole in which to lie. Lieutenant Mac had selected an area where the ground was fairly soft. With a borrowed shovel, I scraped some of the loose soil away from an area large enough for the three advisors and Private Tuan to stretch out. After marking off the edges of our four-man foxhole, I lifted the shovel and rammed it full strength into the ground. It impacted the soft earth and sank into something not earth. The smell radiating from the hole in the dirt immediately told me that buried under our intended foxhole was a badly bloated soldier and I had just sliced a big hole in his distended belly. The gaseous, fetid stench floored me. Gasping and nauseous, I threw the shovel aside and moved away.

I announced I was through digging, that I would sleep on top of the ground. Private Tuan told the soldier whose shovel I borrowed what we had found. We moved over to another spot and set up camp for the night, not in a hole. After dark we lay in the wet mud. The rain had abated somewhat but we were still wet and dirty. Tuan had managed to get some scrap sheets of plastic from one of the destroyed houses. We used them to wrap our legs and covered the rest of our bodies with our rain jackets.

I quietly asked Mac and Bronson what had happened at their human barbecue the night before. Sergeant Bronson explained, with emotion, that all the NVA troops had gotten high on dope, wrapped themselves up in rags, doused themselves with coal oil, lit up, and attacked us like stupid bastards. Lieutenant Mac verified that by saying that this morning when it was light we checked the lines with our medic and found vials of drugs opium, the medic thought. The NVA soldiers were sneaking up to our lines, he continued, all doped up, wrapped in rags. In front of our lines they poured coal oil over themselves. We found those containers also. They just ignited their rags and charged across our concertina wire. They were so high, unless our bullets hit a vital organ, like the brain, or disabled their joints, they kept coming because they couldn't feel any pain. As soon as one went down on top of the wire, another fire freak, using the body as a bridge, ran across his buddy until he was shot down. When they went down many of them weren't dead. They were wounded badly and all tangled up in the wire, burning alive. Mac and his men could hear them moaning and crying, then screaming as the pain cut through the effects of the drugs. He maintained that if it hadn't been for Spooky, they sure as shit would have overrun them.

I radioed Major Haines to say we were set up for the night. I requested the artillery H & I firing remain around us for the night and I would check in again in the morning. As I scrunched around my plastic protection I mused about strange places I had spent some of my nights. When my Marine unit made its amphibious assault on Beirut in '58, our section of the beachhead happened to be the city dump. We secured our section of the perimeter and spent the night there, right smack in the middle of one of the largest garbage dumps I had ever seen. The outpost tonight smelled even worse than the dump did. In spite of the rain, mud, stench, and two-hour shifts, due to exhaustion I did get a modicum of sleep, as this was the first night since we had begun this operation that we could rest without being attacked.

The Seventh Day

Our seventh day at Nong Son began with a flurry of activity. Marine helicopters came in with fresh supplies, and the wounded from the night before last were removed. Early in the morning Colonel Lap and his staff came across the river to Trung Phuoc. The Second Battalion commander and Captain Popps also were present. Colonel Lap brought a surprise with him: Major Van.

Bent over, appearing jaundiced, wrapped in a sweater, field jacket, and wool scarf, he looked like an old man. Major Van had been released from quarters to return to duty, so he had now reassumed command of the Third Battalion. My response to him was cool; I still could not forgive him for what I perceived as skipping out on his duties when danger arose. He recognized my aloofness and did not press the relationship.

Two years later, in 1968, I would have a chapter published in the book *Combat Notes from Vietnam* titled "Memos of a Combat Advisor," in which I discussed this relationship and suggested that a combat advisor use more compassion than I had at the time when dealing with such a situation.

As both battalions were distributing munitions, food, medical supplies, and other assorted sundries of war, the commanders and advisors planned the next operation. The Third Battalion's intelligence NCOs had spent the past 24 hours interrogating the local people who had served as forced laborers for the NVA, learning that the NVA unit was a regiment that had been specifically recruited and trained for this mission, to destroy the Nong Son coal mine.

Even though during the past week the NVA regiment had suffered enormous casualties, we believed that the NVA soldiers remained at the north entrance to the Que Son Valley, hiding in caves and thick jungle about a mile away from Trung Phuoc and were preparing for another attack on the ARVN troops, probably in the evening. From what the villagers said, we judged their total fighting strength now to be less than 300 men and most likely closer to 200. Colonel Lap had scheduled a VNAF Bird Dog to fly over that portion of Que Son Valley, now convinced this was the time to take the initiative and attack the NVA positions before they could mount an attack on us. The ARVN regimental CP was established in the small cluster of wrecked buildings at the bottom of the devastated Trung Phuoc OP. A radio relay team and ARVN artillery forward observers had set up their headquarters on the OP hilltop.

The attack would be accomplished by two companies from the Third Battalion and two companies from the Second Battalion. Captain Popps would be the senior advisor with this task force. Lieutenant Phong would lead the Third Battalion task force elements consisting of the Second and Third companies with Lieutenant Mac and Sergeant Bronson along as the battalion advisors. The First Company would remain behind as the rear guard for the Third Battalion and regimental CP. The remaining company from the Second Battalion would retain its position in the smaller outpost. The Third Battalion would move south up along the ridge line and approach the NVA positions from the high ground. The Second Battalion would move along the valley floor on its right side. The VNAF Bird Dog flight had pinpointed several vital NVA positions upon which ARVN artillery would commence firing just prior to the two-battalion attack. Major Van and his staff would remain behind to work on the preparations necessary to relocate the battalion after this operation. I was asked to stay with the battalion staff to effect coordination with the U.S. air assets.

By 11:00 a.m. the task force was on its way. Just before 2:00 p.m. our troops were in position and the artillery barrage began. After 20 minutes of heavy bombardment the artillery shelling ceased, and the two battalions moved forward. The Second Battalion, on line, moved across the valley floor, the Third Battalion coming on line, down the hillside. Initial opposition was heavy, but the NVA were unable to sustain their resistance due to their poorly constructed defensive positions and lack of decisive leadership.

As the ARVN task force pressed forward, deeper in the valley, the NVA defenses began to fall. No longer were they the elite, well-disciplined, heavily-armed troops dedicated to a single mission. What the South Vietnamese battalions were now facing were the rear echelon support troops who were not as devoted to dying for a cause as the front-line soldiers had been.

Those North Vietnamese soldiers still alive ran back into the valley, retreating behind what turned out to be the last line of defense, a single infantry company that would fight to the death of its last member.

By late afternoon, the operation had stalled in front of a very defiant security force whose mission was to delay the ARVN at any cost. When it became obvious that whatever remained of the NVA regiment was retreating to the south, ARVN artillery was employed to disrupt and destroy as much of the retreat as possible. With ARVN troops smashing down the front door and ARVN artillery raining havoc at the back door, it was only a matter of time before this NVA unit would be history. But the NVA security company refused to surrender. Eventually all were killed or mortally wounded; the ARVN task force took possession of what was once the NVA regimental headquarters.

Captain Popps radioed Major Haines, explaining that the battalion was now in the NVA headquarters and it looked like they were in a big rush to leave. There was a lot of stuff lying around—maps, papers, supplies, weapons, equipment, things like that. Major Haines replied that regiment wanted the battalion to stay there tonight and recon again tomorrow.

As the day was ending, the task force spent the remaining daylight time taking care of the wounded, both ARVN and NVA, and establishing a defensive perimeter, even though we all felt there was no threat of a counterattack.

After supper, before turning in, Colonel Lap, Majors Haines, Major Van, and I discussed the future. The Second Battalion would be reassigned from their An Hoa bunker headquarters back to Hoi An. The Third Battalion would assume the security role of the Second Battalion and occupy their headquarters in An Hoa. One company of the Third Battalion would remain in defensive positions surrounding the Nong Son coal mine area. A second company would remain in An Hoa village as a security force, while the last company would remain inside the small fortress, which would be the battalion headquarters and advisor compound.

The next day, the regimental task force would return, and the following day, Tuesday, 25 October, the Third Battalion would leave here. The Second Battalion would be lifted out by helicopters to return to An Hoa Monday and pack up to move. The two companies of the Third Battalion would go down-river by foot and boat Tuesday to assume control of An Hoa from the Second Battalion.

With all the major details worked out, now I could concentrate on the small ones such as the itches and smells caused by the lack of bathing. Private Tuan and I built a big fire and heated a large pail of water. After a luxurious hot bath using my helmet, even the week-old clothes I put back on didn't seem that bad. I could look forward to another night of tranquility. This night I would even have a straw pallet to sleep on and a roof of sorts over my head since we advisors had set up shop in one of the grass huts that had not been totally destroyed. Tonight, I was bathed, dry, fed, had a place to sleep, and had little fear of any attack. What more could any combat trooper want? I thought as I drifted off to sleep.

Me right after the battle at Nong Son, standing in front of the entrance to a bunker the advisors lived in upon occupying the old French Fort at An Hoa, upon leaving Nong Son.

The Eighth Day

It felt good to wake up knowing that, for the present, at least, it would not be necessary to fight for my life. The morning was spent working out the endless logistical problems involved with relocating a battalion. While the troops were in Nong Son, destined for An Hoa, most of the battalion's equipment and all of its vehicles were in Hoi An and needed to be moved to An Hoa, requiring use of U.S. air assets.

The two-battalion task force investigated what the NVA regimental staff and the walking wounded had left in their rush to escape. At the NVA headquarters, they collected weapons, munitions, maps, equipment, and orders. When the company commanders and their advisors returned with the units in early afternoon, we all gathered around Colonel Lap's CP to listen to their reports based on the information obtained.

We learned that the NVA regiment had been specifically recruited and then trained for a year in the North Vietnam mining area of Lang Son on the Chinese border. The sole purpose of their mission had been to create a psychological setback by destroying the only operating coal mine in South Vietnam to show the people of South Vietnam that their government was helpless to protect natural resources vital to the economic well-being of the country.

The unit moved into South Vietnam via the Ho Chi Minh Trail through North Vietnam, into Laos, and then into South Vietnam southwest of Da Nang, arriving through the Que Son Valley, then moving north toward Trung Phuoc. But they had encountered two major problems. First, the local VC guides who were to assist part of the regiment in crossing the Thu Bon River had never shown up, preventing the regiment from getting across the river on the side of the Nong Son coal mines. Second, the defenders of Trung Phuoc had not fallen as easily as the NVA had counted, allowing the ARVN Second Battalion to enter the battle.

Logs and journals from the NVA revealed that, had it not been for U.S. air support and the ARVN and Marine artillery, they probably would have succeeded. Most of their KIAs and WIAs had resulted from air and artillery, not ground combat. The NVA regiment had consisted of about 1,200 soldiers when it initiated the attack. In the following seven days they suffered approximately 50 percent killed and almost 50 percent wounded. When the remnants

On top of Trung Phuoc outpost looking south toward Que Son Valley, where the remaining North Vietnamese Army troops fled at the end of the battle over the Nong Son coal mine.

of the regiment had departed Que Son Valley the day before, it was no longer even a unit.

Captain Popps pulled out of his flak jacket a large North Vietnamese army flag that he had taken from the NVA security force's last defensive position. Spreading it out on a table, he showed us where every man in the security unit who had been wiped out the day before had signed his name in blood on the flag. His counterpart, the Second Battalion commander, produced several documents. One was the company roster that verified the signatures. He also had a company log that he had taken from the dead company commander, detailing the part the company had played as the regimental security force and describing the pride the entire company had felt at the beginning of the operation, before the battle had been lost. Further on, the log depicted the esprit de corps displayed as the regiment had succeeded in taking over Trung Phuoc, keeping the Second Battalion pinned down in the small outpost, and forcing the ARVN to retreat across the river to the safety of Nong Son. The commander had proudly chronicled his regiment's ability to withstand the "devastating American imperialistic firepower" and survive.

However, as the days passed, a pessimistic tone had crept into his writings. More and more NVA soldiers had been killed or wounded. The civilian laborers had run away, and the regimental hospital had been having difficultly adequately handling the number of casualties. These later writings depicted the digging of mass graves to bury the dead so the enemy could not tell how badly the unit had been decimated.

Descriptions of the preparation for the human kamikaze attacks that night when we had seen running and burning bodies as well as the bitter disappointment at the failure to defeat the ARVN had also been poignantly recorded. The last entry had been written during the artillery attack before the two ARVN battalions had attacked the regiment CP. It stated that the regiment had lost the battle but not its honor. It had fought bravely against superior numbers of American and South Vietnamese government soldiers, but the massive firepower and numerical supremacy of the enemy had been more than the regiment could hold out against. The regimental leaders and the walking wounded would withdraw to prepare for another time, and the security company would die protecting the withdrawal.

No information on this battle can be found in American books on the Vietnam War because no U.S. ground troops were involved. Yet, except for U.S. fire and logistics support, this battle was one of the largest, up to that time, that the Vietnamese had fought on the ground alone. From a historical or statistical point of view it was a major battle because of the number of casualties suffered on both sides.

The "Official Vietnamese Report," certified by Major General Hoang Xuan Lam, I Corps commander and First Military Tactical Zone commander, records the operation as HOA TUYEN 157. The official results list 577 North Vietnamese soldiers killed on the battlefield and 64 assorted weapons seized. Our battalion suffered 53 dead and 127 wounded. None of the Third Battalion advisors received any wounds during the operation. The South Vietnamese Third Battalion endured a 45 percent casualty rate. The casualty rate for the Second Battalion was about 35 percent.

Interestingly, shortly after this battle, in early 1967, all coal mining operations at Nong Son terminated but resumed in 1969, only to operate sporadically until the war ended in 1975, when North Vietnam took control. Today the Nong Son coal mine and several villages along the Thu Bon River are now tourist stops on a guided boat tour out of Hoi An.

CHAPTER 18

Operations Around
An Hoa

The Second Company and headquarters company were now located in the old French fort on the high ground above the USMC base at the An Hoa airport, while the third company was located outside the fort in An Hoa, a community in Duc Duc district. The First Company, commanded by Second Lieutenant Son, remained stationed in Nong Son, responsible for its security. Our operations were limited to the An Hoa-Nong Son area.

The fortress was about 50 yards square and hard to overrun. All sides had clear, open fields of fire. The fort's outside perimeter was protected by barbed wire aprons and three coils of concertina wire, then another barbed wire apron. Inside of this was a minefield. Next was a water-filled ditch about ten feet deep and ten feet wide, its bottom filled with pungi stakes. Between the ditch and the sides of the fort was another minefield.

The fort itself was a walled enclosure constructed of concrete, steel, wood beams, sandbags, and the metal containers in which artillery Howitzer shells were stored, then covered with asphalt. Likely only the basic configurations of the fort remained from the time it had been occupied by the French. Each corner of the fortress had a short tower used as a machine gun emplacement. A 30-inch-wide, four-foot-deep ditch ran all the way around the inside of the wall. Every ten to 15 feet the ditch took a 90- to 120-degree turn so a mortar round exploding inside the trench would only spread shrapnel that short length, protecting most of the other soldiers in the ditch.

Inside the fort were several above-ground buildings. One was the kitchen, a building open on two sides where the NCOs and officers' food was cooked. The troopers bought their own food and cooked it in the trenches. Another structure was the top half of the commo bunker, where the major stayed during the day, and which was his CP. Below it was the battalion's underground communications center. Also scattered around the interior of the fort were some smaller buildings and several underground bunkers used by the officers and senior NCOs for living quarters.

We advisors had our own bunker, a 400-square-foot rat hole we detested. It was a concrete structure with steps leading below ground covered with a plywood and tin entranceway. The bunker was dark, damp, and moldy, stinking of unwashed bodies and mildew, and featuring a collection of creepy crawlies and mice. At first there were three American advisors and two ARVN radio men living in the bunker. Later it had four American advisors and two ARVN soldiers. It became especially bad at mealtime when we had to cook our meals consisting of rice and other vegetables purchased locally with C-ration meats added. The constant monsoon rains made cooking outside impractical, so our food was cooked over a gallon-sized tin can of sand with gas poured on it which produced a noxious, oily smoke that soiled the roof of our bunker and made breathing difficult.

We slept on canvas cots covered with poncho liners (camouflage-colored, ultra-thin, multi-layered, very light-weight blankets). Our clothes were always damp and smelly, and our weapons and other metal implements constantly rusted. After living underground for several weeks, I decided we would move topside, like our Marine neighbors who lived in wood frame buildings with aluminum roofs and screen-covered sides with canvas sides rolled down when it rained. Inside these buildings it was light, airy, and cool, not dark and dank.

I told my team members to start scrounging materials so we could make a structure like the Marines had on top of our bunker. In a couple of weeks, we had collected several panels of plywood, dozens of empty artillery shell containers, 2 × 4s, canvas, and yards of netting material. Using borrowed carpentry tools from the battalion supply and with help from some Marine friends, we began to build our new house. First, we made a floor of the empty artillery-shell canisters laid side by side on the ground. An eight-

Me on my last combat operation for my first tour in Vietnam. This time I did not go as an advisor but as a combat photographer to take movie films of combat.

foot by eight-foot floor became the entranceway to our house which was to be built on top of the concrete roof of the bunker. With the entrance floor finished, we called it a day. The next day we planned to erect the 2 × 4 frame for our house.

However, that night the VC "walked" dozens of mortar shells right down the neat rows of Marine buildings where the Marines were sleeping. The next day Sergeant Bronson, Lieutenant Mac, and I went to the Marine camp to see the extent of the destruction. Six Marines had been killed and more than two dozen wounded. About 15 of the screen-covered frame structures had been hit, some completely destroyed.

When I returned to the fort, I stood in front of our bunker for a long time, staring at the place our framed house was to go and realizing that, although I hated living in the dirty bunker, we were protected in it. I had no right to subject my men to the risks involved with sleeping above ground. Instead of finishing the above-ground structure, we used the materials to enclose the small entrance area to make it our kitchen. We could now cook above ground, but we still had protection at night while sleeping.

Most districts had a U.S. advisory team, but Duc Duc District didn't, so the senior advisor to the ARVN unit at An Hoa also served as the senior district advisor, now focusing mostly on the influx of Vietnamese refugees fleeing from the fighting in Nong Son and relocating in An Hoa. Part of the battalion's responsibility was to collect intelligence from the refugee population regarding any VC activity in the area, especially in the Que Son Valley south of Nong Son.

I was able to get some USAF FACs to fly recon missions over Que Son Valley with me as an observer. The first time up was a unique experience. The captain pilot flew into the An Hoa airstrip where I met him. As he got out of his plane, I walked over to meet him, saying I was Bob Worthington, his passenger for this afternoon.

He said he would be my guide for the next hour or two, asking if I had ever flown in a Bird Dog before, and I replied no, I hadn't. He said he would show me the plane. When we reached the Cessna O-1 (L-19), he proudly walked around and explained the tail dragger plane to me. It was a two-seater (fore and aft) powered by a 213 horsepower Continental O-470, air-cooled piston engine. We would fly low and slow, he continued, with a max cruising speed about 115 miles per hour but we would fly about 90 to 100.

He gave me the history and capabilities of the Cessna Bird Dog reconnaissance plane. It could loiter over a target area for five to six hours, and under ideal conditions, the plane could fly up to 20,300 feet, but it was too hot in Vietnam and this bird (of Korean War vintage) was too worn out to do that. He said we would fly at 3,000 to 4,000 feet until we got to our recon area, then drop down to the ground, if we must, to see what's there. I asked what

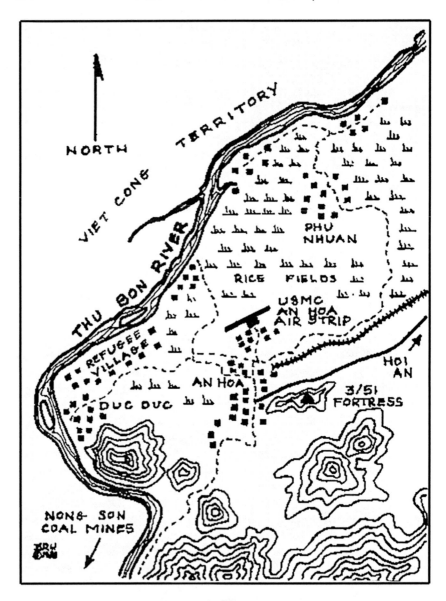

An Hoa

armament the plane had. Pointing to me, he said the weapons we carried and the plane's four target marking rockets.

Opening the door on the right side of the fuselage, he said I would sit in the back, while he would be up front. Pointing to a stick in a holder lying flat on the floor, he explained if he got shot to place the stick in the hole on the floor and I would then be the pilot. I climbed into the back seat. After he made sure I was strapped in, he stood beside me and pulled out a map. Turning it over and around to find the right place, he pushed it in front of me. Putting a finger on the map, he pointed out where we were now, at An Hoa. Moving his fingers southeast he tapped Que Son Valley, where we would go sightseeing. He climbed into the front seat and shut the door. Priming the engine, he yelled, "Clear!" out his window and turned the starter over. The prop in front began to slowly turn and then spun quicker as the engine belched to life.

The An Hoa airstrip was controlled by the Marines and, because of the level of aerial activity, had its own control tower, a rickety wood structure rising 30 feet above the ground, topped with a sandbag-covered platform. The rainy weather had induced the controllers to erect a framework over their heads which they had covered with clear plastic.

The pilot contacted the tower requesting departure instructions. He was cleared to back-taxi the runway for departure. Glancing at the aircraft's instruments he adjusted a couple of knobs, set the altimeter, looked up and down the runway, and pushed in the throttle. He kicked the right rudder, and the light, OD-colored, high wing tail dragger bounced and skidded into a right turn onto the runway. Bouncing along we quickly came to the end of the runway where he gave the plane more throttle and kicked the left rudder to spin us around, facing into the wind, down the runway.

Checking the altimeter, he pushed in on the brakes, and revved up the engine. Turning the ignition, he checked both magnetos, adjusted the gyro to the compass, and pulled the throttle back out to ease off on the power. Wiggling the stick fore and aft, he seemed satisfied with everything, telling the tower he was ready for departure.

The pilot smoothly pushed the throttle forward, released the brakes, and the little plane lurched forward, bouncing down the runway. At 30 miles an hour, he pushed the stick forward, lifting the tail off the ground. At 60 miles an hour, he eased back on the stick slowly as the plane began to lift off the ground. At 70 miles per hour, it was completely airborne. Easing the stick forward again, the small plane, level with the runway, picked up speed. At 80 miles per hour, he pulled back on the stick and we began to rise again at 600 feet per minute. In a few minutes we were cruising toward our target doing 100 miles an hour at 4,000 feet.

This was quite a change from the Hueys I was used to. The UH-1B was a large, massive metal craft that looked and sounded like a powerful war machine. By comparison this Bird Dog was a very small and fragile plane. The Plexiglass windows all around and the narrow sides gave me the feeling of being suspended in the air rather than being inside a plane, a sensation enhanced by the knowledge that the thin aluminum sides of the plane were no thicker than a soda can. It was frightening to realize that my very life depended on such a flimsy airborne vehicle.

Soon, however, my attention was diverted to what I could see. For the first time I was able to study the ground over the Que Son Valley from above. Speaking to me through the headset, the pilot discoursed on how he had been here many times before for the Marines and had seen the valley was full of VC main force units. He explained that we could go lower and they wouldn't shoot at us because they were afraid we had some F-4s just waiting to unload on them. Then we went down as both the plane and my stomach dropped out from under me.

Pulling back on the throttle, the pilot pushed the stick forward and to the left as he gave it hard left rudder. The Cessna tipped over on its left wing, the nose dropped, and it went into a tight spiral down to about 1,000 feet above the ground. Twisting and turning to get me the best view, he pointed out enemy trenches, machine gun positions, and enemy soldiers trying to hide. It was amazing to me to be so close to the enemy, watching them working and moving about in their encampment area, watching me as I observed them, with no shots being exchanged. This was a very hard part of my war to understand: just watching each other. We flew back and forth, making steep and abrupt turns for an hour as I made notes, diagrams, and maps on what I saw. I completed my chores at about the same time my stomach was getting ready to vomit my lunch in my lap. I pleaded for the pilot to return home as I was finished. He pushed in the throttle and we slowly rose back to 4,000 feet and leveled off for a smoother flight home.

Our landing, though, was another frightening experience. Because of the high probability of enemy ground fire on a normal approach, the pilot flew high, over the airstrip and then spiraled down, very quickly, over the end of the runway. At one thousand feet he dove for the ground and flared abruptly, diminishing airspeed rapidly for a perfect three-point landing.

As I climbed out, relieved to be back on the ground again, I thanked the pilot who gave me a thumbs-up sign as he taxied back to depart to Da Nang. I had to sit in my Jeep for several minutes to calm down before driving off.

Later, after going over the data with Major Van and his intelligence people, we realized I had learned nothing really new. I had, though, confirmed that the VC unit was still there and a potential threat to both Nong Son and An Hoa.

Flying in Vietnam was not a favorite pastime of mine. Getting shot on the ground was one thing, as the furthest I could fall was five feet, ten inches. In a plane or helicopter, though, getting shot was only half the problem. Getting down in a safe area was the other half. Flying in combat was too risky for me. Ironically, though, during my second tour of duty in Vietnam I enjoyed flying and did it as much as possible. And when I finally got shot, where was I? Flying in a helicopter! And I was awarded an Air Medal for my combat flights.

Another riveting experience flying on this tour of duty occurred when I was able to hop a ride into Da Nang on a Marine resupply chopper to personally thank the commander of the air commando unit and his crew who flew Spooky, which kept us alive during the Nong Son operation. After accepting my thanks, the lieutenant colonel asked if I wanted to fly in one of his AC-47s that night. I said sure and was told to return at 8:00. As I was leaving his office, he told me to bring a jacket as it got cold up there at night.

Before 8:00 I was back, carrying a field jacket and waiting in the ops briefing room for Puff's crew. They entered and told me the USAF had one possible mission which wouldn't be confirmed until we were on station. While the enlisted crew loaded the 7.62 mm shells and parachute flares, the pilots briefed me on the plane's operations. They showed me the three 7.62 mm six-barreled Gatling guns sticking out the open door and two open windows on the left side of the plane. This was the pilot-in-command's side. Each Gatling gun was capable of firing 6,000 rounds per minute. The pilot "sighted" the weapons by looking through a plastic gun sight on his left window and lining it up with his left wingtip and the target. Pivoting on the target, he would then fire one or more of the three guns, creating havoc on the ground below.

After we boarded and took off, I learned one thing quickly. Even though it might be hot on the ground at 5,000 feet with open doors and windows, it was cold in the plane. Even with my field jacket on, I froze my butt off. The unit that had asked for Puff originally did not have any need for us, so, using the plane's radios, I called all three Fifty-First Regiment battalions to see if they needed any help from Spooky. They were really surprised to hear from me, overhead, but none of the ARVN battalions needed our services this night. We had started back to Da Nang air base when suddenly a Marine unit called for help.

After we reached the unit's position and began orbiting over it, the Marine company commander on the ground oriented the pilot as to what was happening. The crew began to drop flares to light up the area and then the ground commander asked for fire support from Spooky and described where the enemy was. Placing the plane's wing on the target, the pilot began a graceful orbit around it. On the ground CO's command, the pilot let off a rapid stream of firepower from the number one gun positioned in the open doorway, causing an ear-splitting "blurppp" as the Gatling gun spit out each burst. The muzzle flashed in the dark night, and a solid stream of tracers lit up the whole inside length of the fuselage. Empty brass flew all over, covering the floor of the aircraft. After a few more passes, the ground commander said that the VC in front of his unit had left and we were free to go.

This action was enough to show me what it was like in combat, inside Spooky. I was amazed at how accurate the pilot's shooting was from so high up and with no natural lighting. Around midnight we returned to Da Nang and I thanked the pilots and crew for a fun evening.

A big celebration was planned for the birthday of the Fifty-First Regiment on 22 November. The ceremony included the dedication of a memorial for the soldiers killed at Nong Son and military decorations for valor awarded to individual soldiers for their actions at Nong Son. A composite company selected from the Third Battalion was created to represent the battalion. As the senior advisor, I was also to participate.

When I arrived, I realized how elaborate the ceremony would be. The regimental band was there with a 12-man color guard and 20 young, lovely, slim ladies all wearing pretty ao dais in a rainbow of colors, all there to place garlands of gallantry (a necklace of paper flowers) around the necks of decorated soldiers.

As soon as I was put in my assigned place in a large group of soldiers, I realized I was not in with the Third Battalion. Standing next to me on my right were three other U.S. advisors: Sergeant Calder of the Second Battalion, Master Sergeant Wright of Regiment, and Captain Popps of the Second Battalion. Standing there at parade rest, I was trying to figure out what was going on. Sergeant Calder leaned over next to me and, whispering, asked if I knew why we were here. I replied I didn't know, and he said we were going to be decorated.

Soon commands were barked out, and the group of five rows marched out to the middle of the parade ground, drums beating and bugles blowing. Stopping before a reviewing podium, the regimental commander, Lieutenant Colonel Lap, gave a long speech about the fight to save the coal mine. Next Dr. Chi, the Michigan-educated province chief, dedicated the ten-foot-tall concrete obelisk memorial to the fallen soldiers who had given their lives at Nong Son. Then our group was called to attention. The orders were read by the regimental adjutant as Dr. Chi presented each one of us with the South Vietnamese Cross of Gallantry, a medal equivalent to the U.S. Silver Star or Bronze Star, depending on which color star the Vietnamese medal had. I was awarded the Cross of Gallantry with Silver Star as were Lieutenant Mac and Sergeant Bronson.

When all the decorations had been pinned on the soldiers, the lovely ladies placed the garlands of gallantry around our necks. The young lady who stopped in front of me wore a pastel pink ao dai and had long, shiny black hair and a slim, graceful figure. She was at least a foot shorter than me and had trouble reaching over my head. Maintaining my dignity (and trying not to show my pleasure), I lowered my body so she could place the garland of crepe paper flowers around my neck. Now this was the way to recognize warriors, I thought. I felt very proud and honored to be distinguished by the Vietnamese for my actions in combat. A year later, back in the States at Fort Benning, I also received the Bronze Star for Valor from the U.S. Army for my actions during the battle of Nong Son.

During my two months in An Hoa as district advisor, my duties consisted mainly of serving as the USAID assistant for the refugee problem. The main responsibility in this area was determining what USAID supplies were needed and then seeing that they were properly used. More than 5,000 men, women, and children were voluntarily evacuated out of the Que Son Valley– Nong Son area after the Nong Son battle. A resettlement village had been established next to the Duc Duc district headquarters along the shore of Thu Bon River. The district officials worked to set up this village while I ordered USAID materials and food to provide as much USAID support as possible. Working with the Hoi An MILPHAP personnel we held medical clinics every week at the Duc Duc refugee village. In many ways it was a sad job. Realizing the death, disease, and suffering of these people, one couldn't help but be touched by their plight. For the most part they were stoic and uncomplaining, regardless of the hazards and interruptions they had faced. My problem was I felt I couldn't do enough for them.

In addition to serving as the USAID assistant for the refugee problem in An Hoa, I also gathered intelligence for the CIA. The An Hoa complex and its geographical location was of unique interest to our CIA in Vietnam. Because I was the senior U.S. official in the area and fluent in Vietnamese and French, I was recruited to work for the agency while in the area, collecting specified intelligence and providing the information to my CIA contact, which I did until I left An Hoa in January.

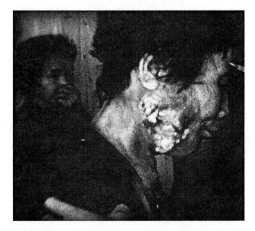

While as an American military advisor I shared the day-to-day danger or excitement or drudgery of war with my fellow Vietnamese soldiers and civilians, I could not share the long-term physical deprivations or the emotional costs of the Vietnamese people. Although during this time I worked to help the refugees and provide intelligence

This woman was seen as a patient during an advisor-sponsored medical clinic held by both U.S. and Vietnamese medical personnel in a rural village. She had her jaw shot off by an artillery strike in her village, was seen and treated, and then medevaced to a hospital for surgery.

that might aid the people of South Vietnam, my ability to connect with these people was limited due to my different position. Without such an ability, I was only a visitor doing a job, a temporary hired hand soon to move on to another job, a fragile status recognized by both the Vietnamese and me.

CHAPTER 19

R & R in Hawai'i

As a member of military personnel in Vietnam I was authorized to take one out-of-country R & R trip during my tour of duty, which I did in November 1966. The destination choices available in 1966 were Bangkok, Thailand, Australia, or Hawai'i. Military personnel were not allowed to return to CONUS (continental United States), however. I selected Hawai'i where I would meet my wife, Anita.

Anita made all the arrangements for our stay in Hawai'i. She would fly to Honolulu on Thursday, 24 November, Thanksgiving Day. I would arrive the next day and be able to stay for six days, leaving on Wednesday, 30 November. Anita would depart the next day.

She made reservations at the Moana/Surfrider Hotel, part of the Sheraton chain at the special R & R rate of $12 a day. The entire hotel bill for the seven days, which included the room, several long-distance phone calls back to the States, room service, six meals for two in the hotel dining room, laundry service, and taxes, added up to $117.46.

Twice a day, at dawn and at noon, the R & R flights from Vietnam would disgorge their loads of GIs on the island of Oahu. Each month 10,000 soldiers enjoyed six days of fun in the sun. My plane arrived at noon, Pan American Flight P208A from Ton Son Nhut, and the other men and I were quickly processed. After being briefed and receiving an orange and red "Aloha R & R Hawai'i" card from the Hawai'i Visitors Bureau, we were released to meet our wives, girlfriends, or families who had been brought out to the airport on military buses.

While the women had been waiting for the plane to land and the men processed, an army chaplain tried to maintain a degree of calm and order by telling jokes, such as "Girls, don't expect too much from your men; each R & R flight carries 65 miniskirted stewardesses because nothin's too good for our fighting men" or "The troops miss hamburgers more than their wives so go get one and kiss him with a little onion on your breath" or "If you grab the wrong guy that's okay—just bring him back and the army will trade him in for another one."

When the men entered the reception area, pandemonium broke out, babies hollering and crying, women screaming for their men and men yelling for their women. Everyone seemed to be searching for someone. Eyes would connect, recognition and disbelief registering on faces with overnight bags and purses hitting the ground as men and women flew into each other's arms, some laughing, some joking, many crying with joy, arms and hands held tight, safely reunited after months of anxious separation.

My wife, Anita, on the balcony of our hotel room on Waikiki Beach in Hawai'i during my R & R.

Anita looked like a dream—tall, slender, shapely. She had her long dark hair held back by a white velvet headband. She wore a knee-length red floral print muumuu. She was positively radiant. I couldn't keep my eyes (or hands) off her. Finally, the chaplains herded us onto waiting buses back to Fort DeRussy, the military R & R center on Waikiki Beach, where we disembarked.

The days and nights passed by too quickly. For a dollar a day plus mileage, we rented a VW bug and drove all over the island. We had our 8 mm movie camera and took several rolls of color film of the island and our activities. Some days we went shopping in the large outdoor shopping center, Ala Moana. We spent other days just lazing on the beach in front of the hotel. One day we went to the zoo; another we took in a Polynesian cultural show put on by Kodak. In the evenings, we went out to eat at fancy restaurants, attended nightclubs where we watched floor shows, or walked on the beach, holding each other close. We enjoyed Hawai'i, its varied activities, and each other.

However, an unexpected problem was that after ten months of a very bland Vietnamese diet, the rich American food made me sick. On the fifth day, I was too sick with stomach cramps and diarrhea to even leave our room, the pain so excruciating that I wanted to die. When I returned to the States eight weeks later, to avoid such circumstances again, I began eating American foods very cautiously, for the first few week, drinking tea, soda, or water, and eating only rice, stale bread, and canned foods before slowly working up to a customary American diet.

When the sixth day in Hawai'i ended, we had to part again. This time the women said their good-byes at the Haluhia Service Club at Fort DeRussy, a single-story, open-walled building surrounded by lush tropical growth, a place the wives called Cupid's Patio.

There were tears, embraces and memories but also the knowledge that our family would be reunited in less than eight weeks. Anita would go back tomorrow to the chilly East Coast, where she and our daughters were staying with her parents in Washington, D.C. I would return to my rat hole in An Hoa. On the flight back to Saigon, I and the other soldiers relived the precious moments we had just spent with our loved ones and prepared ourselves for the contrast of military activities and combat awaiting us in Vietnam.

CHAPTER 20

The Night the Viet Cong Stopped the War

During the two months the Third Battalion had been in An Hoa, we had conducted numerous one- and two-company search and destroy counter-guerrilla operations. Usually these were two-day missions targeting one of the many small hamlets north of An Hoa in the fertile valley alongside the Thu Bon River.

A few days before Christmas Major Van and the Duc Duc district chief planned a "county fair" operation for the small village of Phu Nhuan, about three miles northeast of An Hoa, which had become a regular VC stronghold. The district chief told Major Van that he had information on the identity of some VC leaders and members living in the village, and he wanted the battalion to escort his policemen there so they could locate and arrest them. One way to do this, in theory, at least, was by conducting a county fair operation.

The plan was for the Third Battalion, now consisting of two rifle companies since one company was still providing security at Nong Son, to leave An Hoa at daybreak. It would take the battalion about two hours slogging through the mud to get to the village. The trip would be made on foot initially, along the old railroad tracks and then along a dirt road. By mid-morning, the village would be surrounded, assuming the two companies did not run into any armed resistance.

As soon as the village was secured, the GVN officials, U.S. Naval medical personnel from the MILPHAP office at Hoi An, and USMC civic action officials would arrive with their vehicles and equipment. While the U.S. military and GVN civilian personnel did their jobs within Phu Nhuan, the Third Battalion personnel would provide the perimeter security around the village and search inside for weapons and munitions caches, VC tunnels, and other evidence of the VC using the village. All the villagers would be screened by the civilian police, and VC suspects would be detained.

It was typical winter monsoon weather, cold and rainy, when the operation began as planned on Friday, 23 December 1966. At daybreak, we left An Hoa and for the next two hours trekked through ankle-deep mud, first along the railroad tracks then on a dirt road. Just a few steps rapidly drained our energy reserves, slowing forward progress almost to a crawl.

Encountering no resistance along the way, the battalion reached the village by mid-morning, splitting in half to quickly encompass it. The Third Company went to our left, cutting the village off from the Thu Bon River. The Second Company moved to our right, forming a line separating the village from its rice fields.

As the Second Company was moving into position, a smattering of rifle shots rang out. These sounds were quickly joined by a volley from several automatic weapons. Major Van called for his radio man to contact the Second Company to find out what was happening. Before contact was made, more rifle shots pierced the air, again followed by several automatic weapons.

The company reported that as they had moved upon some open rice fields they had seen several farmers working on the far side. The soldiers had yelled to the men to come over to the company. When the farmers had realized that they were being approached by soldiers, they had dropped their digging tools and run toward a small cluster of trees. At this point, a squad of soldiers chased the farmers who stopped at the trees and picked up rifles hidden there. Grabbing the weapons, bolt-action repeating rifles, they had fired on the advancing squad. The Fifty-First Battalion soldiers, armed with .45-caliber Thompson submachine guns and .30-caliber carbines, had returned fire. In this initial exchange of gunfire no one had been hit. Three of the farmers had dropped their rifles and stood with arms raised in surrender. The other two farmers had run away and had fired again at the soldiers. This time the ARVN bullets hit their targets, killing both farmers. Major Van, grinning at me, stated that we now knew the VC lived here.

In about 40 minutes, we had the village completely encircled. No one could enter or exit without us knowing it. The battalion command group selected a large grass hut built on a concrete foundation for its CP. Inside, tables were cleared off, soldiers moved about setting up radios, covering the tables with papers and notebooks, and arranging a place for the major to use as his "office." With the battalion's functional duties taken care of, Major Van, some of his staff, our radio men, and I walked around the village.

Even by rural Vietnamese standards this village was impoverished, one of the poorest I had ever seen in Vietnam. Few of the smaller children wore a complete set of clothing. Most were covered with threadbare rags stitched together. The adults weren't much better off, dressed in tattered garments that wouldn't have even made good rags with which to wash a car. The attire for the smaller children was only a tattered T-shirt with the genital area left exposed to eliminate the need for diapers. Older children and adults, regardless of sex, were dressed alike in black, lightweight cotton trousers worn with collarless shirts in a variety of colors. Some of the men wore shorts, like boxer-style underwear. Most had their heads covered with tightly woven, conical-shaped straw hats, which provided a degree of protection from rain or sun, while pieces of clear plastic wrapped around their bodies served as raincoats.

The battalion CP was in the only house with a floor other than dirt. All the residents looked emaciated and weak. Most of the grass huts had only the barest of furniture and very few personal possessions.

One hut was set up as the screening and interrogation facility, with interviews to be conducted by civilian policemen who had come with us. All villagers, probably about 100 to 150, would be processed through this place to be identified. Already the bodies of the two dead farmers were stretched out in front of our temporary police station, and the three remaining farmers/VC had been tied to chairs inside, being questioned by the battalion intelligence sergeants.

By noon, the rest of the county fair crew, consisting of about a dozen Vietnamese civilians, including some district and province officials as well as entertainers, pulled up in four-wheel-drive, three-quarter-ton trucks. Now the planned activities could begin. Loud speakers were mounted on poles and portable generators set up. Posters were tacked up all over, proclaiming the benevolence of the government. A large, open hut was converted into a dispensary, where U.S. Navy corpsmen would inoculate the small children first, then treat the ever-present scalp infections most children had, caused by poor hygiene, and the upper respiratory tract ailments common in adults.

We soon realized that even the smaller children in the village understood the implications of death and disease. When they went through the inoculation in our clinic, not a single young child winced or cried when receiving an injection. In fact, the older children, five or six years and up, wanted more than one inoculation, figuring that if one shot was good, two would be better, and three would be much better. Therefore, these children would get a shot and then race to the end of the line for another and another.

We detected this because we were giving all shots in right arms, but some children turned around backward as they approached the medics, baring their left arms. When the children were turned around so they could be inoculated in their right arms, the corpsmen saw the red areas from their first inoculations. Through an interpreter and a district official, we tried to convince the children that one shot was all they needed.

Occasionally some medical oddities were seen. One young boy had a hand that was normal in all respects except it had a second, nonfunctional thumb growing out of the palm. The thumb had bones and a fingernail, but the bones were not attached to the hand as the thumb was joined to the palm only by skin. This child was taken back to the MILPHAP clinic to have the extra thumb surgically removed.

Activities were taking place throughout the village. Patients were seen, medication dispensed, and food and GVN propaganda comic books passed out. The police screening identified a number of suspected VC. More weapons were discovered in various huts, but no tunnels were found.

As the day passed, these activities were interspersed with political speeches designed to convert the villagers to the side of the government. It was pointed out that the day's activities reflected the government's care for its citizens. The problem, though, was that in reality the government representatives only occasionally visited the people, while the villagers coexisted with the VC continually, making the VC influence much greater. The villagers, however, responded to the government officials in the expected ways by bowing and murmuring approval. As soon as we left, I knew the same attention would be accorded to the local VC leaders.

I truly felt sorry for these people. Most of them were apolitical, concerned only with earning a simple living off the land and raising their families. The war between the powers of North Vietnam and South Vietnam had been brought to their village because of its geographical location. Living was hard enough with diseases, infections, and injuries that could not be adequately treated locally, shortening the peasants' life spans in comparison with city dwellers. The continual fighting just added another dimension of violence and the potential of death to their already precarious existence.

As darkness descended and the generators came to life, their muffled "putt-putt-putt" gave light to the night's activities. Sick call ended, and the give-away shifted to clothing. Then singers and dancers performed government propaganda shows for the villagers.

While this was going on, I was taking movies with the 8 mm Kodak camera Anita had brought to me in Hawai'i, part of a plan to make a movie of what a U.S. combat advisor did in Vietnam. During an argument between a villager and a government official over an item of clothing, a brightly colored dress, I filmed the heated exchange. The clothing being distributed had been given to the government officials by me. My mother had headed a church drive in Roxbury, Connecticut, which had collected clothing for me to give to needy Vietnamese. When I showed the movie back home after this tour, my mother exclaimed, "That's my dress!"

Since the initial firefight that had greeted us in the morning, the enemy had been quiet. However, as the activities ceased for the night, shots came from the side of the village facing the rice fields as some VC probed our defenses around the village. Thirty minutes later, more shots were fired. This time our Marine liaison team called in artillery fire on the tree line from where the shots had come. The shells crashed in, and the shooting ended. But shortly after this, more rounds came in from a different direction. It looked like we would encounter sporadic shooting all night long, although we didn't expect an attack, and the VC undoubtedly knew we would not leave our defensive positions around the village.

About this time, an old peasant man came to our perimeter and said he had to talk to the battalion commander. He explained he lived outside the village in the area from where the VC were shooting and a baby girl had been wounded and needed medical treatment. The man was escorted to Major Van, who talked to him while I listened. He said that a small baby had become a victim of the firefight, with both her feet shot up badly, and she urgently needed medical treatment. If the co van my (American advisor) could radio for a phi-co thruc-thang (helicopter) to take the baby to a hospital, the VC would agree not to shoot during the evacuation of the baby, the old man claimed. Major Van turned to me and asked if I understood what the man wanted.

I said that I was not sure but thought that he said the VC would stop the war now but questioned if this was some sort of a trick. The major admitted that he didn't know either.

I told the major to tell him I don't know if we could get a medevac, but first we needed to see the baby. He had to bring the baby here so we could examine her and then decide what to do. I emphasized that the old man should realize I couldn't order a helicopter to come here. All I could do was ask. The Marines in Da Nang would make the decision whether to send a helicopter. After a long discussion with the major, the man agreed to bring the baby and her mother to us.

After the man left, I had the Marine liaison team relay the information to their headquarters, making sure that they conveyed my feeling that we didn't know enough yet to make the request. When (if?) the baby arrived, our corpsmen would examine her and then decide if immediate medical care was required beyond what they could provide in the field.

Thirty minutes later the Marines radioed back that they could fly a medevac in if we could guarantee a cold LZ. I told them I'd let them know. About 45 minutes later, around 8:00, the old man returned with a young lady and what resembled a picnic basket with something wrapped up inside. Moving aside the cloth, I saw a female baby, about a year old, with both feet torn apart by shrapnel. Facing a man across gun barrels who is shooting at you is one thing. Facing a small child whose only contribution to her condition was the fact that she was born got to me. Looking at the baby's condition and then at the mother, I was reminded of my wife and our two young daughters and vowed to get the helicopter that night.

The young mother was visibly distressed about her child, but she readily relinquished her to the American corpsmen, knowing these men would help her baby. While the corpsmen were examining the baby, I was filming their work on her. When finished, the corpsmen stated that both feet had been severely lacerated by shrapnel fragments, and even though they removed most of the fragments, cleaned the wounds and stopped the bleeding, both agreed that the damage to the muscle and tendons required immediate surgery to repair the torn tissue or the baby girl would probably never walk.

Consequently, I told the Marines to immediately make the official request for the medevac, providing the map coordinates of our location.

I explained to the major that we needed to set up an LZ for the helicopter and needed to get a couple of squads to secure a place next to the village for it to land. Speaking to one of his staff officers, Major Van sent out orders for his soldiers to find an LZ and secure it.

I then asked how we would know the VC wouldn't shoot down the medevac. The man and the mother both said that no VC would shoot if a helicopter came in. I told the man he had to go back to the VC and tell them I would have a medevac coming for the baby and her mother and not to shoot. One of the Marines using the radio called me over and said his unit wanted to know how we could guarantee the VC wouldn't shoot the helicopter when it came in.

I responded by saying that I couldn't guarantee anything except I would personally be out there on the LZ to guide the medevac in and I did not believe we would have any trouble. The voice on the radio said he would see what could be done.

While I waited for a response I went out to check the LZ and found that the soldiers had one surrounded adequately in the open area next to the village. I checked and rechecked its position against the map, verifying that there was no wind, so the helicopter could land from any direction.

Then I went back to our CP to wait.

Thirty minutes later, the voice over the radio said the medevac was on its way, with an echo tango alpha (ETA) of two-five minutes. I told the old man to go back to the VC and tell them the helicopter was on its way and not to shoot it.

I asked the major if he could have his soldiers bring the woman and her child to the LZ as soon as it landed, because I wanted her on board immediately. I didn't want the helicopter to stay on the ground. He nodded in agreement.

I then explained what I had planned to the Navy corpsmen. As soon as they heard the helicopter inbound, they were to get the baby ready to go and give it to one of the ARVN soldiers escorting the mother to the helicopter.

Grabbing my helmet, flak jacket, web gear, and flashlight I picked up my PRC-10 radio and went out to the LZ to wait. Squatting in the bushes, I remained silent, straining to hear the noise of the incoming medevac. The handset of the radio was hooked to my helmet chin strap which was dangling alongside my ear. I could hear the Marine back in our CP talking to the medevac pilot, who was about five minutes out, approaching from the northeast.

Next the pilot reported being two minutes away, asking if I was sure the Victor Charlies wouldn't shoot. I confirmed that was what they told us. I guessed that we would just have to wait and see. While I had faith that the VC wanted to save the baby and would not shoot at us, I still held my breath, ready to react instantly if something went wrong. A minute later I could make out the muted whup-whup of the chopper. Because of a light rain and low clouds, it wasn't very high. I asked the squad leader where the baby and mother were, and he replied here as he pointed to her about ten feet away.

I radioed the pilot to say I had him in sight, explaining the best way to approach and land. I moved into the center of the small clearing and coached him down. God, was this scary. My thoughts centered on the danger involved in what I was doing, I hoped like hell the VC would keep their word and won't shoot me.

The next few seconds seemed like hours as I waited for the helicopter to maneuver around to come in for a landing. Slowly moving my flashlight in a small arc, I talked it down, giving the pilots directions left and right as well as calling out their height above the ground.

The squad leader ran over with the mother and child, and I handed the basket with its precious cargo to the crew chief. Next, I lifted the mother into the helicopter. The crew chief buckled her in as I ran swiftly to the side.

Slowly the large, dark Huey rose waist-high and pivoted around. Building up to full power, the Lycoming gas turbine engine whined as the helicopter nosed over, tail up, and began its forward movement. Skids almost touching the ground, it picked up speed and altitude simultaneously. Climbing high, it banked over the village and struck a northeasterly course back to Da Nang, to a hospital where the baby girl's feet could be saved. Then, calling the security back in, we moved into the village.

I felt good. Taking my helmet off, I raised my face to the sky, letting the soft rain wash away the sweat that was running off my forehead, into my eyes, and down my cheeks. An hour or so later the firing began again from across the rice fields, but it was more of a nuisance than a problem.

By the next day, the operation was over. We had collected 23 VC suspects. Most were middle-aged men, but there were also some young women in the group. With their athletic-looking young bodies, long shining dark hair, bright white smiles, and flashing brown eyes, the young women were used as messengers for the VC. Pretending to be innocent, young peasant girls visiting relatives, they were able to freely move about, carrying messages or documents for the VC. Even the ones we had captured on this operation seemed far removed from the war as they coyly flirted with the South Vietnamese soldiers. Seldom were they detained long or treated harshly by the U.S. Marines as they traveled from one village to another.

Returning to home base was a slow muddy walk, a repeat of the one the previous day. With us we had the VC suspects, arms tied behind their backs and roped together in a chain. They would be interrogated again at Duc Duc district headquarters before being sent to Hoi An for more processing. At least at the end of our two-hour hike we could relax. It was Christmas Eve.

A week or so earlier I had received a large Christmas package

A pretty, young Vietnamese woman used by the Viet Cong to transfer messages as U.S. Marines would not suspect (or detain) pretty Vietnamese women. This photograph was taken during a "county fair" combat operation.

Viet Cong suspects detained after a combat operation during a "county fair" operation.

Me and PFC Thuan, Christmas, 1966, in the advisor bunker at An Hoa.

of goodies from my hometown Congregational Church which I looked forward to sharing with my team. Starting in the early fall, two women from the
church had begun collecting items for Christmas packages to be mailed to
Roxbury servicemen stationed in Vietnam. Contributions of homemade
cookies, cheese and crackers, dried fruits, presweetened iced tea, Kool-Aid,
cough drops, writing paper, and envelopes had been boxed up. Each Roxbury
serviceman would receive an 18-inch by 10-inch by 16-inch box full of goodies.
My wife sent me a photo the local paper ran of one of the church women
holding a box with my six-year-old daughter, Suzi, holding a framed picture
of me in uniform.

What was supposed to make Christmas Day different from the others
was the holiday cease-fire. For 24 hours, all participants in the war agreed to
maintain their present positions and not engage in any combat activities. We
thought this was unlikely, however, as we could not envision a day without
fighting somewhere.

We felt the 24-hour cease-fire would not last because the VC would try
to use the time to gain any advantage possible. Not wanting to be caught off
guard, we kept our radios tuned to the various Marine battalion nets in our

area. What we ultimately heard confirmed our belief that the VC were on the move.

Sure enough, in the night, only 90 minutes after the truce began, one marine company, in a defensive position just outside of An Hoa, was hit with VC mortars and small arms. During the attack, the VC fired 20 mortar rounds into the Marine position and fired more than 1,000 rifle shots at the Marines. The fight lasted the entire day, ending in the early evening. The Marines finally retaliated with artillery fire until the VC disengaged and left. The Marines suffered several casualties. VC losses were not known.

Throughout the day, we listened to the Marine company commander requesting permission to go after the VC or to have reinforcements go after the VC despite the cease-fire. Both requests were denied all day long. The only recourse was the use of Marine artillery, but even that was withheld until late afternoon. The official report of the cease-fire violation as printed in U.S. newspapers stated that the incident with the Marine company was "brief" and Marine casualties were "light." It was not considered to be a major truce violation. So much for the truth.

Then again, both sides distorted reality publicly. Sometimes in the early evening we could pick up Radio Hanoi's *Voice of Vietnam* program. Thu Huong, an attractive North Vietnamese disc jockey, better known as Hanoi Hannah, played popular U.S. music and attempted to propagandize U.S. troops with her sweet, seductive, English-speaking voice. As serious as Hanoi Hannah was, her news broadcasts were actually hilarious. When describing combat operations in I Corps that had occurred in Quang Nam Province, the U.S. or Vietnamese losses she detailed exceeded the total number of helicopters, planes, trucks, or men we had, and sometimes she reported U.S. vehicles destroyed, such as tanks, which U.S. units did not even possess at that time.

It was not uncommon to learn about a U.S. Marine battalion that had fought an NVA or VC main force unit and then hear Hanoi Hannah describe the battle on the air. For example, she would state, "A battalion of the U.S. Ninth Marines suffered a serious defeat four days ago when they encountered our People's Army in the mountains of western Quang Nam Province. Our forces lost 15 men, but the Marine battalion had 860 men killed and 100 tanks destroyed. They also had 300 helicopters shot out of the sky." Next, a tirade would follow to persuade the American Marines to leave South Vietnam. "Vietnam is not American soil, and the U.S. warmongers have no business being here. American Marines should refuse to do battle and cause useless deaths of Vietnamese people. American Marines, we have done you no harm, why do you persist in encroaching on the property and lives of the South Vietnamese people?"

At times, propaganda tapes made in America by members of the Student

Nonviolent Coordinating Committee, using phony names, were aired urging all U.S. servicemen to defect. Other times U.S. newspaper articles or editorials critical of the U.S. involvement in Vietnam were read. Hanoi Hannah's music was outstanding, her sexy voice captivating, her news broadcasts ridiculous, her American tapes and editorials sickening. Still, we tuned in to her every night we could.

Such are the vagaries of war; one day the enemy might decide to violate a cease-fire to gain a tactical advantage and kill an unsuspecting foe, while on another, they would keep their word and stop the war, if just for a while, to save a wounded child.

CHAPTER 21

Going Home

My final orders for departure directed me to report to Koelper Compound in Saigon on Tuesday, 17 January, for out-processing and then to leave Saigon for the United States the next morning. Sunday, 15 January, was the last day I would spend with the Third Battalion, Fifty-First Regiment. It was a cold, rainy day but a memorable one for both me and the battalion.

In early January, we had vacated the old French fort we had occupied in An Hoa since the battle at Nong Son. By the time the entire battalion was finally relocated to Hoi An, it was Monday, 9 January. My replacement had arrived, and I planned to spend the week showing him around and helping him meet the other American advisors and the Vietnamese soldiers in the battalion.

The next night, though, a rampaging NVA unit resulted in the Third Battalion, the Second Battalion, and an ARVN mechanized infantry battalion combining forces to react. Normally I would have stayed in Hoi An while my replacement went on the operation as the senior U.S. advisor. However, this was an opportunity I couldn't miss. For the past six weeks, I had been making an 8 mm color movie of what a combat advisor did in Vietnam. However, I had encountered one problem, which I had not been able to resolve. Previously, during all combat operations on which I had gone, I had been able to film the beginning and the end, but I was too busy during the fighting to shoot any footage, so I planned to tag along on this operation as a combat photographer.

The units left Hoi An at 4:00 a.m. and moved south down Route 1. The bridge crossing the Ba Ren River had been blown up and was lying on its side in the river, partially exposed on top of the water. Carefully moving on top of the twisted metal framework, the foot soldiers crossed into the combat zone. The armored personnel carriers (APCs) of the mech infantry unit swam across the river. The APC (officially designated an M113) was a tracked vehicle which carried a crew of two and 11 combat soldiers. It could float in water

215

and its armor exterior provided small-arms protection for the soldiers. Powered by a V-8, 215 HP engine, it had been designed by Chrysler Corporation in the late 1950s.

At daybreak we were in position to move west off Route 1 toward the NVA unit and the local VC main force with them. From the minute we left the highway until the operation ended 12 hours later, we were constantly under enemy fire. We moved with three battalions abreast, with each battalion having one company in its rear as reserve. The Third Battalion was on the left, the mech infantry battalion in the middle, and the Second Battalion on the right.

I got some excellent footage of a combined infantry and mech infantry combat operation. At one point, the Third Battalion command group was crossing an open rice field. We thought we were behind the advancing line of one of our companies. Because the mech infantry had become bogged down assaulting a hill (on our right flank, they were the center battalion), the Third Battalion had to pull back to stay even with the APCs. Twice we had to pull back. On our third movement forward, the assaulting lines of our two front companies had become separated, and now the battalion command group was part of the assault.

Advancing across this open rice field, we came under heavy automatic weapons fire from the tree line 20 yards to our right front. Luckily, right next to our group, in the ground, was a large hole, about 15 feet by 15 feet and three feet deep, so everyone jumped in.

I whipped out my movie camera and began filming the machine gun shooting at me. Not every Vietnam veteran has a home movie of the enemy shooting at him. Major Van, the battalion commander, stood up and, using arm and hand signals, maneuvered some troops of our adjacent company against the tree line. In a few minutes, the firefight was over. I had gotten it all on film, so coming on this operation had been a good idea.

On my last combat operation this young lady was found with some Viet Cong but did not have her proper identification, so she was detained as a messenger for the Viet Cong.

Feeling a tap on the shoulder, I turned to face the battal-

Me test firing the AK-47 (captured from the North Vietnamese army) I carried on combat operations. Every seven to ten days the advisors would test fire their weapons and ammo in the moat surrounding the French fort they lived in to insure they worked okay.

ion sergeant major. Grinning broadly, exposing several gold teeth, he told me to turn around … and follow him. Pointing to the ground, he explained that I should backtrack exactly in my footsteps, backward. Following his orders, not understanding what he was doing with me, we backtracked to the spot where we had all stopped when we had been shot at.

He said for me not to move as he walked in front of me and crouched down by my legs. I watched as he reached between my feet and picked at the damp ground. In a few seconds, he had recovered five enemy military full-jacketed machine gun slugs. He had been right behind me when the shooting had begun and he had seen a stream of bullets tear up the ground at my feet. When the VC had seen us coming across the field, I guess they had all gotten buck fever, but they had fired too low—every single shot had missed us by just inches.

By nightfall the operation was over, and it had been successful. We had recovered several weapons and documents and had killed many of the enemy. I also finally had plenty of combat footage for my movie.

On Sunday, 15 January, the regiment held an awards ceremony for the three battalions. Several Vietnamese soldiers and officers and some of the

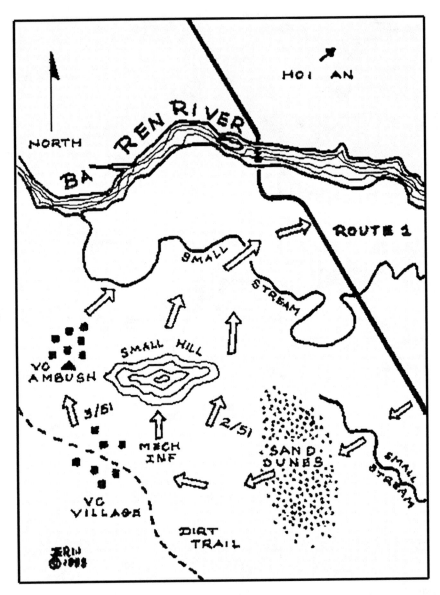

Ba Ren River

U.S. advisors were decorated for valor on the battlefield. During the ceremony, I received the Vietnamese Gallantry Cross with Silver Star by the commanding general of the I Corps Tactical Zone, Brigadier General Hoang Xuan Lam. Assisting in the presentation of the award was USMC lieutenant general Lewis M. Walt, commander of the III Marine Amphibious Force, and Dr. Nguyen

Huu Chi, the province chief of Quang Nam. This was the second award of the Vietnamese Gallantry Cross I had received for valor and the second award ceremony I had attended. In spite of the bone-chilling wind and rain, the ceremony was impressive, a fitting finale to my Vietnam tour. I concluded my good-byes that day to the men and officers with whom I had spent the last six and a half months.

Lieutenant Mac was the only "old timer" still on the advisory team (and his tenure would end in less than 90 days). Staff Sergeant Bronson had already returned to the States. His replacement, Staff Sergeant Pellham, was being reassigned to an advisory staff position. He was being replaced by another staff sergeant who had joined us in late December just before we had pulled out of An Hoa.

Leaving was a bittersweet affair. It's hard to shut the door on a period of your life that has been so intense, so close to the fine line that separates living from dying. Parting, though, is a way of life in the military. One can perceive the event as the termination of a rich and meaningful relationship or the beginning of a new and exciting future. I chose the latter. My job was over, I had done the best I could, and I had survived. If asked whether I would be willing to repeat the tour, there would be no hesitation in my response. Yes, I would.

As a career infantry officer, I had had two main objectives by volunteering for duty in the Vietnam War. First, I had wanted to earn the coveted blue and silver badge, the CIB. Second, I had wanted to experience sustained combat with an infantry unit, to know how I would react, if I would be an effective officer, whether I would be able to perform in combat situations, if I could honestly call myself a competent infantry leader. My tour in Vietnam had produced the results I had hoped to achieve. I had spent a year assigned to various Vietnamese infantry units. I had survived intensive combat operations, and I had earned the CIB. I had not earned the Purple Heart, since in a year of combat operations not a single enemy bullet or piece of shrapnel had touched my body (I would get my Purple Heart 19 months later). I would return home older, wiser, but still intact physically and psychologically.

Monday morning, I moved to Da Nang to out-process the I Corps advisory headquarters. Driving around the city, I couldn't help but wonder at the changes the war had brought. A year ago, with Vietnamese troopers from Da Nang garrison, where I had first been assigned as the senior tactical advisor, we had conducted combat operations in the rural area of East Da Nang across the river from the city. Now the area was occupied with temporary wooden buildings of the U.S. Marines. Personnel billets, offices, storehouses, PX, clubs, and everything else common to a large military force dominated what had been fields and jungle.

Talking to a young Marine officer, I couldn't believe that the khaki summer uniform was required in the officers' club in the evening. Less than a year ago Vietnamese soldiers had been swapping bullets on this same ground with the VC, contesting its ownership during the night. Now night usage required a uniform I never wore in Vietnam. Such is progress in a war.

I spent the day getting debriefed, signing forms, and packing clothes. Except for the M1 carbine I had been issued in Saigon, I only had one personal weapon left, the Smith & Wesson stainless steel .38 special revolver. I had sold the .45 to an advisor in Hoi An. At that time in Vietnam, we could bring home souvenir weapons such as some rifles or handguns. I had one of the ARVN regiment officers complete a Vietnamese war item form authorizing me to bring my Smith & Wesson .38 home as a souvenir. Most of my clothes, especially socks and underwear, were too worn and moldy to bring home and were discarded. The next day I boarded a C-130 for the trip to Saigon.

The day in Saigon was a repeat of debriefings, signing forms, turning in my carbine and field gear, and repacking for the trip home. I renewed friendships with several men with whom I had attended the MATA course. Two of the men I was with in Hawai'i were there. We learned that a friend, an airborne captain, had been killed about three months before. Rumors were flying that another MATA classmate had been wounded halfway through his tour and medevaced back to the States. Again, I felt fortunate I had survived without injury.

I looked like a combat veteran going home. Dressed in my summer uniform, it was obvious I was not just arriving in-country. The baggy uniform hung on my lean frame, testifying to my loss of 20 pounds during my tour. My skin was dark from the sun, and my chest bore two rows of ribbons topped by the CIB.

Waiting for our boarding passes at the MACV passenger terminal was like old home week. Most of us were together again for the first time since we had arrived at Travis AFB a year ago en route to Vietnam.

Martin Rodriguez and Dan Walther, two more MATA classmates, called me over. We were swapping war stories and lies when we simultaneously saw another friend walk in the door. As if on signal, our eyes popped open when we saw the decorations he had earned. The CIB, Distinguished Service Cross (DSC—the second highest decoration a soldier can earn for valor in combat), Bronze Star, Purple Heart, and Vietnamese Cross of Gallantry were displayed in addition to the numerous other service ribbons we got for just being in Vietnam. As he came over to our group, we exchanged greetings then got around to asking what we all wanted to know … where our friend had been, and how had he earned all those medals? One man said that to have all those medals he must have seen a lot of shit. Glancing around at us, cheeks blushing with embarrassment, looking at his feet, he quietly said he had spent the year in Saigon, assigned to a staff position, shuffling papers all year.

We couldn't believe him and pressed until slowly he revealed his story. Upon arriving in Saigon, a year ago, he had been assigned to a Vietnamese unit manning an outpost. On his fourth day in Vietnam, he had arrived at his new assignment. The advisor he was replacing had been eager to leave so spent an hour showing him around the outpost and then departed by the same helicopter. Late that night, before he had even unpacked, the outpost had been attacked. He had spent all night fighting for his life. At daybreak a relief unit had fought its way to the outpost. He had been shot several times.

A month later, in Japan in the hospital, he had faced a choice: return to the States and be eligible for another tour in Vietnam or return to Vietnam then and complete his tour. He had elected to return to Vietnam but was not allowed to go back to a combat unit, so he had spent the rest of his tour as a staff officer. In spite of being awarded all of the medals, he had felt cheated. His entire combat experience had amounted to ten hours and he couldn't even remember most of what had happened. Looking at each of us, he said he would gladly trade his medals for our experiences. Most of us had spent between six months and a year with combat units. While we didn't have the medals he had, we certainly had had more combat experience.

A young airman with a bullhorn announced that Flight Tango Seven Four Zero would be boarding in 20 minutes. A tug maneuvered a massive silver USAF C-141 Starlifter toward us. The tug stopped, and several men swarmed around the aluminum giant, stuffing chocks under the tires, hooking up cords from portable engines into its belly, and angling the pickup with the steps to a door near the tail. Supplies, which I hoped were food, were loaded through the forward door.

Fifteen minutes later the young airman requested all passengers for USAF Flight Tango Seven Four Zero to McGuire Air Force Base in New Jersey line up with their boarding passes in the order of their pass numbers. Because I would start 30 days' leave the day after the plane landed in the States, my flight home would go to McGuire AFB in New Jersey, 125 miles from my parents' home in Connecticut.

Oh boy, I thought, with pass number two, I'll be second to go on board. If I had thought back about being bumped by a colonel from my intended jet ride at Clark AFB a year ago, I might have realized that any field grade personnel, regardless of their boarding numbers, would go before me.

Sure enough, when the airman called for all O-6s and O-5s to come forward, three full colonels and five lieutenant colonels appeared out of nowhere and boarded. Next came a call for majors, and then the rest of us boarded—now by the boarding pass numbers.

After another 20 minutes, four Pratt and Whitney 21,000-pound thrust turbo fan engines roared to life. At the end of the runway, waiting for clearance to depart, the pilot explained our trip. We would fly first to Wake Island,

3,800 miles away, six hours and 55 minutes' flight time with the tail winds. Next, we would fly to Hickam Air Force Base in Honolulu, 2,300 miles from Wake, taking four hours. The last leg would be the longest, Honolulu to McGuire, 5,000 miles and, if the tail winds held, taking eight hours and 30 minutes. We would be on the ground at Wake for one hour and at Hickam for another hour. The total time en route would be approximately 21 hours and 30 minutes. By departing Saigon at 11:30 a.m. on 18 January we were scheduled to arrive at McGuire about 8:00 p.m. the same day. Even though we would spend almost a day en route, we would also lose a day by crossing the International Date Line.

At 8:15 we touched down at McGuire AFB, just outside of Fort Dix, New Jersey. Before we left the plane, we were told we would go inside the terminal building and clear customs and complete processing. As the aircraft doors were opened, we were hit with a shocking blast of arctic air for which we were unprepared as we were wearing our short-sleeved summer uniforms. Almost as soon as we had entered the room, our baggage was delivered. We were told to place it on a table for a customs inspection.

The customs agent asked to see my papers. Without saying a word, I handed him the forms. An Air Force NCO took my travel orders and waited. The customs man inquired if I had anything to declare. I replied no. He asked me to please open the bag and remove the contents. Taking a small key from my pocket, I opened the padlock on my duffle bag, pulled out dirty clothes, underwear, field gear, my air force survival knife, toilet kit, boots, and odds and ends of personal gear, and I spread it all on the table. The Smith & Wesson pistol was at the bottom of a smelly combat boot, so it was not checked, and I didn't mention it (in spite of the war souvenir paperwork). Looking at the mess and then glancing at the Air Force NCO, the customs man told the sergeant I was okay to go. The sergeant gave me some copies of arrival papers and saying I was free to go, then welcomed me home and wished me a good leave. Pushing my gear back into the bag and slinging it on my shoulder I walked to the door leading into the main terminal building.

On the other side of this door, pandemonium reigned. Wives, children, sweethearts, parents, relatives, and friends excitedly awaited their soldiers. Standing tall, off to one side, was my beautiful wife. Wrapped in a warm, full-length coat, only her face visible, with just a hint of her short, pixie-style hair—she sure looked nice. We recognized each other simultaneously, she squealed and flew into my arms, while I dropped the bag and grabbed her. After a few minutes of hugging and caressing, she led me over to a counter, where she had a warm field jacket for me.

She and the two girls were staying at my parents' home in Connecticut. Glancing at my watch I said we should be in Roxbury in about four hours, about 1:00 or 1:30 a.m.

Anita and I celebrated a delayed Christmas in Roxbury, Connecticut, 19 January 1967, with our daughters Julie (left) and Suzi.

Looking up at me with her pretty smile, she softly said, "No, we won't be there until tomorrow morning. I told everyone you'd be too tired to drive so late at night, so we'd stop somewhere on the way, so you could get your rest." Smiling again, she added, "I have reservations at the McGuire Inn, just outside the main gate." This portended an unexpected welcome in contrast to the nights I had so often spent on dirt floors of grass huts and bunkers during dark nights of combat throughout my tour of duty in Vietnam, sometimes wondering if I would live to see another morning.

Epilogue

After my leave, I attended the Armor Officers' Career Course and then the Classified Nuclear Weapons Employment Course. I spent a year as an infantry company commander at Fort Benning, by far the worst year in my military career due to an overbearing and over-demanding battalion commander. Consequently, I decided to leave the Army to attend graduate school, but I needed money, so I volunteered for another tour in Vietnam as a combat advisor. Meanwhile, in April 1968, our third daughter, Karen, was born.

In the summer of 1968, I was promoted to major and returned to Vietnam. I had three assignments. The first assignment was as a district advisor on the Cambodian border in III Corps, where I immediately got hookworm and then got shot. While recovering in Saigon I had a second assignment as the advisor to the unit responsible for the security of the bridges in and around Saigon. My third assignment was to train two ARVN light infantry companies to become commando units for conducting raids in the Rung Sat Special Zone in III and IV Corps south of Saigon. By the time I had completed my third, and last, combat tour, I had earned the USMC Combat Action Ribbon for combat in Lebanon, then the Army Combat Infantryman Badge, seven decorations for valor, the Purple Heart and the Air Medal for Vietnam.

In September 1969, I left active duty (but remained active in the reserves) to begin graduate school. I first received an MA in counseling and psychology and then a PhD in counseling and clinical psychology. Upon entering the PhD program, I was selected to return to active duty while obtaining my PhD. After receiving my degree, I was assigned to be an Army clinical psychologist, which was my profession for the next eight years. I also graduated from the U.S. Army Command and General Staff College and then earned another master's degree in business administration. As a psychologist, I engaged in considerable research, focusing on the adjustment of Vietnam veterans, earning an international reputation as a pioneer in that area. I also ran a five-year psychological evaluation program for U.S. Army Vietnam POWs. I retired in 1981 as a lieutenant colonel, having served as the psychology consultant for the U.S. Army Health Services Command (HSC) since 1975.

For the next 16 years, I was a business professor, then a journalism professor and a nonfiction writer. In 1997, at age 60, I retired from my position as a journalism professor at New Mexico State University. In addition, over the years, my wife and I have owned and managed several small businesses.

Today, I continue writing with more than 2,400 publications to date, mostly articles related to general aviation. In 1975, I became a pilot flying my own plane as the psychology consultant for HSC. In 2015, with more than 7,000 flight hours, flying my ninth plane, I was diagnosed with a defective aortic heart valve. Emergency open heart surgery replaced the valve, the result of Agent Orange, after spending two combat tours in Vietnam, but also ended my career as a pilot. The heart now functions in the normal range. Our three daughters are grown, with children of their own. My wife and I live in southern New Mexico.

Bob Worthington
Military History

Elliott Robert "Bob" Worthington retired from the U.S. Army in October 1981, three and a half month months shy of 25 years of service as an enlisted man, NCO, and officer. His military career began when he dropped out of college to enlist in the U.S. Marines in February 1957.

After his infantry training he was assigned to the 10th Marines, an artillery regiment in the Second Division at Camp Lejeune, North Carolina. He ended up in a 4.2-inch mortar battery and went on a six-month Mediterranean cruise as part of the USMC Reinforced Marine Infantry Battalion trained for combat assaults as needed anywhere in any countries facing the Mediterranean Sea.

On 15 July 1958, his unit completed a combat assault on the city dump of Beirut, Lebanon, as part of the U.S. Operation Bluebat to stop the war being fought in the country by outside countries. The war lasted several weeks, and by the fall, Bob returned to the States. While in the Marines, he met Anita Elliott, a Washington, D.C., college student.

As a corporal, he left active duty in February 1959 to return to Dartmouth. He and Anita married in September 1959 as he entered his junior year. During his senior year at Dartmouth, he was employed as a regular, full-time police officer with the Hanover, New Hampshire, Police Department. Majoring in art, he graduated in June 1961 as a ROTC distinguished military graduate. He was also an Army ROTC student (as well as enlisted in the Army Reserves). Due to a mix-up in his ROTC records he was not commissioned in the infantry, but in the chemical corps. After completing the chemical corps basic officer course, he remained at Fort McClellan, Alabama, where he became a platoon leader in a smoke generator company.

He requested a branch transfer to the infantry, transferring to the 2nd Infantry Division at Fort Benning as a rifle company platoon leader in early 1963. That summer he attended jump school. On his third jump he broke his hip, was hospitalized for two months and then received a one-year medical profile, prohibiting his return to the rifle company. He became the battalion assistant personnel officer. An additional duty was as the battalion OIC for its pistol and rifle team. During the Fort Benning post matches, one of Bob's pistol shooters was unable to shoot so Bob took his place, winning the post pistol championship. This lead to his becoming the XO of the division marksmanship detachment, and as a professional pistol shooter, he earned the highest competitive rank of Master. He held this position until his one-year profile expired and was assigned as the assistant operations officer in an infantry battalion. During the summers, the battalion was trained by a Special Forces team in unconventional warfare tactics and it also trained in helicopter tactics. Bob was promoted to captain in mid–1965 and then received orders to Vietnam as a combat advisor.

Bob attended the Military Assistance Training Advisor Course at the Army John F. Kennedy Special Warfare Center at Fort Bragg, North Carolina, and then the Vietnamese language school at the Defense Language Institute at the Presidio of Monterrey in California.

He served in Vietnam as a combat advisor in 1966–1967. After Vietnam, he was assigned to the Armor Officers' Career Course at Fort Knox, Kentucky, and then attended the army classified Nuclear Weapons Employment Course. He was then assigned to Fort Benning to command a basic combat training company, which became the worst job he ever had because of overbearing battalion and regimental commanders. The assignment was so bad he decided that if these two men represented what he would become he decided to get out and attend graduate school, which required money. He knew if he returned to Vietnam as a combat advisor, he could save a lot of money. He was promoted to major, which ended his command tour and returned to Vietnam as a combat advisor from 1968 to 1969. At the end of his tour he was released from active duty and began school at Northern Arizona University. He received his MA in counseling and psychology in May 1970 and joined the university as a staff counselor. After a year he entered the University of Utah counseling psychology PhD program. At the same time, the Army was anticipating difficulty with senior officers and NCOs when it transitioned from a conscript force to an all-volunteer force. The solution was to locate former combat arms officers and return them to active duty to receive doctoral degrees in the behavioral sciences to help the Army move into an all-volunteer force.

He graduated with a PhD in counseling psychology and a minor in clinical psychology in August 1973 and received a one-year post-doctoral fellowship in community psychology at William Beaumont Army Medical Center in El Paso, Texas. While in the Army Reserve and on active duty, Bob attended the Reserve Command and General Staff College, graduating in the fall of 1974.

Assigned as the clinical psychologist for the Army hospital at Fort Polk, Louisiana, he had only served about nine months when he was selected to become the first psychology consultant for the Army Health Services Command, a flag command at Fort Sam Houston in San Antonio, Texas, overseeing all health care, health facilities and personnel in CONUS, Hawai'i, Alaska, and the Panama Canal Zone. During this time Bob became a member of the DOD Operation Homecoming, a five-year project following up on the adjustment of all military Vietnam POWs and a member of the Center for POW Studies (Bob headed the program to do the psychological evaluation of all army Vietnam POWs). He served as a sports psychologist with the army's Olympic modern pentathlon team and became a pioneer researcher on the adjustment of Vietnam veterans. Because of his considerable traveling to work with Army medical facilities and personnel in the States, Bob became an instrument rated pilot and the Army paid him to fly his own plane. This led to his becoming an aviation psychologist, working with Army aviation. Because a lot of his work required management consulting within and outside the Army, Bob earned a master's degree in business administration from Webster University in 1979. He ended his Army career as the chief of the Fort Sam Houston Army Mental Health Service (while also serving as the HSC psychology consultant). Bob retired from the Army as a lieutenant colonel in October 1981.

Bob became a university business professor, a full-time writer and then a university writing professor, from which he retired in 1997. As a writer Bob has more than 2,400 publications, including several co-authored books, and journal and magazine articles. He and his wife live in Las Cruces, New Mexico.

Index